#WhatIf ...
So I dared

A memoir of agymcha

ANN GUSTAVSSON

First published in Australia 2015
By Ann Gustavsson

Copyright © Ann Gustavsson 2015
All rights reserved. No part of this book may be reproduced, stored or transmitted in any manner or in any form without written permission of the author. Copyright resides with Ann Gustavsson.

Book cover image by Maurits Gustavsson

National Library of Australia Cataloguing-in-Publication data

Creator: Gustavsson, Ann, author.

Title: #What if... so I dared... : a memoir of Agymcha / Ann Gustavsson.

ISBN: 9780994399304 (paperback)

Subjects: Gustavsson, Ann.
                Women artists--Australia--Biography.
                Koreans Australians--Australia--Biography.
                Women immigrants--Australia--Biography.

Dewey Number: 759.994

Printed by: InHouse Publishing
                www.inhousepublishing.com.au

Disclaimer: This book is based on the author's personal experiences. It is written from the author's memories, journals and letters, every effort has been made to express the essence of a moment in time. Although this story is a work of non-fiction, some of names have been changed. No discourtesy has been intended towards any person or event mentioned in this book.

Author's website: www.agymcha.com

Acknowledgements

I could not have written this book without the understanding and the support from my relatives and my family, especially my husband Rolf. I would also like to thank to Trudy Zussino and Glenda for your attention to detail copy-editing the book and to Robyn Ferguson for your constructive criticism.

My life is enriched by your love and support, thank you ALL very much from the bottom of my heart.

FOREWORD

When I was asked to write a foreword for Ann's memoir I was reminded of the day in 2011 when I opened Ann's first solo art exhibition and explained what her signature, *Agymcha,* on her paintings meant. *Agymcha* represents the whole of Ann as it gives the initials of her married name and her birth name.

Her latest achievement, her memoir, reflects Ann's complete personality written in her inimitable style. As in her art work her determination to succeed to the utmost of her abilities is also reflected in her written work. But there is more in the book as she is sharing her knowledge on how she achieved and developed her talents, whether it be in art, writing, work, bringing up a family, fitting in with the culture of the countries she visited and enjoying the rich experiences that were offered to her. One of the most emotional and beautiful part of the book is how she came to marry her husband and how she coped with the initial hard life in the outback of Australia, rearing a family. She uses tension in her style of writing when relating how she and her husband created their strong relationship while traversing Australia. It is exciting when she reveals how she found work, bought houses, getting her younger brother to Australia and even more interesting how she became proficient in whatever task she took up. It is also rewarding reading when she vividly describes her impressions of Sweden and her husband's family when she and her husband with their two young sons visited her husband's country of birth and how she adapted to the customs of that country without losing her own identity. Family relationships are important to Ann which is strongly portrayed when she visited, for the first time since she left, (a span of some 18 years) her own country Korea. Meeting her own, in a *way,* estranged family and re-learning some of the customs are described with compassion but also with humour. At times I laughed out loud at some of the antics created due to intercultural encounters.

My husband and I treasure the friendship that was spontaneously created when we all lived in Mount Isa some 40 years ago. And, like many people in Mount Isa, we were very sad when Ann decided to leave the City.

The book offers encouragement, having a go when opportunities arise, *dare to go beyond* what is required and listen to your heart as well as be honest with yourself and others. The book is a reflection of Ann's life, her own successes, disappointments, overcoming deep tragedies, self-doubt at times but always optimistic about eventual success. Her experiences, whether sad, happy, funny, frustrating, are told candidly and show Ann's wonderful achievements through her determination, optimism and believing in herself- following her heart. It is a great story that reflects how she always gives of her best and at the same time let readers know that ***dare to do*** when opportunities are given and ***follow your heart*** - are acts for achieving.

Trudy Russino
12/07/2015

Contents

Acknowledgements	III
Foreword	V
Chapter One	1
Chapter Two	9
Chapter Three	27
Chapter Four	39
Chapter Five	61
Chapter Six	115
Chapter Seven	159
Chapter Eight	175
Chapter Nine	213
Chapter Ten	269

Chapter One

"Hi Ann, just wondering if you are free on Sunday afternoon, mum and I may come for a visit". Regards, Julie. – (Tuesday, 5.40pm)

I was happy to read Julie's text message on my i-phone and I was looking forward to seeing my friend, Frances, whom I hadn't seen for a few months, so I texted Julie back.

"What a lovely surprise, we are free on Sunday; let me know what time you are coming we'd love to see you both". – (6.10pm)

"Lovely, it will be around 12.30ish I will let you know if different as mum is doing an open house beforehand". – (6.30pm)

"I will have lunch ready by 12.30pm. Look forward to seeing you both on Sunday". – (6.32pm)

"Lovely, see you then". – (6.33pm)

"Hi Ann, leaving Noosa now see you soon". – (Sunday, 12.33pm)

Just after 1.00pm they arrived at my place. It was very nice seeing them both and catching up with what's been happening in and around of each other's life since the last time.

Frances is a close friend of mine we have known each other for over 36 years. At times, months pass by without being in touch but we can pick up on our conversation from where we left as if it were yesterday. Frances was a chef at the hotel restaurant called "Copper Grill" in Mount Isa where I worked as a hostess. She is now sixty-eight but still working, selling real estate from her home, about half an hour from us by car. Her eldest daughter Julie lives in Noosa and works for one of the car sales yards there.

A cold smoothie I made for all of us with frozen mango, banana and yogurt was just right thing to cool us down on a very hot and humid day. The Korean dish, *bibimbap*, I prepared for lunch was also delicious. Julie brought her Laptop and Tablet PC to show me and Rolf many of their lovely images from their recent family get together for two weddings in the family in one week. One of Frances' granddaughters got married and in the same week, Julie at the age of forty-three was married also. Having known them for so long I feel close to them and we had a wonderful afternoon together catching up.

It doesn't matter who we talk with lately the main topic of conversation is the extremely dry and hot weather we are having at the moment and it dominates most of our concerns.

Clouds are rolling in fast on a sweltering day; there is a good chance of rain soon. It's been almost eight months since we had good rain. It is like back in the days when we lived in Mount Isa, a mining town in the outback of Queensland in Australia. It rarely rained in winter and waiting for rain for 6 months was pretty normal. We lived there for most of our young and productive years, until we retired from the work force in mid 2001 and had moved away from there, 1,800 kilometres south-east to the greener pastures of the Noosa hinterland on the Sunshine Coast. It is now only 30 minutes away by car from the beautiful South Pacific Ocean and within two hours by car we can get to the best hospital in Queensland perhaps in Australia and the museums and art galleries have world class exhibitions. Pomona is a small town, a peaceful community of a population of less than 3,000 people. A paradise to live in especially when we have sufficient rain falls as we had originally expected.

But when the dry spell continues for so long, as it has been lately, living on a large acreage property where much water is needed, waiting for the rain day after day is exhausting and weakens our mental spirit. No amount of long hand watering will replace a good soaking rain. There are a couple of small orchards of mango and citrus, a bamboo plantation, some exotic edible trees, veggie and ornamental gardens on our property with two dams. We have a dream to create a self reliant property where we can grow ourselves most of the things we need.

Since our children have grown up and have left home and we have retired from the work force, we now have the time to try to make such a dream come true. We chose this area as we had believed that it usually has the rain falls we need being close to the Coast. But as the record breaking dry weather continues more and more areas in Australia are now drought declared; almost every day from the TV news we see, how terrible the situation is for people and live stock in the outback and it is heart-breaking to hear how they are suffering because of the drought. Last night television news confirmed that 80% of Queensland is now drought declared, up to 38 of its shires are in drought all at the same time, and it is the biggest drought on record.

At least we still have some drinking water left in our tanks and water in the dams for the garden however not knowing when the next good rain is coming is stressful, the summer is almost gone without filling up our water reserves as in previous years by this time of the year.

The climate change is so great, this last year, 2013, the first time ever since we moved here we harvested fully ripened oranges and mandarins in summer followed by poor harvest in the winter. It sure was very unusual, not only we human and animals are having difficulties to adjust to climate changes but also plant life such as the citrus trees seemed to be very confused indeed. There has been significant increase in many different natural disasters all over the world and the disasters are getting worse, breaking many records. In recent years the extreme bush fires, floods and droughts in Australia have dominated the news and political issues.

The fact of the matter is that we do grow older from the minute we are born and everything changes including the climate. As the world population increases inevitably the consumption increases and how we live creates a lot of pollution thus, the increasing pollution would increase the effect on our environment for sure. The reports from scientists show enough evidence that the temperature is rising. It is hard to understand why there are some skeptics who still refuse to believe that global warming is real. Developing a new way of life to reduce and slow the greenhouse gas emission is indeed a very important issue for the future.

Starting to rain now and the sound of the rain is so good, feeling relieved and refreshed! I hear the sudden burst of laughs of Kookaburras, a chorus of magpies and butcher birds, as though they also feel happier and energized by the rain. Everything in the yard is getting rain washed and shined; in their true colours, everything looks much more alive again. The weather forecast, maybe, was right for us this time; it actually is raining here, here at last, not just an empty promise. Too many times lately it rained nearby but not here, it was patchy, it seemed so close yet so far. My longing for rain has been developed over many years having lived in the rain deprived mining towns like Mount Isa in far North West of Queensland and Kalgoorlie in Western Australia.

There is huge construction work of a $590 million dollar Highway upgrade of the Bruce Highway near our place, upgrading from a two-lane highway to a four-lane highway expected to be completed in 2016. It is devastating to witness the destruction of such a large area of beautiful nature, stripped to bare land to make way for the upgrade of the highway, many beautiful native trees are knocked down and even some people's loving homes had to go. Nevertheless the upgrading was necessary as there have been too many fatal accidents in the past on that particular stretch of the highway as it didn't have enough lanes for the increasing volume of traffic. We are living in a material world of throw away cutting edge technologies and the good roads are essential to transport more and more things to where they are needed thus it is inevitable more and more of nature is destroyed to make faster and wider roads.

I was brought up in an era before a lot of the modern technologies and can't help but wonder if our life is better off now? The life before so many of the modern throw away technologies perhaps was neither convenient nor comfortable but we were able to repair a lot of things to re-use which was surely far better for our health and the environment.

The shower of rain didn't last long and instantly I feel anxious for more rain. It is very disappointing, most of it evaporated as fast as it came down in the hot atmosphere without anything much in the rain gauge to be recorded. It has been like that lately for months. It certainly is a very unusual weather pattern for this time of the year.

This week has been an extra emotional week for me, being the anniversary of the week of my arrival in Australia. At the very young age of twenty, I, all alone, left the country in which I was born. I left behind my family and friends and came to this far away foreign land Australia, to meet a man whom I had met as a pen-pal and had fallen in love with. That was 44 years ago! Engaged to be married and dreaming to start a brand new life with him. Too young and naïve to comprehend what life was all about but very much in love, full of curiosity and determination, so determined that I didn't let anyone have a say in my decisions.

Life then was very different to now; grown up without most of the modern things like refrigerator, television or telephone which were then a luxury not a necessity as they are now, a simple transistor radio had then played a huge part in our lives. Most people thought travelling overseas in an aero plane was possible only for the rich and very famous – not for a young girl like me brought up in a working class family in South Korea and to get the chance to travel to Australia in 1970 was unheard of let alone coming to Australia to live.

The "White Australia Policy" in Australia still played a big role in immigration law which was not yet completely dismantled until the Whitlam Government in 1973. It was literally one in a million opportunity for a non Anglo Saxon like me from a country like Korea, not included in the Commonwealth Countries, to be allowed to enter into this country to live. Indeed Australia was a very different society then! In fact the whole world was very different then, there weren't any internet or World Wide Web services like now. Urgent messages were sent by telegrams as international telephone calls were expensive and many couldn't afford to get a phone connected at home. Australia was, not yet known to Korea in those years, perhaps not yet known to most of the world as it is a, relatively speaking, very young country. The only thing I knew about Australia was a vast island where lots of kangaroos hopped around. The only kangaroo I had ever seen was the picture on the lid of my father's shoe polish tin which had the trade mark with a picture of a kangaroo on it. The preconception most people had then of Korea was merely a war torn country in poverty; most people didn't care to know even where it was located on the map of the world.

I was completely cut off over night from everything what was dear and familiar to me and literally reborn in another world, where, not only didn't I speak the language well but a place where people, climate, food and the culture was so very different to Korea. Moreover starting the new life with the man I hardly knew and who was also new to Australia and brought up in a very different background not only to mine but also to Australians had indeed many difficult challenges to overcome.

YES, I was extremely ISOLATED and very LONELY in a totally unfamiliar world! Far away from home for the Very First Time in my life, could never have guessed how much I would miss family and friends and the food I was brought up with.

Perhaps I wanted to believe the life would be far better in Australia and took it for granted that there would be lots of better things to eat in Australia. The last thing I would have thought I would miss was such an ordinary thing as *kimchi*. The spicy vegetable pickles I had at breakfast, lunch and dinner. But oh boy! Didn't I Miss it! It's an understatement! Having a bowl of steamed rice and *kimchi* became literally only a dream over night. The first couple of years were very hard to adjust and the loneliness was unbearable. I would stand by the window often gazing at the unfamiliar environment lost in thoughts feeling very lonely and intimidated. I wondered how I was ever going to manage to learn all and adjust. Often I cried when Rolf was not around, to release all my emotions to be able to cope. Yet, had I ever once regretted that I came? I wanted to succeed in what I came for, create a happy life together with the man I fell in love with; the tears were not on any account of sadness, they were of the loneliness, and it was a way to cope.

I will be turning 65 years this year, a new mile stone in my life. I felt the profound need to pause and take some time out to reflect and re-assess where my life journey is taking me. My inner voice has been telling me that I must translate into English for my family the story, I had written in Korean more than two decades ago about my earlier experiences in life. So that they can read about how I had grown up in Korea and what it was like to start the migrant life in Australia with a foreigner I knew so little about. And how I had tackled the unexpected and difficult firsthand challenges the life had thrown at me and how I had learned to create a brand new life in Australia.

Looking back I have always trusted My Intuition and followed my OWN heart! I have been able to stand outside of myself and look in, to take the necessary steps toward what I wanted in my life by listening to my own inner voices. And, that, deep down, I haven't changed.

A couple of weeks ago I had the radio on while I was painting a portrait in my studio as I often do these days. There was an ABC radio program on and it was about the stories written by 2nd World War Australian brides who went to America to live.

My tears were running down my face listening to the stories, in empathy with some of their experiences.

Those compelling stories took me back to the memories of all those years ago when I first came to Australia to live and made me Put Down my Paint Brushes for a while and Write...

CHAPTER TWO

A few months before I graduated from high-school, I was one day with a friend I grew up with; her name is Young Yi and she is one year younger than I am. We were just talking about how we were going to make use of the English language we had learned at school. We figured out that there could be a way not to forget English as well as improve it if we had a pen friend from an English speaking country. So we agreed to go into the city next day and to visit one of the Pen-Pal Groups to find an address of such a person.

There were a lot of Pen-Pal Groups in Seoul, South Korea in those years. Having pen friends within Korea was very popular amongst high-school students. In fact it was encouraged especially for senior grade students to write to the Korean soldiers in many places to comfort them and help them to find solace in reading. For a little membership fee we could get as many addresses as we wanted. And the information for overseas pen pals was also readily available.

We went to the Pen-Pal Group nearest from the bus stop where we got off in the city and paid the membership fee to join the overseas pen-pal group. Once we registered as members we were given a book to have a look - a book full of information of overseas people who were looking for a pen friend like we were. The book was pretty thick and looked identical to a small Oxford-English-dictionary. As I DIDN'T HAVE any idea who in particular I was looking for, without any thought I opened it at almost in the middle. I was slowly reading the information on that page written in English as I ran my finger down, reading the details of each one of the contacts with concentration.

My finger stopped about half way down the page, as I read about the information of a Swedish man who was living in Kalgoorlie in Western

Australia. Who wished a pen friend to improve his English and so on, and best of all I read in it was that he needed to study English, and he was an older man. Very Old! Ten years older than I was! When we were that young, a one year older person was an old person, a person ten years older was indeed Very Old! Very old means there won't be any Marriage Threat. How naïve I was then! Only a couple of lines below on the same page there was another address from Western Australia and that one was from Geraldton. Surprisingly it was of a similar aged man but he was from West Germany. There was no need to look any further. We left the place with an excitement with the new found contacts for each of us after Young Yi decided to choose the address of the West German in Geraldton.

Not knowing that my whole life was about to change, it surely was a profound pivotal moment of my life!

As soon as I returned home I started to write the letter. It was a brief introduction of myself and a wish to become his pen-friend but it took many hours to construct the letter in English. Then I had to help Young Yi to write hers given she was in one lower grade than I was and her English was not as good as mine. I took both letters with me to school and used the typewriter to make them look neat and mailed the letters on the next day, in the hope of receiving a speedy reply *as quick as yesterday*, and waited for it every day but nothing for weeks then into more than a month, the wait was like an eternity!

I remember very well like yesterday, how excited I was the day when my father brought me the letter from Australia that I was waiting for, for so long. My heart is pounding with a thrill even now after 44 plus years just thinking of that moment! Had my strict father only guessed what was about to happen! But how could he have ever guessed it? Even I had no way of knowing what was about to happen! My father was only proud of me, thinking that my English was good enough to communicate with an English speaking foreigner, not knowing that he would take his precious daughter away from him forever!

I was very lucky indeed that it was written in English he couldn't understand. A letter from a strange man for his well respected daughter would never have been acceptable to my father! I never had anyone from overseas to write to before and I didn't have any clue how long the letter would take to and from Australia. In those years international mail services between Australia and Korea were slow we were lucky to receive a reply letter within a month. However it was not uncommon even during those years, to hear about someone who had a pen pal in the U.S.A. because of the military ties Korea had with the U.S.A. However it was pretty much unheard of for anyone to have a pen pal in Australia. The world we had grown up in was very small and closed in, not the World Wide Web exposed internet driven world we are living in now.

When I read the very first letter I'd ever received written in English I felt the whole world had its doors opened to me. The horizon was extended beyond my imagination. It gave me a whole lot of new meanings to life, being connected with a person who lived a world away from me but accepted me as a friend! His letter was also brief. He wrote that he had been in Australia for less than three years from Sweden and that he was working as a mechanic for a diamond drilling company in a small gold mining town. He said he would like to exchange photographs and get to know more about me.

Brief as it was, I Felt like I had just ENTERED a brand New Universe!

It was such a spiritually up-lifting moment being connected to the unknown and my curiosity was beginning to run Wild!

I wrote that evening in reply, about my family, my father's garage business and the climate in Seoul and also suggested, we exchange postcards and stamps as well to see and learn about the different cultures of each other. I wrote that I would like to know all about him as well. I wrote it and rewrote again and again for the next couple of days until I was satisfied with my grammar and spelling. I enclosed a photo I had of myself and a postcard which was a picture of Deok Su Palace in Seoul, a glimpse of 5,000 years of Korean history. Within a week Young Yi had also received a reply from the German friend. We were so excited being in this together to dream on to become one day really fluent in English.

Then came the next letter that I was waiting for in anticipation, enclosed in it was a black and white passport photo of him. He looked so handsome with big eyes and he didn't look at all OLD even though his age was a decade older than mine! I couldn't take my eyes off him! My heart was racing even faster as I read the letter written about his overwhelming happiness of seeing my photo and that he couldn't take his eyes off it. He wrote that his hair is blond and his eyes are blue, and he will prepare a good full sized colour photo of himself and enclose it in the next letter for me. Although I found out that his command of English was far better than mine, it was a secondary issue and no longer the main focus as I realized our hearts were already in touch with each other as if it was meant to happen. It was so unexpected and surreal as if I was dreaming it all.

He wrote about Kalgoorlie where he lived, the weather was very dry and hot during summer time 35 plus degrees and it goes up a lot more some days and in winter it can drop at night to a single digit but never cold enough to snow. Most people who were born and lived there have never seen snow. It is so dry, there are no natural water reserves and water supply had to come from Perth almost 600 kilometres by pipe line.

Camel trains used to carry the water to town before the pipeline was built 50-75 years ago. Many of the streets were made very wide for a camel train to be able to turn around in those years and remained wide still. He also wrote that there were plenty of kangaroos and emus around the place. He wanted to know when my birthday was and what my interests were. Enclosed in the letter there was a postcard with a magnificent picture of a huge Poinciana tree in full bloom in an intense orange-red colour.

The picture was amazingly beautiful! Being brought up all my life in a big city, population of three million plus, I have not yet seen much of nature anywhere other than cityscapes given I have had almost no travel experiences. To see a photo of such a beautiful tree blew me away. He wrote that he was waiting in anticipation to read more about me and the letter was signed with Sincerely Your Own. I read it again and again until I could fully understand his English correctly given some of the things he wrote weren't easy for me to comprehend.

I replied to the letter as soon as I could; I wrote about how happy I was also to see his photo and couldn't wait to receive the next photo of him. I wrote to let him know that I had shown the beautiful postcard he sent me to all my family and friends who had never seen such a beautiful tree before and it was rather strange to learn that the seasons were opposite to Korea. I wrote more about our climate in Seoul. The beautiful four distinct seasons it brings, spring, summer, autumn and winter and wrote about our national flower called in Korean, *Mu-gung-hwa* which is the Rose of Sharon and is a kind of hibiscus. I let him know when my birthday is and I asked about his. I also wrote that I didn't have a hobby in particular but I was interested in many things and I enjoyed very much listening to the western pop songs even though I didn't always understand the full meaning of the songs written in English.

I have many favourite singers and unlike many of my friends I liked Cliff Richard more than Elvis Presley, I could almost sing along his songs like "The Young Ones" and "Summer Holiday" because I listened to them so often from the pop music programs we had on radio.

I enclosed a picture of *Mu-gung-hwa*, our national flower and a postcard which had a synopsis about picture of a group of ladies in old Korean costumes doing the laundry by the stream and a lady carrying an urn on her head to bring water home with her. I also signed the letter with Sincerely Your Own. Before I mailed the letter I put on as many stamps of different images as I needed for the postage for him to see.

Once again I had to wait for many weeks for the reply, thinking of him every minute every hour of the day and couldn't wait to read more about him and most of all I couldn't wait to see another photo of him.

A few weeks later as I expected, but not soon enough, the letter arrived. I almost tore the envelope to open it and found the colour photo I was waiting for. Yes, he is truly a Handsome looking man, he sure Looks Young and he has both Arms and Legs! A blond with blue eyes! What's more he looks so HEALTHY! It felt as if I had just met him in person.

The letter was hand written not typed like the last one and he wrote that he wished that I would hand write also. I agreed with him instantly in my mind given how much more intimate I felt reading his hand written letter. His handwriting was as neat as typed and easy to read. By reading it I sensed deeply that he was an Honest and Sincere man. He wrote that he too didn't have a hobby in particular but he was interested in many things and when he could he liked to go for a drive out to the country in his little car and enjoy watching animals, birds, flowers and whatever he could find around Kalgoorlie which was all very new to him. Although I enjoyed very much having a ride on public buses, trams and trains, which were very convenient and readily available in Seoul, it made me dream how great it would be to have my very own car and be able to drive wherever I wanted to go. It sure was an amazing thought!

He let me know his birth date and he wrote that he was in good health but he was very lonely until he met me. He wrote that he couldn't explain earlier because he didn't know how I felt about him but he thought he might be in love with me even though we hardly knew each other as yet and he still didn't know how I felt about him but he was hoping that our feeling was mutual. Because he believed we could be very happy together he would try very hard to win my heart if there was a chance. He asked if I could think about Marrying a Foreigner. I didn't have to answer him immediately but he was very SERIOUS about it. I couldn't believe what I was reading, and my heart was pounding so hard it was almost Hurting me!

He continued that it seemed we were very far from each other but that it was only about 8,000 kilometres by a modern plane and would take about 16 hours which wasn't much, he thought, given it took him 36 hours from Sweden to Australia three years earlier. He also enclosed a photo of red roses in full bloom taken from his mother's garden in Sweden which his mother had sent the year before and explained also about the tiny blue flowers in the photo. Red roses are the colour of love and when you receive three red roses, Swedish people perceive the first one to mean "trust" the second one "hope" and the third one "love" and the small blue flowers, pansies in the photo, are translated into English "Love-in-idleness". He wrote that he would be waiting for my reply and wished me to write back as soon as I could and he signed that letter differently to the last one, Sincerely with all my love your own.

I was Very young and not yet prepared for a Marriage Proposal from him or any one for that matter. I was nineteen not long since I had graduated from high-school.

Those years in Korea we started elementary-school at age 7, and 6 years after we graduated elementary-school we had to pass a hard entrance exam for the secondary school of our choice to be able to enter for the junior years, similar to grades 7, 8 and 9 in Australia. We then graduated after the 3 junior years. Students who wanted to go further had to pass another entrance exam to enter the senior years which was like the senior grades in Australia years 10, 11 and 12. Those entrance exams were known to be very hard and difficult to pass as there weren't enough schools in Korea for everyone to enter in those years. It was even harder to enter universities not only because the exam being more difficult to pass for the same reason but also the fees were much higher and not affordable for average families. Many children couldn't attend even junior-school let alone university because of the high cost. Those years Korea was still in Recovery Mode from the many Wars they had been through, the last War being the Korean War which ended in mid 1953 when I was three years old.

I am the eldest child in a family with five children; father and stepmother, one full sister who is three years younger, two half sisters seven and ten years younger and my half brother who is seventeen years younger than I. We have lived most of our lives together with our grandma who is the mother of our father as it was a Korean custom, my father being the eldest son, that it was his responsibility to take care of his mother once he got married. My grandma was a chief in the family who was the overseer and my father was the financial provider. He had a garage, a business of automobile repairs and was able to provide our basic necessities in life. We were never allowed to talk back to our parents, we were only to listen and obey; I don't remember if I was ever included in the adult discussions of any kind, we were just children to my parents, even when I was nineteen years old and had graduated from high school. Being born a girl was not much help in the way of being included in the adult discussions.

No one ever talked about things like puberty or discussed anything about sex with me; it was a taboo topic, treated as somewhat dirty and degrading, even between friends. We were very naïve for our age being brought up in such a protected children's world not exposed yet to television or internet like now. At least I was in those years! The day when my period started, innocent and naïve as I was I thought I was going to die soon. Yet, I was hesitant to tell my grandmother about it because I was afraid to make her sad given we may not be able to afford to get help from a doctor. I was very scared of dying and worried sick for many hours and when my friend, Young Yi dropped in to see me I had to tell her. She rushed me with her to see her mother straight away as she also got scared that I might have a bad disease and I might die soon.

I still remember, like yesterday, how surprised we both were to see how unaffected Young Yi's mother was even though she heard all about our dreadful fears, yet her face had no sign of worries at all and she looked at us both with an affectionate smile. She calmed us down and in her soft motherly voice explained kindly to us all about what was happening with my body.

I was about thirteen years old then. Too young to comprehend what it was all about but what a relief it was to find out that I was not sick at all and not going to die soon.

I lost my mum when I was very little and grew up searching for a photo of my mum all my life because I wanted to remember her face. No one ever wanted to talk to me about why my mum drank bleach to kill herself when I was only four and my sister was barely one. That would have been 1954 not long after the Korean War ended (1950-1953), when the country was still very much in turmoil from the war.

Although I can't remember my mum's face I still have the agony of the faint memory of the day my mother killed herself.

My mother was then, I believe only 25, in extreme pain lying by the doorstep banging an empty aluminum bowl against the door frame to get someone's attention to get help for her burning throat and trying to put a word together for "I - C E D – W- A- T E R!" I was shocked and frightened to find mum in such a state, took the bowl off mum's hand and very scared ran down as fast as I could to a corner store down the hill near our place. Crying loudly with fear I tried to explain to the store keeper that "My Mum is-Very sick- and she Wants- some Ice". I do remember someone in the store had sensed the urgency and quickly put some ice in my bowl from the pile of large ice cubes spread thick on top of fresh fishes kept cool in the store, grabbed my hand and ran up the hill to our house as fast as we could run together.

My memory has been blocked right there since. I don't even remember who the person was that ran with me to my home or anything else that happened after. The shock has destroyed the rest of my memories of my mum as well; it wiped out my mum's face forever from my memory. I wanted to remember so badly but I still cannot remember my mum's face to this date! In the 1950s in Korea, I believe, the photos were taken only by a professional photographer with a studio camera looking like a big wooden box and it was very expensive to have photos taken. No one owned a camera of any kind at that time. Moreover if my family had any photos at all they could have been destroyed during the Korean War and if there were any photos of my mum since the War they would have been destroyed deliberately after my father got remarried.

Many years ago when I was still a child I had managed to find a photo which had been the official traditional formal wedding photo of my parents taken by an expensive photographer but it was only of my handsome looking young twenty-three year old father. Someone had deliberately cut my mother off. I still have that photo as I had brought it with me when I came to Australia and I get sad even now when I look at it in my album.

I remember also how different life was already by the time I went to junior-school in the 1960s; it became affordable for some families to have a camera of their own. Even though I never owned a camera during those years, I had managed to have some photos taken and I still have those photos from my junior-school days and onwards but there were only two photos from before my junior days. One is the wedding photo of my parents with my mum cut out and one with our grandma in our garden of marigold and sun flowers when I was about seven years old.

My parents were born and brought up in the midst of the years Japanese colonial rule reigned in Korea which started in 1910 and ended in 1945. Almost 36 LONG HORRIBLE Years! They were born in mid 1920s and had grown up under the Very Oppressive power and Ruthless <u>Japanese Colonial Rules</u>. They were never sent to school. They were not included in the privileged circle of people who had the chance to attend school. They had to learn by themselves to speak Japanese instead and learn whatever trade they could to survive in a VERY controlled and forced environment. They didn't have any freedom as Korean nationals in their own birth country. The painful stories I have heard from my father are too many. The scar on my father's face, made by a large burning hot nail was one of the painful reminders. I was the very first person in all of my father's side of the family to be educated at high-school and I knew how lucky I was and I studied very hard.

My stepmother passed away with cancer when I was fifteen years old. I was devastated loosing another mum. She was a warm and kind person and I still do remember my stepmother's face with loving memories which I hold close to my heart. Within a couple of years after she died my father remarried again, he was still young at thirty-nine years of age.

Yes, I had a dream, a simple dream, about becoming a good mother one day when I grow up, getting married to a good man and having lots of children and a loving home. Come to think of it now, given all my life growing up with envy of friends who had a normal family with their own parents, a dream to find a good man and be a good wife and mother was always in my thoughts.

But never had I imagined he would be a Foreigner who lived in a Far Away Land called Australia and So Soon!

I remember how my whole perspective on life took a SHARP turn! All of Sudden, I was put on a spot to think about Marrying Someone I was only beginning to know – a man I had not yet met who lived far away in another part of the world I hardly knew anything about. It was hard to contain all my emotions. But I couldn't mention it to anyone as it felt unreal, I was having huge issues myself to take in it all.

I had to think very carefully about everything what it meant to accept his proposal before I gave him the answer in my next letter. I needed help but I couldn't think of anyone who could guide me to a right direction in MY Interest not in their interest. Not even my family who probably would try to stop me to protect me from the dangers, most of all the danger of uncertainties. After a few days of serious thinking I figured out that no one would understand how I was feeling and what I wanted for my life better than myself, - it had to be MY OWN decision no one else's!

The decision was relatively easy to make when I came to think about, if I didn't go I would have to live the rest of my life wondering **WHAT IF** *I went…*

I may never be completely happy, no matter what were to happen in my life in the future. I knew then I had to go, even if I had to come back with nothing but the disappointments. If I didn't go I may regret the rest of my life and thinking **WHAT IF** *I went then…*

I wrote to him that although I was too young and was not thinking of marriage as yet, but then I must confess that all my thoughts were beginning to be consumed with the idea of becoming his wife. I think that I, maybe, was also falling in love with him. I wrote that I was somewhat stressed out but at the same time felt free as if I had found a set of Wings to Fly. Strangely enough, my intuition tells me that it was meant to happen and must have been already decided for us and ordained by the heaven's Almighty God! Because I know it couldn't have happened even if I had planned it and I was trying to look for a man like him to marry.

Our English was not perfect but we were communicating without much misunderstanding. In fact it was rather more exciting having the challenge of learning as we went.

Our letters became truly love letters, the love letters between two strangers yet to meet!

Every minute of the day he was in my thoughts and I felt emotions I didn't know existed! Knowing that I was in his thoughts was unbelievably wonderful!

To make it all happen we both had to trust our OWN feelings and follow our own hearts no matter how many people tried to discourage us. There were many who discouraged us. Even the Australian government officials had tried their best to discourage Rolf not to go ahead. He had to take a day off from work and drove 550 kilometres to have an interview with immigration government officials in Perth for my visa. Yet they kept him in the office all day deliberately, trying very hard to convince him not to go ahead.

They finally gave up when they realized he was so serious that he would not leave without the permit and would wait for it as long as it took, even though he had to drive back that late night 550 kilometres all the way to Kalgoorlie to work the next morning.

It wasn't easy for me either to get my passport. It took months to get it, after many interviews and checkups. I guess it was largely due to having constant issues to be cautious with North Korea. Moreover in those years anyone going to Australia with such case as mine was so very rare.

A short time after my graduation from high-school I was very lucky to find a couple of part time jobs. The first one was at a small firm for translating services. There I was able to learn how to translate Korean census registration and to put it into a right format in English as well as preparing documents for visas and passports. Those documents had to pass for notarization of a true translation of the original documents by the district public procurator's office in Seoul. I was so lucky because of this job I was able to prepare all the documents I needed by myself with much of help from the office and I didn't have to pay the expensive fees. The office staff was only too happy to help me in any way they could as they thought I was very special and were excited for me to have the chance to go to Australia to live.

I was very busy while I was preparing all the documents I needed, and I became busier when I was granted the visa and passport as there were too many other things to do, not only what I had to do but many things I wanted to do before I left.

First of all I knew I had to learn fast to speak English, although I could read and write English reasonably well my spoken English was very poor. Because we were taught only to read and write English by a Korean teacher at school and hardly had any practice at all in spoken English.

I knew someone who was working at the education centre in one of US military bases about 20 kilometres away from Seoul. I asked him for help to find an educated American soldier who worked at the centre, who might be interested in teaching me and a few of my friends spoken English, and in return we would show him around Seoul.

I was introduced to an educator at the center who hadn't been long in Korea and who was a graduate in literature from Washington-University and very interested in my ideas straight away as he wanted to learn to speak Korean from us. We soon became very good friends with him. His name was Lawrence, Lev in short. We got together whenever we could, as often as we could. I always made sure I was with a couple of my close friends whenever I had a chance to spend time with Lev and I made sure that we didn't put ourselves into a situation of being misunderstood or misled into other than teacher and pupil relationship. My first objective was to practice English conversation with him as much as we could.

Fortunately, Lev was a very intelligent young gentleman with a very good teaching ability and also was very cautious to remain as an English teacher to us and as a student learning Korean from us. Together we visited teashops, cafes, strawberry fields, and palace gardens. Sometimes we went to concerts in the city together and we were always busy talking and laughing. It was so much fun we couldn't wait until the next meeting. We didn't want to be looked down on by the public or our own family mistakenly as if we were prostitutes of American soldiers just because we were with an American in military uniform and I had to make sure we were extremely cautious of our behaviour. I had to insist no matter how heavy it might be; we needed to look as students and not the prostitutes and I made all of us carry a notebook and Korean-English dictionary as well as English-Korean dictionary in our arms not in a bag, whenever we were out about with Lev.

Only about three months prior to leaving the country I became very concerned about what am I going to do if all is well and I got married and have to live in Australia. I was thinking about the fact that I couldn't speak English well enough and worried about what sort of job prospects I would have, what would I do if I couldn't find a job.

I have always admired the portrait painter whose portrait work of the visiting international delegate was displayed in front of the city-hall as a welcome. I decided to find that well-known artist and learn from him if he would teach me to paint portraits like he could.

I thought it would be nice to be able to paint portraits and keep myself occupied whilst I needed to improve my English in Australia. He was a photo realist working on silk and had a studio in a quiet area of Seoul. At first he ridiculed me and didn't want to take me seriously when I told him that I wanted to be an artist like him but I had only 3 months to learn because I was leaving the country for Australia soon, - Australia of all countries, - he probably thought. He perceived me for a liar and told me to go away with a saying that to learn what he does would take at least a couple of years full time study.

Although he was too proud of himself and had not shown me any interest at all to teach me, I promised to myself that I would go back to him as soon as I had all my documents to show him and convince him that my reason was real, and how desperately I wanted to learn from him everything he cared to teach me in such a short time frame. When I went back to him with my passport he was very much surprised and reacted in amazement, he looked at the passport as if he never ever had seen a passport before let alone expected to see such a document from a young girl like me. It was only then he asked me to draw a portrait of President Johnson of America from a little black and white picture of the president which was cut off from a news magazine.

He was rather surprised to see that I did have some drawing skills and told me that I may come and learn in whatever time I had left. I was very grateful and went to learn from him as often as I could in the evenings. From his lessons of painting every eyelash of a person's face I have managed to train my eye seeing things in detail, which was a huge influence on painting the traditional realism style of paintings I do now.

YES, every step I have taken was like putting together a Jigsaw Puzzle, and amazingly, it did FIT all together in the end, and coming to Australia was the Ultimate Prize.

My family had been aware that I had a foreign pen friend in Australia and my English was improving by the letters and they were all happy for me and proud of me for that. But not to the extent that I was engaged to be married and that I was getting the documents ready to leave the country, as I was extremely cautious not to disclose any details prematurely to many people who loved me. Because I was worried they might stop me from going as they would worry about the danger of the uncertainties, and try to protect me especially my father who would never allow me to go, let alone let me marry a foreigner. I knew my father was always proud of me even though I am only a daughter not a son.

The day was getting closer for me to say good-byes and leave everyone I loved behind for the uncharted territory where the man of my dreams was waiting for me! I couldn't sleep or eat; troubled with mixed emotions for many days and nights very scared how I was going to break the news to my father. I had been very lucky to manage to organize everything without any of my parent's financial help because I was working a couple of part time jobs and I had some money left from the money Rolf sent me for my engagement ring. I had bought a cheap ring as I needed the money for getting ready to leave and Rolf paid for the airline ticket. The Australian dollar value was very high in those years, much higher than even American dollars, if my memory is correct, $1 AUS to $1.20 US, and 300 Korean Won to $1 US.

It was a week before I had to leave for Australia when I was sure there was absolutely no chance of anyone or anything stopping me that I felt safe enough to find the courage to face my father with the news. I waited until my father finished his breakfast and then I put down my passport with visa and the airline tickets in front of him where he was sitting down with his legs crossed interlocked on the floor to read the morning papers. He looked at me and he could sense that I was scared with some kind of guilt and wondered what all the documents were about. I calmly explained to him that I was leaving in a week for Australia to meet the pen-friend I had been writing to. Most importantly I assured him that my visa was only for three months which meant that I would come back within three months if I didn't like him or the place and the passport was the permission from our government for me to leave. I pointed to show him where the visa was stamped in my passport and in particular the validation and explained the others were my airline-tickets.

He was totally astounded listening to such unexpected news, his eyes were shock-ridden, didn't know how to react, he picked up the documents and put down the documents without even looking in or without saying a word he just remained seated like a statue just staring at me with a numb face, couldn't make up his mind to react in anger or in excitement for me and he got up and walked outside for a few minutes. I never ever saw my father in such a helpless state before. In a few minutes he came back inside the room with a lit cigarette in his mouth to where I was still sitting in the same spot, Guilty as Charged, waiting for his verdict and he stood right next to me and looked down at me and said in his calmest voice, "That means it is already too late for me to stop you or anything else in that matter, I guess" he sighed and murmured as if he was talking to himself.

I responded very quietly but quickly in a guilty voice "Yes, dad" didn't dare to look up at him.

But how relieved I was to hear that from my father!

I don't care to remember what else he said that day because I heard what I needed to hear and I was set free to go! I remember very well how I was profoundly grateful to my father for letting me go and I Thanked God!

I processed in my mind that what I heard my father say was "I am very shocked with the news but you have my permission to go." I was so very relieved and happy that I actually got my father's permission. My stepmother was aware of what was going on with those letters from Australia more than she showed but she must have preferred for me to leave. She kept her suspicions to herself which was luckily in my favour. Soon after my first-stepmother died my father moved his business from Itaewon to Norangjin, further away from home to the other side of the river, to get more of the road exposure and to expand his business.

Our father lived away from us to be at the business premise 24/7 with his new wife. We were still with our grandma at Itaewon until about the time my new stepmother was ready to give birth to our little brother. Even then I was the only one who was told by my father to move down and live with them and help out our new step mother who was pregnant, perhaps more so to keep his eye on me as he was aware that I was at that age attractive to boys. My younger sisters moved in with us about a year later whilst our grandmother remained in our Itaewon home living with our younger aunt who was engaged to be married.

Our new-stepmother was a young and modern person from the southern province, spoke dialect with an accent and her way of doing things was not the same as how we did them in Seoul and my father was protecting her from my grandmother's old ways and decided to live in a different place. The relationship I had with the stepmother was more like friends not mother and daughter. Age old Korean tradition of living together with mother-in-law had brought a lot of unhappiness for many families but very fortunately it was beginning to change slowly in favour of the young people.

We had a wonderful grandma but she was not an easy mother-in-law to live with, given she had endured many Wars and the Long and very

Oppressive Years of the Japanese Colonial Rules. Her beliefs and values were very different to younger generations. I have witnessed too many problems growing up in that environment I didn't want to end up in such a predicament marrying into a family and have to live with a mother-in-law. It is fair to say that it was one of the reasons that encouraged me to leave when I had the chance and explore a different world!

CHAPTER THREE

One very cold winter morning in February 1970 whilst it was just another day for most people it was a very special day for me and my family and close friends.

Despite the cold morning many relatives started to arrive early to send me off at the Kimpo International Airport that day. As the hour passed by my feelings were turning numb, indeed I didn't know what I was supposed to feel on such a day.

Seemingly my father had accepted the situation and was in peace with himself. He looked proud that his daughter was going overseas in a big plane. He was pleased with himself that he was able to organise a mini bus and a car through his business connections to transport all our family, relatives and my friends who wanted to go with us to the airport to see me off. It was a very first time for all to go to the airport as there had been no reason for anyone to go there before. I was the first one ever of family and all the people we were close to go overseas in an aeroplane.

The Kimpo International airport was about 20 minutes by car from where we lived in Norangjin. As soon as we walked inside the airport the atmosphere in there was so different to anywhere else I had ever been before and I felt a huge stress lift off my shoulder knowing that I was leaving with the support from my family and friends and most importantly with the loving support of my father.

Something significant that I will always remember, what my father said to me at the airport, "If I only knew earlier that you are going to Australia I would have taught you to drive a car." seeing his eyes filled with love I was overwhelmed.

It made me emotional, responding in tears "Thank you father and I am Indebted to you for all you have done already for me and I am Very Sorry being stubborn, but I will be back to see you As Soon As I can".

Until that very moment I never had expected my father would talk to me like I was an adult. It was indeed a significant moment of a validation from my father that I was an adult after all, not a child anymore and I will treasure not only what he said but how he said it for the rest of my life.

Those years in Korea the only people who had the licence to drive were the occupational drivers, you had to be rich to own a car of your own and if you were rich enough to own your car you could afford to employ a driver. I had never seen or heard of any of my friends who had the licence to drive a car, even friends from a wealthy family thus the thought of obtaining the drivers' licence was not on the radar of our thoughts. It was totally unexpected to hear someone would like to teach me to drive a car let alone my father.

The last few minutes before I boarded the plane the emotion got so over whelming, especially seeing my full sister, Kyung Hee crying uncontrollably and walked away from the airport without even saying goodbye. Even though with all my heart I empathized with her sorrow and felt like I was abandoning her ….I had to go…..leave everyone I love behind….for the ONE I love far away.

I walked away bravely toward the departure gate with a smile and hands waving Good-Bye, the reality has not yet sunk in and there were No tears.

I walked inside of the big airplane of Cathay-Pacific airline with an equally big curiosity as to what it would be like to have a ride in a plane and found my seat. The atmosphere inside the plane was a little airy to start sitting amongst total strangers and closed in. I looked out the window, questions flooded in my mind as I thought about for the very first time that I was there all alone disconnected from all my family and friends outside. What was I doing? Was I making the biggest mistake of my life leaving all those people who cared for me? What is going to happen to me from here on? All of sudden I was getting stressed out with the fear of not knowing the fate of my future! At last I have a Touchdown of Reality, and facing the facts so to speak!

The plane is starting to make loud noises getting ready to take off. My heart started to churn as the wheels starting to move, my tears started running down my face as if I was waiting for that very moment and pouring down as fast as the wheels on the runway as though a flood gate forced itself open. I couldn't stop my tears until I was too exhausted to think about it anymore and fell asleep. I woke up with puffy eyes and a big headache many hours later when the plane was making the changes to descend toward the Hong Kong airport. Stepping out of the plane for the very first time into a foreign land, I first noticed the big change of the outside temperature to the cold temperature in Seoul. It was very warm and humid, thinking that I was REALLY FAR AWAY from home and all alone. I followed the fellow passengers and through airport check in and found the guide who was holding up a board with my name written on it and I followed him out of the airport to a bus.

Thousands of different neon lights were lit up welcoming me in its brightest form and the place was busy with people and cars, it was identical to the beautiful city of Seoul at night yet an unfamiliar place and I didn't know anyone and no one knew that I was coming. I was all by myself, I felt Brave and I felt Helpless all at same time.

The bus stopped at the front of the grand looking hotel, the Park International Hotel in Kowloon where I was booked for one night. My next flight to Darwin in Australia was late at night next day. I have managed with my poor spoken English to check in the hotel without any help and I felt proud. I followed the porter dressed in a smart uniform who carried my suitcase and a makeup case to my room. I felt GREAT! I felt rich for a moment in fact as Rich as a Movie Star or a Millionaire! As soon as I entered my room which was on the fourth-floor, I locked the door and made sure it was well locked again. I checked the windows also to ensure they were locked, remembering what my grandma taught us, *"giving others the temptation or the reason to harm you is a greater sin than the sin of offenders, and prevention is far better than the cure."*

I walked around the room inside and thinking what a beautiful place to sleep, there was a large bed in the room which looked too big for one person to sleep on, and rather intimidating. It was going to be the very First Time in my life to sleep on a Bed. I was brought up all my life sleeping on a bed made each night with quilts on the floor, and most of the time slept with my little sisters.

I stood by the window gazing out at the neon lit big city outside spread out before my eyes glittering like a huge jewellery store. It was a sublime moment. I stood there all alone lost in thoughts, in utter fear of not knowing what the future will hold for me, tears running down my face. I was contemplating all that had happened to bring me to that very moment.

I had a long hot bath in the luxurious bath room and tried to forget and wash away all my worries. I never before had such bathroom to myself in my entire life, that being said we never had a bathroom in our place, we washed ourselves with a container of water every day and every now and then we did go to a public bath house nearby where there were separate wash houses for females and males. The place had many taps; we had a wash first before going into a huge hot tub together to relax. I have a lot of fun memories going there with my sisters, mum, grandma or aunties and I will never forget how light I felt as we walked home. It felt so light as if I was walking on a floating cloud and my body was so warm the freezing temperature outside didn't worry me at all.

I crawled onto the bed and laid myself down Right in the Middle of the bed with the hope that I would not fall off the bed while I was sleeping. Tried to bring some sleep but couldn't relax so I switched on the little bed side light again and staring at the ceiling wide awake thinking of each face of my family one by one and I was already missing everyone so terribly. It's been a mere half day since I left them but it felt like years! I couldn't help but wonder, would I ever see them again especially my dear old grandma, the thoughts made me very sad and I began to weep again. I prayed that everyone would stay well and wait for me until I return. I fell asleep mentally exhausted with the chain of thoughts filled my head. When I woke up in the morning I was relieved to find myself STILL on the bed and not on the floor and injured.

There was plenty of time before my next flight and as I didn't need to get picked up by the guide until late that evening. I got dressed up in my favorite dress, the knee high well cut red one piece polyester dress with a collar and a black tie, my long shiny black hair brushed down and put on my pretty red high-heels and went out for a walk to look around. I felt great all dressed up in a made to measure dress and shoes. In Seoul late

1960s, there were a lot of small boutiques with good dress makers, where you could get your dress made to measure with the fabric and the design of your choice and also shoe makers where you can get your shoes made to measure and there weren't many pre-made dresses or shoes in the stores to choose from if you wanted something really nice.

Most housewives could sew the basics and we were used to the clothes passed down from family and we didn't need a lot of new clothes or shoes to be happy. But Seoul being the large capital city, we were accustomed to live the life style of a city, it may be only one good outfit or pair of shoes to wear to go out but we have to dress up to go out as well as we could afford because looking our best was necessary living in a highly competitive society of a very heavily populated city.

It was still early morning when I got out of the hotel. It was not too warm for what I was wearing and just right. Soon I arrived at a small open street market place; no one seemed to notice me as a foreigner as I didn't look any different to the majority of the people there. I was just one of them until I wanted to buy something from a stall; the vendor was talking away to me in Chinese as she would to any other locals interested in buying things from her stall. I asked for a price in English that's when she realized I wasn't a local and looked at me with curiosity and asked me if I was Japanese. I replied that I was a Korean she looked at me rather puzzled that I was a Korean not Japanese, and made me think that she had not seen many tourists from Korea.

I managed to buy a set of eight embroidered cotton table placemats and a matching table cloth as well as a beautiful folding hand fan made with a thin sandal wood. I liked it as it had a good smell and I liked the delicate patterns carved on it. I was even able to bargain the prices as I could at the markets in Seoul which made me feel so proud. The vendor was very quick at working out the conversion from Hong Kong dollars to American dollars, but so was I. I also bought from another vendor an elegant white blouse with a stand up collar in Chinese style made with fine cotton.

I was getting hungry, given I had nothing to eat since the meal I had in the plane the night before. I asked around if there was a Korean restaurant nearby. I walked away from the noisy vendors and walked toward the direction where I was told I would find a Korean restaurant that had authentic Korean wooden doors. I walked passed often tall and large people with light coloured hair and big nose. Breathing the same air as those people from all over the world made me feel good and more confident. I was happy when I arrived at the place with authentic Korean wooden doors. I got hungrier thinking about Korean food I was going to have very soon, *kimchi* and rice was all I needed. As soon as I walked in a lady smartly dressed in Korean traditional dress greeted me and asked me if I was a Korean, it was so great to say in Korean "Yes, I am from Seoul." It felt like it's been years since I spoke Korean with someone else who could. I ordered the delicious marinated BBQ beef called *Bul-go-gi* with *kimchi* and steamed rice. Not only did I enjoy the delicious food but I enjoyed the lovely conversation I shared with a couple of people while I was there. I left the restaurant with the pleasant experience. The early afternoon sun was warm and my feet were starting to ache so I walked back slowly to my hotel. Even though I was reasonably used to walking on heels, they were brand new shoes not yet broken in and it had been many hours on my heels. I was very relieved when I finally arrived back at the hotel in my air conditioned comfy room and could take the high heels off and rest.

I hopped on the bed right in the middle again lying down fully dressed feeling very satisfied about the pleasant day I had and had a good rest. After I got up, there was still enough time left, so I freshened myself up and went back to the Korean restaurant for more chat and company. I was welcomed back by the lady I met earlier and I was introduced to a lady who was having a cup of tea by herself, she was an air hostess of Qantas airline and she was very interested about how I got to go to Australia and I was very interested in her experiences as an air hostess who flew all over the world.

It was in between lunch and dinner, there were only three of us in the restaurant and we were so into the conversation as if we had been friends for a long time. We exchanged some contact details and I left first to get back to my hotel to get ready for my next flight to Darwin, Australia. I felt another boost of confidence having had such a satisfying day, very unlike the night before; I didn't feel any fears on the day. Things were only starting to look up and a little more clear. I slept most of the night flight to Darwin by Qantas airline feeling calm and relaxed.

Arriving early next morning at the Darwin international airport in Australia as the plane descending through the mysterious clouds toward the airport my heart was churning in a whirlpool of curiosities. I will be flying out again in a few hours to Perth nevertheless it was such an exciting moment to arrive actually at a city in Australia. The plane was on the end of the tarmac and the first thing that caught my eyes was the very unusual uniform the airport attendants on the ground were wearing and they looked Ever So Odd! They were wearing a khaki coloured uniform, short sleeved shirt with a necktie, shorts with long socks and sandals. I never ever have seen anyone wear a necktie with such strange outfits. I was only used to seeing people wear a necktie with a tailored suit or on a shirt tucked in a long pair of trousers and closed-in shoes never with open sandals. I knew then I was for sure in a somewhere strange foreign land FAR AWAY from home!

The second I stepped outside of the plane the hot and humid air almost choked my air-ways. It was hard to breathe, walking into the airport building expecting a relief from the heat outside and much cooler inside but only to find out it wasn't much different inside. A huge floor standing fan was pointlessly working very hard blowing the hot air around and the queue for the custom check-in was very long and very slow. In no time the taffeta lining of my polyester dress was saturated in sweat sticking onto my skin and made me unbearably uncomfortable.

The standard of Darwin international airport was very primitive; certainly nothing like the standard of the other two international airports I had been to as neither Kimpo airport in Korea or Hong Kong airport was that primitive. I couldn't help but wonder if I had arrived at the right place. Added to my disappointment, was the terrible realization that I had to stay there at such an uncomfortable place for many hours until my next flight to Perth. I bought a glass of iced orange juice to quench my thirst and found a seat in a lounge room to cool down and then thought about what I had to do next - rationally.

I had the plan to change into a Korean traditional costume at the Darwin airport given it is the last stop before I met Rolf at the Perth airport as I thought it would be the best outfit to stand out in the crowd and to be noticed quickly by Rolf. But it was a daunting task not only because there was no cool room to get refreshed and changed but also I knew how uncomfortable and hot the costume would be to wear in such a hot place. The costume was made of thin layers of see through fabrics thus I had to wear two layers of long sleeved tops over two layers of fully gathered long skirts with a pair of long baggy pants under them as well as wearing normal underwear. Nevertheless I must follow my plan and I must get changed. It was imperative for me to stand out in the crowd and easy to be found by Rolf at Perth. Perth airport would be very crowded with lots of people and there would be other Asian young girls like me and may confuse Rolf, - I thought.

I got changed in the public ladies room with lots of difficulties pinned my long hair up as well to be cooler. I came back out to the waiting room to dare to look one of its kind, looking very authentic Korean in such a place. Stand out is an understatement! Sat myself right down on the tiled floor against a wall, not on a chair because I worked it out that tiled floor would be much cooler to sit on. Yes, I was desperate to cool down! As I expected, many people did stare at me. They may never have seen such a beautiful and colourful costume or maybe they were amused seeing a person in such an improper outfit in hot weather, or they may be gossiping seeing a young girl dressed in such a way sitting on the floor not on the proper seat in the airport lounge room. But that was all OK for me I couldn't care less what other people thought about me. I had to do what I had to do to survive and the only thing that mattered to me was that I was well prepared to be found quickly by Rolf at the next airport. I was very relieved when I finally board on MMA (Mac Robertson Miller Airlines), my last flight to meet him, which was a small domestic airline.

I heard the announcement that we would be arriving shortly at Perth airport. My heart was racing like crazy and my eyes were glued to the window, this time my eyes were only looking out for him, nothing was more important than to spot him in the crowd.

Before the plane was at the end of the Tarmac I spotted a man on a balcony who had the camera set up on a tripod and standing by it all alone and staring only my way.

That's HIM! There He Is!

It was as if someone had drawn a straight line with a ruler from my eyes to his.

I didn't expect to find him so easily and so quickly and what's more the airport was not at all crowded as I had imagined.

My heart was racing with the joy of spotting him and I exhaled a huge sigh of relief! I felt so ridiculous the way I was dressed and how unnecessary it was.

Stepping out in scorching mid afternoon 40 degree heat in such a costume, long sleeved white top over a red long skirt with lots of white roses embroidered on it. I was hoping such a colourful and beautiful Korean costume would catch his eyes straightaway and I looked up his way. Sure enough the second I stepped out I saw him waving both his arms in the air and looking toward me but I couldn't wave back because in one hand I was carrying a beauty case and the other hand was holding the bag of my clothes I had changed from so as I walked on I kept on looking in his direction. I could almost hear his camera clicking away for every step I made. I felt happy! Although the sweat was pouring down my face, with the extreme heat almost choking my breath, everything was all good since I was sure, that he was there waiting for me.

As soon as I came out to the arrival lounge Rolf was waiting right there for me and we hugged and kissed. When our eyes met and locked Hard on each other's for the Very First Time, the way he looked at me with his big blue eyes I Felt Such a Strong Force of Magnetic Pull Right Through My Heart, as if all of me got just Vacuum Sucked into his big blue eyes, and all the way to His Heart and Soul! I felt such a relief and felt very safe in his arms as if I had been lost for a very long time and finally re-united with the man I was searching for. But the strange thing was that I never had been lost nor was looking for a safe place.

How I felt then was that strong it's got complete hold of me for all those years!

Forty-four years on even now I am feeling it! It is the feeling, strong enough to carry me through all those lonely times I had endured and any other difficult challenges I have had and I only hope it will be with me till the time I am no longer able to think.

I don't remember much about the conversations we shared on that day, he spoke too fast and he had a strong Swedish accent I never heard of, it surely was not like the American accent I was mostly used to. And of course, I was rather preoccupied with my own thoughts since I finally met him.

I had the answers to myself, the definite assurances to spend the rest of my life with him.

When he asked me if I would like to look around Perth city before we head off for Kalgoorlie, I remember saying to him "No, I just want to go home." Not comprehending the distance is almost 600 kilometres away. He loaded all my things into his little old Mitsubishi colt four-cylinder sedan and we headed off home. It was wonderful to sit in his car! He drove and drove for hours, large flocks of sheep grazing peacefully in the vast land and I was very excited when I first spotted a few kangaroos hopping rather strangely in the distance and we saw also some emus but I was somewhat surprised there weren't as many kangaroos around as I had imagined.

We drove past a lot of farming lands of wheat fields but the peaceful scenery was spoiled badly by the bad odours of lots of road kills, dead emus, kangaroos, cattle, sheep and more on the road, the decomposing odours of the road kills under the hot sun was so intense and unbearable we had to hold our breath and hold our nose tight while we drove past them with the car windows down. Cars didn't have the air conditioner in those years. Having been brought up in a big city, I had not seen many live animals let alone so many dead ones. It was unbelievable and sad.

I felt tired from the jetlag and given the huge stress was lifted off my head; my body was starting to relax. As the darkness fell I too fell into a deep sleep. It was almost eleven o'clock at night when Rolf woke me up as we were getting closer to Kalgoorlie. I couldn't believe how long we had been travelling to get to his home from the airport. I learned a few days later that the distance we had travelled that day was a longer distance than from the top end to the bottom end of South Korea.

I was wide awake by the time we arrived at the township of Kalgoorlie. I could see here and there where the street lights were shining; to my surprise what I saw was not what I had imagined of a place in Australia. There were many old corrugated iron fences around what seemed very old houses and there was no living soul on the street and it was dead quiet as if no one was alive anywhere.

Rolf parked the car at the side of a dark street and helped me out of the car. I was startled when I heard an old man's voice that came from nowhere. It was so dark I could hardly see him but someone wanted to shake my hand. He seemed to know Rolf well and had been waiting and was very pleased to meet me. His voice was thick and loud and his English was even harder to understand what he was saying except that his name was Bill Baker. Bill followed us in and didn't leave for a long time. I learned next day that Bill is an Australian born and in his 60s and lived alone in the flat right beside us and he is a winder driver at one of the gold mines.

The three of us all sat by a small table in the kitchen, while the two men were busy talking and laughing and the only thing I could do was look around whilst I was sitting with them at the table. The place was very old and tacky, just the basics at the most of living conditions. There was a small portable gas stove sitting on what could be an old wood stove but looked as if it hadn't been used for a while. On the shelf above it many of the large sauce bottles looked covered in dust and lost their true colours. They too looked like they hadn't been used at all for some time. The simple curtain on the small window by the table where we were sitting just inside the door where we came in was a vinyl curtain and had a few cigarette burn holes and felt greasy.

The old wooden floor had gaps big enough to lose a pen if I were to drop one. I could see a part of an old wooden dressing table with a large mirror and some shelves just inside the bedroom where the kitchen light managed to reach. I walked in there to find out what was on those shelves and I was delightfully surprised and it brought tears to my eyes to see the display of photos of me, all the ones I had sent to him. There was a high wooden bed in the middle of the room its legs were high enough that I could see a couple of pairs of his shoes under it and one side of the bed there was a pair of wooden cabinets matching the dressing table.

The other doorway from the kitchen was to the living-room. In there was a set of homemade metal shelves with a small LP-player with radio built in it and small speakers on either side of it and some other things like books and records on the shelf. And there was an old worn out fabric bench lounge covered mostly with an old blanket. In a small space behind the lounge room was a free standing old bath tub with the taps on the wall above the tub and above it there was a small unit of a gas heater. I knew he had been in Australia for only three years and he was not a rich person but I didn't imagine his living condition would be like what I saw then; I expected the living standard in Australia would be somewhat a little more luxurious than what I was used to.

I was more surprised than disappointed and I told myself that it shouldn't be any matter as I got there safe and I was with him at last. I made up my mind that I would do my best looking after him and make him happier.

With that, the new chapter of my life had begun at a place called Kalgoorlie in Western Australia, Far, Far away from my families and friends, - AGAINST all ODDS!

CHAPTER FOUR

The temperature next day went up to 43 degrees Celsius, Fahrenheit 110 degrees! The inside temperature was not any cooler than the outside and nowhere to escape to cool down, - the heat was so unbearable! 34 degrees in Celsius would have been the hottest summer day for us in Seoul and moreover merely three days prior, I was living in the cold winter temperature of February in Seoul.

Rolf drove away early Monday morning to start work at 8.00am, and until he returned home after 5.00pm, those were much too long hours to have no one to talk with. There was a little church across the road from our flat but most days except Sundays no one was coming or going there and the streets were very quiet with very little traffic even though it was only walking distance to the main street. The hardest thing still was to cope with the LONELINESS. I stood by the window and cried for hours gazing out to the totally unfamiliar environment missing family and friends beyond measure, wondering when I would see them again. Thinking of everyone's face and the good times we had shared together, not only did I miss the people but I was hungry for the food I used to have.

I played my LPs of pop songs I brought with me, and singing along to them one by one, missing home I sobbed badly. Sometimes I heard my own sobs had got louder than the volume on the speakers. Thank God, I brought those records with me they were my salvation and the only things that were familiar to me in the entire new world I landed myself in.

I was allowed by the airline, to bring only 20 kilograms with me in my suitcase to Australia, how very wise I was to opt to bring all my records of pop songs and a set of classical music I had. By the time I filled my suitcase with all the records I had and some note books, a small photo album, some of my embroidery works from school days, a set of traditional red lacquered flower vases, a box of oil paints, it was already so heavy, I could only bring one traditional costume for me and one pair for him and three pairs of new tailor made outfits and two pairs of shoes. How silly was I thinking then that any comfy clothes or shoes other than tailor made would be not good enough to wear in Australia?

I dressed up in my tailor made fully lined outfit walking on high heels to town with my long and thick hair down saturated in sweat; people on the streets stopped and stared at me in amazement. Gave me the look that they had never seen anything like me before and they probably were wondering what I was doing at a place like Kalgoorlie dressed like that? Although I have seen a small Chinese restaurant in town I never have seen any Asian persons on the street.

It was so obvious of the effect of so-called "White Australia Policy". Most of the people who lived there those years were the senior age group of Anglo Saxon back ground-white Australian people who probably were born there and had lived there all their lives. The majority of the employees in the stores or offices were made up by those elderly white people who seem to have been in the same job most of their working lives. They looked at me with the very reserved look of *"what are you doing here?",* when I entered the places.

A young Asian girl like me was indeed very rare to see there and my overly well dressed look created strange reactions more often than I was comfortable with. It made me feel really out of place in many ways and didn't fit in their close-knit community! One day Rolf suggested to me to cut off all the taffeta linings of my outfits to make them cooler to wear and it was good that I took his advice. They were much cooler to wear without the lining sticking onto my skin saturated in perspiration.

We didn't have a phone in our flat; neither did anyone I knew have a phone in those years and I was completely isolated, hardly had anyone but Rolf to talk to. But seeing Rolf very exhausted came home from the hard day's work in such harsh environment, covered in dirt and saturated in sweat was enough to know that I was not the only one having a hard time to adjust, and I tried to focus my energy to learn to speak English fast and adjust as quickly as possible for both of us.

But not without obstacles, letters from different Asian girls seeking to be a pen-friend with Rolf kept on arriving at our mail box even after I had arrived. Rolf explained to me that originally he gave his address and personal details to "Australian Post", the weekly publication magazine, after he read an ad about pen-pal in the magazine, to find pen friends. It was soon after he had moved to Kalgoorlie in 1968 and he was very lonely. He had no control over where his details were exposed. He believed it was exposed all over Asia at the same time as it was in Korea and he was happy to agree with me to destroy them unopened as he no longer needed another pen-friend. And I was very pleased when finally the letters stopped coming.

I tried to get some silk and other materials I needed to paint portraits but it was very difficult to find the right things not only because of my poor spoken English not being able to explain about them properly but also because of where I lived, a place like Kalgoorlie. I wasn't able to find the pure white silk I needed for the support for my portrait painting so I tried on the white taffeta instead. But the ability of the taffeta to absorb the oil was not as good as the silk thus it leaked the excess oil no matter how little I used to paint with. Nonetheless I continued to paint on taffeta and practiced painting the faces of the covers of TV magazines to keep myself occupied.

We decided to hire a television, a black and white one, no colour TV back then. Our family in Korea never had a TV when I was in Korea so I was very excited to have TV at home. But everyone on TV spoke much too fast for me and the Australian accent was not easy to understand moreover most thing broadcast on TV in the day time those years in Kalgoorlie was horse-racing or trotting, which was even worse, in fact I couldn't understand a single word they were saying and it was just boring. Listening to the music was the best thing I could do and as the records played on and filled the place with the familiar tunes I felt at home a little more day by day.

At the beginning even cooking simple things such as steamed rice was difficult. The only way I knew how to cook steamed rice was not possible. Because the specially designed pot we had in Korea in those years with a heavy bottom and heavy lid to cook rice in the absorption-method was nowhere to be found in Kalgoorlie. I didn't know how to steam rice with an ordinary pot with thin bottom with a thin lid, the ones Rolf had. I was told that everyone just boiled rice in lots of water in such pots and drained the water out and no one seemed to have ever heard about steamed rice in the absorption-method like we did in Korea.

I tasted such boiled rice but I didn't like it, the taste was not right to me and it was very important to me to find the way to steam rice the way we did back in Korea as steamed rice was something I wanted to eat every day. How easy and wonderful it would have been if there had been an electric rice cooker like we have nowadays! I tried to steam rice by just adjusting the heat in different stages of the gas stove while it was cooking but many times it turned out the bottom was too burnt to eat, middle was almost edible and top was still raw.

It took days but in the end I worked it out how to steam the rice in absorption-method in such a pot. Lift the pot up about 2 centimetres from the flame once it reached rapidly boiling point and turn the heat right down to the simmer and with a heavy rock placed on top of the lid to keep the lid down to air tight for about 20 minutes until all the water in the pot was absorbed. After many tries I got it perfectly right and I was able to enjoy the properly steamed rice again.

But, soon enough I found out that Rolf had grown up with potatoes instead of rice and wished for potatoes as much as I for rice and whilst I was missing the hot and spicy food with steamed rice or soft boiled noodles, he was hungry for bland food prepared in butter and milk with herbs and served with potatoes or hard crunch bread. He preferred hard crunchy textures and I for the soft textures and he was grown up with dairy food whilst I never ever had a glass of fresh milk growing up. Moreover Rolf never ever had eaten garlic or chili in his life he just couldn't handle the hot and spicy food that I so enjoy.

How terrible to realize that yet it was another hurdle to overcome. A monumental problem at that indeed! Given we have to deal with it every meal time of every day of our lives.

I remember how nauseous and sick I felt just by seeing Rolf eating rice with milk and sugar. Hurdle is an understatement indeed we had some life changing tasks in our hands, and it was only the beginning of the discovery of not only how different appetites we have but also how very different we were as people in every way. The good communication skill was paramount and to be able to communicate better not only did we have to improve our English fast but we also realized that we had to start to learn everything from scratch like a new born baby, if you will. But we were obviously not babies and we were already used to eat certain things and set in certain habits, it was much harder to change because our preferences for certain foods and tastes were so strong. And neither of us was any good at cooking to make the transition smooth.

All meals and the rent was provided for Rolf by the company he was working for thus he was lucky that he didn't have to cook at all at home only after I came to live with him he was having meals at home. I was so hungry for *kimchi*, I wanted to buy the ingredients and try to have a go at making it myself and I went shopping to look for the ingredients many times. But there was nowhere I could find things like Chinese cabbage or the particular ground chili powder I need for *kimchi* and only the cabbage anyone knew about in those years in Kalgoorlie was the white cabbage. Even the fruit and vegetable shop keepers didn't know what I was talking about, and fresh garlic and ginger were hard to find. In those years most Australians were brought up by a simple diet, meat and three vegetables, which was mostly boiled or baked. The variety of food was very limited especially at a place like Kalgoorlie; too dry a place to grow anything in commercial quantities and too far away from the growers.

Many difficult challenges we had faced at the beginning of our life together was at the very basic and fundamental level such as eating and talking and I must add the challenges were beyond measure.

One day I heard a very loud and strange dialogue going on right outside of our flat and I could smell an equally strange strong unpleasant odour I have never experienced creeping inside through the gaps of the wooden floor and opened louvre windows. I looked out of the window and I saw a group of indigenous people drunk and lying down right outside our flat and I got very scared as to what they might do to me if they saw me inside. I locked the doors and kept my eyes on them the whole time while they were outside, I couldn't even walk around much inside of my own place because the floor creaked at many places. There were a lot of Australian pure indigenous people living around Kalgoorlie, the race of people I hadn't heard much about until I came to Australia. I saw them mostly naked and intoxicated at any time of the day and staggering in town or sleeping under a tree just like the dogs they had with them. Sometimes little children were with them as well; their life style was hard to comprehend for me and their look was somewhat scary to me.

Rolf was working as a maintenance fitter for a diamond drilling company called Associated Diamond Drillers (ADD) an exploration drilling company contracting for various mining companies, and was drilling mostly for gold or nickel around north of Kalgoorlie in places like Menzies, Leonora, Agnew, Sandstone and further north Meekatharra. He had to go to all those places whenever something was broken down on the drilling rigs. He could be away in the middle of nowhere in a very harsh environment for days and sometimes weeks until he repaired the problems and came home. I was very scared and lonely when he was away and left alone at home at night but I had to remind myself how horrible it would be for Rolf to be doing what he was doing in such hard conditions far away from home. I had to learn to cope just as he had to and started to go with him instead of being left alone at home.

Rolf had three close friends, Carl, Jim and Henry. Carl was the friend Rolf came to Australia with from Sweden and Jim was another Swedish friend Rolf met in Kalgoorlie and Henry was a German friend whom he had met in Victoria. They were all single men working together for the same company and we spent time together often in the weekends when they were in town and not working. And they were the only guests for our wedding day!

Our wedding was a mere registration at the Kalgoorlie Regional Registry Office, followed by a simple but formal exchange of marriage vows witnessed by a few strange onlookers and those three friends, and there were absolutely no relatives from either side of our family. We were too far away from everyone and didn't even have a phone to receive the calls on such a day.

Rolf was wearing a hired black suit and I was in my favorite red dress with a black tie. His hair was cut very short and my long hair was clipped back ear to ear with a long hair clip and brushed down. No one will ever guess when they see the photograph, that it was our wedding photo! Nonetheless it was one and the only photo of our wedding day! I saw a cuddly blue and white toy teddy bear and a little cute brown toy koala bear sitting together on the window sill of a toyshop as we were walking past it on the way to the photo studio where our wedding photo was to be taken. Rolf noticed that I was admiring them and asked me if I wanted to have them. I nodded my head with a big smile like a child. I was feeling the emptiness not having my family around and their blessings on such a day. Nevertheless I felt a little better cuddling them tight in my arms and I saw in Rolf's eyes that he was pleased for me.

After the photo was taken we met again with his all three friends at one of the local hotels best known as a good steak house called Palace Hotel, where our grand wedding reception table for five was reserved! It was the very first time in my life I was about to have a steak. I was not brought up eating much meat, let alone a big steak to myself.

We were brought up with lots of vegetables either pickled or fresh as a salad with rice and more fish than meat of any kind and meat dishes were prepared meat in small pieces or well cooked in a broth not a big piece like a steak.

The waiter asked me how I would like my steak done, given I didn't have any idea what was the meaning of the question; I probably just nodded my head to get by. When the meals were served I couldn't believe what I saw on my plate and I shut my eyes in shock! A huge thick rump steak hung over the plate it was served on and bleeding pure red blood into a heap of fried chips! Visually it made me nauseous. I tried not to look at the plate Ever Again and concentrated to try to compose myself as if nothing was wrong. When Rolf asked me why I wasn't eating my meal I told him that I was not hungry.

Of course it was a big lie but he believed me. I have told Rolf the next day how hungry I was in truth, but it was easier to pretend that I was not hungry than trying to complain how unsightly it was, in front of his friends, I couldn't even look at it let alone eat it. Rolf was genuinely surprised to hear that and told me he was sorry he didn't think that far and he could have ordered another meal for me had he only have guessed the truth.

Every time I see a rare steak sitting on a pool of blood reminds me of the dinner of my wedding day how hungry I was on the day of all days on my wedding day!

Kalgoorlie goldfields had a rich history of gold mining for over 70 years. About 9 kilometres to the east, there was another gold mining township called Boulder. Between the two townships there were many pubs that I lost count and there was ongoing competition between the pubs for the coldest beer. Beer drinking culture was very strong and it was a way of life in the goldfields. Most workers rushed to a pub for cold beers as soon as they knocked off work before they went home, whilst their wives patiently waited at home with cooked dinner for them.

Rolf heard from local people, that in those years, when hardly anyone had a refrigerator at home and the hotels closed the business early at 6.00pm, the men had to rush to hotels before they were closed, to have a few cold beers after work. Even though in later years the pubs started to close a lot later at 10.00pm and most homes had a refrigerator to cool their own beer the tradition stayed on. Rolf only stopped going to pubs after I arrived and came straight home to me as soon as he finished his work. A couple of times we went out for a pub crawl together with friends for fun and they intended to have just one quick drink at each pub, but we could never visit all the pubs in one night because there were too many, nevertheless it wasn't bad fun trying.

Often in the weekends we went fossicking around gold fields, I didn't enjoy it at the beginning any outdoor activity in such harsh environment was not easy for me to adjust. I didn't have much knowledge about minerals and didn't know where to look for then but I got more and more interested in it as I read books Rolf had about them. Once we were very lucky and we discovered a small area had milk opals not far from Coolgardie, 44 kilometres south west of Kalgoorlie. It was great! A huge achievement! Another time we had sifted out from a pan a couple of gold pieces just big enough to identify them, on the edge of a dry creek bed, however small may they be, I too was then bitten by the gold bug like Rolf was. Over the weeks and months we didn't find any more gold or opals but we ended up collecting a big box full of gemstones; many different agates, amethyst in pretty violet colours and crystals of many different shapes so we bought a tumbler and the tumbler was working to polish them many days and nights.

The landscape was very dry and harsh, the spinifex country semi-arid scrubland with gray salt bushes, we had to make sure we took enough water to drink with us every time we went out. Some of the abandoned old mine shafts had some water but most likely it was poisonous as arsenic was found in such water. I have heard that a person got lost in the past in the goldfields near Kalgoorlie in summer time and died within a day from heat exhaustion and thirst. Although I have seen a few water holes called billabong and the famers had dug dams to hold rain water for their cattle, I wondered how any of those animals I saw, many cattle, sheep, emus, rabbits, horses, kangaroos and more could survive in such a harsh environment. We saw a few different varieties of lizards as well and must not forget to mention there were many different flies, we had to spit out the tiny bush flies that had managed to fly into our mouths while we were talking and sometimes we had to cough them out and they were not shy to crawl into our eyes or nose and kept us busy brushing them off.

Sometimes I went with him out to the places 200-500 kilometres away from home in the goldfields north of Kalgoorlie where he had to go to repair a drill rig in the middle of nowhere. Many of the roads were unsealed and badly corrugated; we got covered from top to bottom in so called bull-dust, so fine dust there was no way to protect ourselves from it.

And when we got to the place, only the broken down drill rig and men in stress were waiting for Rolf. There wasn't anywhere we could get cleaned up or shelter to get any kind of relief, apart from the vehicle that took us there which was usually a dirty truck or a Ute. The food we could have in such a remote place so far away from any township was very limited to what could be kept without a refrigerator. Eating mutton and tin veggies had never been in my diet, but as the time went on I was able to eat a little. It took me many trips to find the appetite for such bland and odd tasting food, and we had to get used to eating amongst many flies, mosquitoes and many other insects once the sun went down.

Those were the experiences I never ever had guessed that I would have when I came to Australia. The life in Australia was very different indeed to what I had ever imagined it would be like and it was terribly hard to cope at the beginning but once I got to know what to expect I was gradually able to adjust to the new life and found joy in it all.

I was very happy when I found out that I was pregnant. The thought of becoming a mother was so very wonderful and I was very much looking forward to it. I got very sick with terrible morning sickness at the beginning of the pregnancy. I couldn't smell food let alone eating any. Very Strangely I craved for Cooked Cold Prawns and it was the only thing I could eat and keep down. But prawns were not easy to find in such places. I was around 48 kilograms in weight before the pregnancy and getting thinner by the week and weaker and I wasn't sure if I would ever get better lying in bed alone and feeling sick and abandoned while Rolf was away in the goldfields working. But about the third month I was starting to feel better slowly and by the end of that month I was fine, fine enough to go with Rolf to the bush again.

Our life was starting to take its shape and there was a certain routine happening in our lives and things were getting clearer and easier to comprehend as the days passed by. It would have been 4 months or more since I left Korea but it felt like many years since I was in touch with my family. I had much to learn and adjust to and I thought there was no point worrying anyone by writing about my loneliness or the difficulties I had. It took so many months but eventually I got in the frame of mind to write letters to my family and friends to let them know that all was well with my new life in Australia. Also let them know that I was married and expecting to have a baby and I was learning to cope with life a little more each day and how much I missed them and hoping that all was well with them also.

It felt like I was a million miles away and hadn't seen them for thousands of years, and each reply made me realize how truly I missed them. No one in my family was used to writing letters as our family all lived close and not having the communication for a long time with the relatives living far away in the country was a pretty normal part of our lives in those years.

I remember how emotional I was when I opened the very first parcel from home, in came a letter written by my stepmother who wrote about how my three year old brother was missing me, when a plane flew past our place she saw my little brother looking up to the sky and shouted as loud as he could, "Drop my BIG Sister off RIGHT NOW please!" I burst into tears reading it. Because I adored him and I too missed him badly.

I remember some of the things that were in that parcel, there were a packet of dried seaweed, a couple of large packets of ten of instant noodles and a small bottle of sesame oil together with a few other light items (because of the expensive postage) but I don't remember now what else was in that first parcel but I know I will never forget reading the letter and receiving those items in particular. It was so great to be able to cook and eat my favorite food that I so missed. The two-minute instant noodles called *raymen* originated from Japan I believe; it was a relatively new thing for us in the late 1960s.

It was an instant hit for especially young people of my age, it was like a cooking revolution from the traditional way of preparing food, we were not yet exposed to any other fast food before as we grew up eating only natural organic food prior to it. It was an extremely cheap junk-food, but tasty and was simple to prepare, and ready to eat in just a few minutes, anyone could prepare it as it only needs boiling some water. We had it for lunch even at the office as it was that easy and quick to prepare. Many decades on we now see them here in Australia on our supermarket shelves; I must admit I still enjoy them every now and then as nothing beats the taste especially the ones made in Korea.

I couldn't wait to cook, *Miyuck Gook*, the seaweed soup, and I cooked it that afternoon straight away. I soaked a handful of dried sea weed in warm water for an hour and rinsed it a couple of times and then squeezed all water out and cut into bite sizes and stir-fried them with little pieces of beef, salt, pepper in some sesame oil, and then added a few cups of water and simmered it for an hour. The smell of cooking was So Good and I had tears in my eyes with feeling homesick. When I was eating the hot soup whilst my favourite record was playing, I was in a MESS with tears streaming down into the soup bowl together with the sweat dripping into it from my forehead but I was in heaven! It was that delicious for a moment it felt like, I was back at home in Korea.

I always loved *Miyuck Gook*, the seaweed soup that was the special soup we had on our birthdays and it was the soup for the mothers who just had a baby. Back then I never saw any new mothers after child birth eating anything else other than *Miyuck Gook* and steamed rice for the first three weeks after they had a baby. The soup was known for low in calories and fat, and high in calcium, iron and protein, good for healthy breast milk for the newborn baby and good for fast recovery from childbirth for the mothers.

I have sent a letter also to the American English tutor, Lev, to explain where I disappeared to. And to apologize about not telling him for all those months I have known him that I had a pen friend to whom I was engaged to be married in Australia and that I was preparing to leave the country. But I didn't get a reply from him for months. Later the envelope with his name on it had arrived in my mail box and I was very happy to receive it. I tore the envelope open and read. Hand written in upper case printed letters very neatly on the front and back of an A3 paper, two half pages on each side. The first sentence of the letter was written in large Korean characters which translate to *"Happiness will come to those who wait"* which is a quote from a well known Korean proverb and he continued the letter in English.

DEAR MISS LEE!

I HAVE WANTED TO WRITE TO YOU FOR SO LONG! EVERY DAY FOR MONTHS I HAVE THOUGHT ABOUT YOU, WONDERED ABOUT YOUR NEW LIFE IN AUSTRALIA. HOW I WOULD ENJOY SEEING YOU AGAIN! HOW I WOULD LIKE TO TELL YOU ABOUT ALL THAT HAS HAPPENED TO ME AND ASK ABOUT YOUR LIFE WITH YOUR HUSBAND. YOU LEFT KOREA IN FEBRUARY ONE-HALF A YEAR AGO. BUT TO ME I REMEMBER YOU AS IF YOU DEPARTED YESTERDAY… YOU ARE PERHAPS THE MOST FASCINATING LADY I HAVE EVER MET IN MY TRAVELS AND I WILL NEVER FORGET YOU. I CAN NOT STOP THINKING ABOUT

YOU, MISS LEE. AS I THINK ABOUT YOU RIGHT NOW, I SEE YOUR LOVELY FACE AND I HEAR YOUR SWEET AND QUIET VOICE. I'M ALMOST CRYING. I MUST SEE YOU AGAIN SOMEDAY MISS LEE!

I AM NOW IN AMERICA AGAIN. I, LIKE YOU, HAVE ALSO LEFT KOREA BEHIND. IN TWO WEEKS I WILL BE IN EUROPE (IN WEST GERMANY) BUT ALREADY I AM THINKING ABOUT KOREA I WILL COME BACK. I LOVE KOREA AND I KNOW THAT SOMEDAY I WILL WALK THE STREETS OF SEOUL AND RIDE THE BUS THROUGH NO RANG JIN AGAIN.

Again he wrote in large Korean characters quoting a verse from a pop song then in Korea which translates, *I want to live in Seoul, the beautiful Seoul...*

I HAD A MARVELLOUS TIME FROM THE FIRST DAY TO THE LAST IN KOREA. AND I OWE YOU A GREAT DEAL OF CREDIT ... YOU INTRODUCED ME TO THE PEOPLE, FOOD, DRESS AND WAYS OF KOREA AND THEN JUST AS I BEGAN TO KNOW YOU, MY LOVELY HOSTESS YOU FLEW OFF TO ANOTHER WORLD IN AUSTRALIA. THAT WAS A TERRIBLE SHOCK FOR ME AND PROBABLY WAS THE PAINFUL MEMORIES FROM THOSE DAYS WHICH KEPT ME FROM WRITING TO YOU FOR SO MANY LONG MONTHS NOW.

YOU WERE RIGHT WHEN IN YOUR LAST LETTER, YOU ASKED ME NOT TO JUDGE YOU HARSHLY AND YOU WERE RIGHT WHEN YOU SAID, "I WAS NOT SO BAD TO YOU". YOU WERE VERY GOOD TO ME, TOO GOOD IN FACT. BUT YOU MUST UNDERSTAND HOW I FELT. I AM SORRY THAT I DID NOT WRITE TO YOU FOR SO MANY WEEKS, EVEN THOUGH I WAS THINKING OF YOU EVERY DAY. I WAS VERY BUSY WHILE I WAS IN KOREA. BUT MOST IMPORTANTLY, MY HEART WAS STILL HEALING! BUT I WANT HEAR FROM YOU NOW MISS LEE. I WANT TO WRITE TO YOU OFTEN NOW AND I WANT TO HEAR FROM YOU AS OFTEN AS I CAN. YOUR HUSBAND SHOULD NOT BE JEALOUS AND YOU SHOULD EXPLAIN IF YOU THINK IT IS NECESSARY TO DO SO, THAT I WAS A FRIEND AND A TEACHER.

I REALLY HOPE YOUR LIFE IS VERY GOOD AND FILLED WITH PLEASURE. YOU MUST TELL ME ABOUT IT. YOU MUST FEEL QUITE COMFORTABLE SPEAKING ENGLISH NOW AFTER SIX MONTHS OF DAILY PRACTICE, AND I SHOULD BE ABLE TO KNOW THE IMPROVEMENT BY READING YOUR NEXT LETTER. PLEASE WRITE TO ME QUICKLY, LOVELY LADY. WHAT ARE YOUR PLANS? I KNOW THAT YOU WERE THINKING OF LEAVING AUSTRALIA AS SOON AS POSSIBLE AND I DO HOPE YOU HAVE NOT ALREADY GONE. OTHERWISE THIS LETTER WILL NOT REACH YOU. WHERE DO YOU PLAN TO GO? ARE YOU PERHAPS TRAVELLING BACK TO SWEDEN OR TO EUROPE? ARE YOU STUDYING SWEDISH LANGUAGE OR DO YOU SPEAK SWEDISH WITH YOUR HUSBAND AT HOME? TELL ME ABOUT AUSTRALIA? HOW IS THE WEATHER? ARE YOU MEETING INTERESTING PEOPLE? WHAT DO YOU DO ON WEEK-ENDS? ARE YOU DRAWING PORTRAITS? TELL ME EVERYTHING, MISS LEE. TELL ME QUICKLY.

WHEN YOU LEFT KOREA, I WAS LEFT WITHOUT MANY THINGS AMONG THEM, A FINE FRIEND, A CHARMING HOSTESS AND A LOVELY AND CAPABLE INTERPETER. I WAS A BIT LIKE A MAN WITHOUT EYES, EARS AND HEART FOR SOME SEVVERAL WEEKS, BUT IN TIME I REGAINED CONTROL OVER MY ENVIRONMENT. I WAS INTRODUCED TO NEW PEOPLE. EVEN LEE DONG SUN CAME AGAIN TO MY HELP. LIKE YOU, THERE ARE MANY KOREANS WHO WISH TO MEET A FOREIGNER WHO SPEAKS ENGLISH. THANKS TO THIS FACT, I WAS SOON INTRODUCED TO TWO UNIVERSITY GIRLS FROM DONG KOOK UNIVERSITY AND KON KOOK UNIVERSITY AND ALSO I WAS INTRODUCED TO A FAMILY OF FOUR WHO LIVED NEAR ANYANG AND WHO WANTED ME TO TUTOR THEM IN ENGLISH CONVERSATION. I ACCEPTED THESE SIX STUDENTS AND REFUSED TO TAKE MONEY FROM THEM.

I BECAME FRIENDS WITH THE TWO YOUNG LADIES, PARTICULARLY. JUST LIKE YOU THESE TWO GIRLS COULD SPEAK ALMOST NO ENGLISH WHEN I FIRST MET THEM, BUT

WITHIN A FEW MONTHS WE HAD BECOME GOOD FRIENDS AND THE GIRLS WERE ABLE TO SPEAK ENGLISH EASILY THOUGH NOT ALWAYS WITH PERFECT GRAMMAR. THEY COULD EVEN MAKE JOKES WITH ME JUST AS YOU COULD. OUR CLASSES WERE NOT FORMAL, THAT IS, THEY WERE NOT HELD IN A CLASSROOM WITH THE TEACHER STANDING BEFORE HIS STUDENTS. IN ADDITION TO WORKING AT MY REGULAR JOB IN THE ANYANG EDUCATION CENTER, I WAS TUTORING MY STUDENTS FOUR NIGHTS EACH WEEK AND WE CLIMBED MOUNTAINS (DO BONG SAN AND BUK HAN SAN) AND WENT TO THEATRES IN SEOUL, ATE STRAWBERRIES IN SUWON ETC. ON WEEK-ENDS, MY STUDENTS AND I WERE ALWAYS TOGETHER.

MANY TIMES I TRIED TO MEET YOUR FINE FRIENDS KIM KWANG SOON AND YI YIN YE AND MANY TIMES I WROTE LETTERS TO THEM PROPOSING THAT WE MEET IN SOME TEAROOM IN SEOUL BUT ALMOST ALWAYS WE FAILED. KOREA IS A SMALL COUNTRY AND PUBLIC TRANSPORTATION IS GOOD BUT THE TELEPHONES ARE HORRIBLE AND YOUR FRIENDS WERE BUSY. I WAS ALSO VERY BUSY WITH MY WORK. MY COMMAND OF KOREAN LANGUAGE WAS IMPROVING BUT I COULD NOT USE TELEPHONES EASILY. AS YOU SURELY KNOW THERE ARE MANY PROBLEMS BEING A FOREIGNER. I WILL WRITE TO MISS KIM KWANG SOON VERY SOON. SHE WAS A FINE INTELLIGENT GIRL FROM A GOOD FAMILY.

I HAVE SENT YOU THREE PICTURES WHICH I KNOW YOU WILL REMEMBER. THEY WERE TAKEN DURING THE WINTER IN SEOUL. I HAVE OTHERS, BUT THESE ARE THE BEST PHOTOGRAPHS WHICH I HAVE FOR YOU. I HOPE YOU LIKE THEM, MISS LEE. I HAVE SOME PICTURES OF MYSELF AND I WILL SEND YOU ONE IN MY NEXT LETTER IF YOU WISH. I WOULD LIKE YOU TO SEND ME A PICTURE OF YOURSELF IF YOU CAN. PLEASE SEND ME A PICTURE.

I HAVE BEEN AT HOME FOR THREE WEEKS ALREADY. ON AUGUST 10 I WILL FLY TO NEW YORK AND THEN TO EUROPE. I WILL BE LIVING SOMEWHERE NEAR FRANKFURT, WEST

GERMANY. BUT I DO NOT YET KNOW WHAT MY ADDRESS WILL BE. I WILL SEND IT TO YOU AS SOON AS I LEARN IT. BUT DO REMEMBER THAT YOU CAN ALWAYS WRITE TO ME USING MY PARENTS ADDRESS IN SEATTLE, U.S.A.

WHILE I HAVE BEEN HERE AT HOME I HAVE BEEN VISITING MY OLD FRIENDS FROM HIGH SCHOOL AND UNIVERSITY DAYS, MOUNTAIN CLIMBING AND JUST RELAXING FROM MY BUSY YEAR IN KOREA. BUT MY MIND KEEPS THINKING ABOUT THE WONDERFUL PEOPLE AND THE INTERESTING FOOD, WAYS, MUSIC AND SOCIAL CUSTOMS OF YOUR HOMELAND, KOREA. I WANT TO GO BACK TO KOREA AS SOON AS POSSIBLE AND I THINK THAT AS SOON AS MY ARMY DAYS ARE FINISHED I WILL RETURN. KOREA IS A GOOD BUT POOR LAND WHICH NEEDS HELP. I WOULD LIKE TO HELP KOREA IN ANY WAY I CAN … PERHAPS AS A SOCIAL WORKER. I AM IN LOVE WITH THE EAST WITH ASIA. AND I KNOW THAT I MUST COME BACK.

AND YOU KNOW, I THINK QUITE SURELY THAT I WILL SEE YOU AGAIN SOMEWHERE, MISS LEE. IT MAY BE IN EUROPE IT MAY BE IN ASIA …. BUT I THINK WE WILL MEET AGAIN. I HOPE SO. I CAN NEVER FORGET ABOUT YOU, NEVER.

UNTIL THEN, I WILL KEEP THINKING ABOUT YOU, LOVELY LADY. PLEASE WRITE TO ME QUICKLY. WRITE ME A LOVELY LONG LETTER. I WILL WAIT EVERY DAY.

He wrote *Love* in Korean and signed his name, *Lev*, also in Korean.

I was very glad to hear from him at last and I was somewhat pleasantly surprised reading about his reason why it took that long for him to reply. He had been very cautious not to express those feelings he had for me just as I was cautious not to disclose to him what was going on with my personal life. I was very proud of how respectful we were to each other.

The letter was unlike any other letters I had received from Korea given it was written in English and written about the very final year of my life in Korea, I made sure that I kept it as a kind of validation of who I was and where I came from and to remind me of my good upbringing in Korea. The letter holds a piece of my past I will treasure for a long time and I wanted it to remain as a past and not let it complicate my thoughts because I was moving forward into the new chapter of my life. And I made sure it was the first letter I received from him and the last by not replying.

One of our neighbours gave me a cute little puppy one day. He was a multiple breed with brown fur, only a couple of weeks old. We named him – "Buster". I never had a pet before in my life; many people in Seoul had a watch dog chained up at the gate to deter the burglars and the intruders but I don't remember anyone who had a dog for a pet as such in my neighbourhood in Korea in those years I was there. Buster was just adorable and a very good company for us both. One of the trips for Rolf's work on a very hot day Buster and I went with him; I was then about 8 months pregnant.

While we were on a very dusty road Buster got suddenly very sick with distemper. We were so helpless didn't know what to do and too far away to get any help in the middle of nowhere. We stopped the car by the dusty road and helplessly in sadness in extreme heat we had to watch our poor little puppy die. While we were waiting helplessly an echidna came out of the bush and surprised us, I had never heard about echidnas let alone seen one before. It was small in size but looked very tough with all those many sharp spines which made me think that any life would have to be tough to survive in such harsh environment and thought how sad and vulnerable predicament we were in then.

When finally Buster died we buried him in the bush near the road. We were very sad and exhausted in the heat but we had a long way to get to where the machine was broken down and hurried to find the place before it got too dark. No one had told us and neither of us knew Buster had to be vaccinated against distemper. We both were heartbroken losing him in such a way; it took a very long time to get over our sadness and to want to have another dog for a pet.

A couple of times when there were long weekends we went fishing 375 kilometers south to Esperance - a little seaside town was a beautiful place by the ocean- so different to the dry goldfields. We drove past a large salt lake called Lake Lefroy, which once was a beautiful big salt water lake with lots of wild life but unbelievably the water had almost all dried up over the many years and became a dry salt pan covered with crusts of salt. We also saw varieties of different native plants on the way, banksias and grass trees (used to be called black boys) and more which I have not seen in the goldfields. There were many road-kills by the road and they reminded me of what the road from Perth airport to Kalgoorlie was like. It was very hard to believe that so many animals large and small were killed by colliding with cars passing by. Couldn't help but thinking about what kind of damages would have been done to the human lives. The rotting smell was horrible we had to hold our breath as we drove past.

Esperance also was the place where we spent our honeymoon. It was the very first time in my entire life putting my feet on the sand by the ocean. I know I will treasure the beautiful time we shared on our honeymoon as long as I live, the week in a tent on the beach by the pristine ocean where there was absolutely no one else but the two of us.

It was in April the seaside was very cool and windy at times but it was a lot cozier than the hot temperature in midsummer. I didn't realize then but I know now very well that Rolf doesn't feel comfortable to be in a crowd of people he doesn't know, he much rather prefers a quiet place.

We caught some large king-salmon and were proud to bring them back with us to a friend and he was very kind to cook "fish and chips" for all of us. It was delicious everyone enjoyed it very much. Gradually we became friends with a few people, especially a couple from Seychelles Island, Gilbert and Georgette. Gilbert worked with Rolf and they were very kind and friendly to us. They had a six years old daughter and a son four years old. They were all bi-lingual spoke French at home and spoke fluent English with others. Quite often they invited us around to their lovely home and shared delicious meals with us and when I was getting close to having the baby, as their children had grown up, they gave us all of their baby things they had and helped me in any way they could without being asked. They could tell that neither of us had much of an idea what to prepare for the baby. I was very grateful for their kindness.

Once I passed the morning sickness I had a relatively speaking, trouble free pregnancy and I enjoyed being pregnant. To know and feel our baby was growing inside of me was one of the most profound experiences I could ever have. I felt very comfortable arriving at my womanhood and looking very much forward to becoming a mother. December that year, 1970, our baby was born at the maternity ward in Kalgoorlie Regional Hospital. I had some idea about the labor pain but never to the degree of the pain I had. I was in labor with excruciating pain over ten hours through the night. I felt alone and abandoned not having Rolf there with me even though I had agreed with him that he should go home and catch up with some sleep as he had to work the next morning.

Baby was born early in the morning and I was so very exhausted that I fell asleep. When I woke up Rolf was back in the room and I could see the overwhelming joy and relief on his face. He was a proud dad and glad that all had gone well. The nurse brought our son to us and I held my baby in my arms, and when my baby looked at me for the very first time, it was Just Magical! Words cannot describe how I felt at that moment. And there isn't anything that I can compare the feelings to. I wanted Rolf to experience the magnificent feeling but Rolf was rather reluctant to hold baby at first and told me that he was very afraid he might drop our baby. The wait until he was ready was like eternity for me but a little later when he cautiously held our baby in his arms; I was in tears with overwhelming joy! It sure was a beautiful moment to share!

The first time when a nurse came to take my meal order and gave me the menu to choose from I was very concerned that there wasn't anything on the menu that I could eat. Because all new mothers who just had a baby in Korea eat *Miyuck Gook*, the seaweed soup and steamed rice for the first three weeks. Even though I expected the custom would be different in Australia I didn't think I should eat things like, scrambled eggs, ham salad, corned beef, sausages or cake. I was expecting some sort of healthy soup instead.

When I asked the nurse if it was really Ok to eat such food so soon after one had a baby, not having any clue where I was coming from, she looked somewhat puzzled and said "OF-CO-URSE?" and gave me a silly look. I had no choice but to order what was on offer and I was rather surprised that nothing bad happened from eating such food.

I had enough time while I was in the hospital to write to both sides of our family and informed everyone about the birth of our first son and I didn't forget to write to my family about the kind of food I was having and that I was fine.

During the time I was at the hospital I tried to learn as much as I could about how to take good care of baby. They also taught me about postnatal care of myself and gave me some instructions to follow after we left the hospital. I promised to myself that I would do everything as I was taught and always follow through the instructions properly.

It was very nice to bring baby home but the flat was unbearably hot and uncomfortable. Moreover there were lot of nappies to wash by hand everyday but there was only one set of cement wash tubs in the common laundry for all 4 flats, disposable nappies were never heard of in those years. Only one toilet for all as well and there was a huge tangle of old and dried up bush in front of the toilet door and around the laundry which was a perfect place for many different insects to breed including the dangerous red-back spiders.

I didn't know anything about red-back spiders. When Rolf tried to tell me such little spiders were dangerous I didn't take it seriously. The first couple of times when Rolf was on his knees and crawled back in fear after he had been to the toilet and asked me to check if there was any red-back spiders on his back, ignorant as I was, only judging by the mere size of it, I thought Rolf was rather silly and over re-acting. Such a grown up man to be so scared of such little spiders, and I thought that I would have just squashed it without any fear if I ever saw one.

However, having lived there almost a year by the time our baby arrived not only did I come to understand that red-back spiders were fairly dangerous but that I had to be vigilant for our baby. And one day when I actually saw red-back spiders on the old hoist clothesline I had our washing on, I was petrified. Moreover baby red-back spiders are white and they were very hard to see on the white nappies, I checked and rechecked but, still had nightmares worrying I may have missed seeing one. It sure wasn't a safe place to live and I had to convince Rolf for us to move to another place to live as soon as possible. Within a couple of weeks, Thank God, we did move out of there for good!

We found another place to rent reasonably quickly. It was a lot further away from town. But we liked the house which had three bedrooms and a big back yard had a dunny at the far corner with a high fence around it. It was a much safer place for our baby to grow up and play. It had a big fire place in the lounge for cold winter days as well as a lovely big wood stove in the big kitchen. Best of all it was a house not a flat we didn't have to share laundry room or toilet with anyone.

We loved our new place and found our new neighbours were much friendlier as well. I heard lots of different interesting stories about the life in the goldfields and I was very well informed what was going on in the neighborhood. Even the days when Rolf was away from home with his work I was not so lonely anymore having our baby to look after and those ever so friendly neighbours around.

Rolf bought me an old *Singer* sewing machine and I enjoyed sewing things for our baby. I had brought with me from Korea nine pieces of 20 centimetres x 20 centimetres squares of embroidery I had done when I was at junior school and to make the best use out of them I made them into a nice little quilt for our son, even though many of the squares were in a soft pink colour. I was very proud how it turned out. Having an infant, there was always a lot more to learn and do. Even though I had to push the baby's pram about 2 kilometres each way I visited the baby clinic in town as often as I could, learning to take good care of our baby and meeting other mothers at the clinic and interacting with them was all very interesting for me.

Our little car, Mitsubishi colt became too small and we had to change our car to accommodate our baby's needs. We bought a Holden Kingswood HK 1968 model station wagon for $1,950 which was a lot of money for us then. Later we bought also an 8 foot x 5 foot box-trailer so we could cart around our fire wood that we chopped from the bush. We were slowly adjusting to our new way of life and always tried very hard to improve the way we lived.

I tried to write to both of our families to stay in touch despite the fact that I found it wasn't an easy task writing to Rolf's family because of the language barrier and a lot of feelings I had were lost in translation. So I bought a set of tapes and from time to time I tried to learn to speak Swedish but it was only an ambition as I didn't have much chance to practice it with anyone and moreover I have yet to improve a lot to speak English.

Every now and then I had to meet Rolf at his workplace in Hay Street while I was out in town. Hay Street in Kalgoorlie was very well known to many as it was the place where many prostitutes operated their business and his workshop was very near there.

They lived close to each other in shack-like places with doors painted in bright colours, you couldn't miss them. I used to feel awkward walking past there with our baby in a pram. It was surprising to hear that they were reasonably free from interference from the law to operate and more surprisingly so close to the main street of the town. I heard about many single men going there when they were back in town for a break from working in the goldfields. It was quite common that some of them would spend their entire hard earned money there before they went back out to the goldfield again to work.

Most people believed that having those prostitutes in town was rather necessary for stopping those single men interfering with married women.

In November 1971, ADD asked Rolf if we wouldn't mind to move up to Darwin to live. There was a boom in exploration for Uranium in the Territory and the maintenance fitter they had in their workshop in Darwin was not coping with the increased demands. We both thought it was a good opportunity to move to live near the ocean; Rolf didn't hesitate to tell them we wouldn't mind going. The company promised to pay all the costs to fly all of us to Darwin as well as all the costs of moving our things to Darwin by a transport company. But Rolf opted to drive there so we would have the chance to see more of Australia. I was told it would be almost 5,000 kilometres by the route we were planning to take but I agreed with him to go by car only thinking about how nice to be able to see so much of Australia. But not comprehending what the distance actually meant for travelling with an 11months old baby in a hot car in the middle of such a hot summer. We both were just excited to move out of the harsh dry inland and looked forward to the life of living by the ocean. We sorted out all our things; having lived in a fully furnished rental property we didn't have many things of our own to send by transport. A lot of things we owned weren't worthwhile keeping or taking with us on such a long trip. We either gave them away to friends or threw them away. Whatever we thought important and could fit in our box trailer we took with us. The car space had to be free because we were planning to sleep in the car all the way.

We farewell our dear friends and the neighbours and with a box-trailer full of our possessions, we drove away from Kalgoorlie, a very special place in our hearts!

Chapter Five

We headed west to Perth; we had to get there by early next morning to get the back seat of our Kingswood modified to be able to lay it down flat to make it possible for all three of us to sleep in the car.

The vast landscape was changing fast and interesting to see as we drove on the Great Eastern Highway, from the vast arid goldfields to the huge farmlands of ripening wheat fields that stretched before us for kilometers. Often we drove alongside the pipeline, stretching all the way to Perth, 530 kilometres. I heard it was the longest fresh water pipeline in the world! Many flocks of sheep were grazing, kangaroos and emus far and near, the hawks and the crows by the roadside scavenging off the road kills were certainly not a pretty sight but they all made up the vast Australian landscape – the beautiful and unique! Many different flocks of birds showing off their dances in the sky and on the road side many beautiful wild flowers were in full bloom; large orange flowers of banksias and handsome grass-trees stood out always and captured our attention. It was such a different experience to the last time we drove on the same road 21 months earlier. Having lived in that part of Australia all that time I was able to comprehend a lot more about the nature around us. I felt close to many things I saw, a sense of belonging and not so strange anymore. I even got used to Rolf's accent which was no longer hard to understand.

We stopped for short breaks whenever we arrived at a township and treated ourselves to cold drinks and nibbles. We had been on the road about seven hours and the sun was going down. We needed to stop and wash and sterilize baby's feeding bottles and teats in boiling water as well as feed and bathe our baby and prepare our dinner, all before nightfall.

We parked our car under a big gum tree not too far from the road for the night. We managed to get everything done and we were ready for the night. Inside the car with all the windows up to protect ourselves from the mosquitoes was very hot and uncomfortable. But it got cooler as the night deepened and we felt cosy and happy that we were on our way to a better place to live. Thousands and thousands of stars shone brighter as the night set into pitch-darkness. The vehicles passed by on the highway at times were very loud and broke the silence of the starry night. In the distant, cattle bellowed repeatedly *MOO...* and informed us that we were not there all alone.

We were back on the highway at the break of dawn and arrived at Perth in the early morning. We walked around the place while things were getting done to our car at the garage. The city I saw then was somewhat like what I had imagined Australia would be like before I came to Australia and it felt so good to be back in the city life. After we picked up our car we drove a short distance to Fremantle, we had lunch at a lovely café by the ocean before we were back on the highway to the north to Darwin.

The scenery was different to what we had seen before and it felt as if we were travelling through different countries. How vast and wonderful Australia is, seeing was believing!

I thought of my dear friend, Young Yi as we drove past Geraldton and wondered how she was as I hadn't heard from her for almost a year. Unfortunately I read in her last letter that she hadn't been able to continue the friendship with the German pen-friend who lived in Geraldton because of her poor English. Not just Young Yi but almost a year had passed by without much contact with anyone back home. As we were driving on the highway for hours my thoughts were on my family and friends in Seoul and I wondered how everyone was and hoped that everyone was well. Ever since our son was born I was so busy I haven't had much time to think about my family and friends in Korea.

We saw many different wild flowers like daisies in full bloom at times some kilometres wide on the side of the road. We drove each day from dawn to dusk. Some days were very humid and we would stop at road houses wherever possible to have a shower and get our urgent laundry done as well as top up fuel and our water containers. Many of those road houses were not clean, so much so that in some places I had to leave my shoes on while I was having a shower but we were very hot and at times covered in dust and no matter how dirty the public facility was we were just thankful that we could have a shower and wash the dirty nappies and our soiled clothes.

Every late afternoon we had to find a place suitable to stop and try to get all the chores done before dark. Most nights were very bad with mosquitoes and we couldn't have survived without the mosquito spray. Since we had the car modified we had a much bigger space to sleep on but it was very hot and sticky to sleep in the car with the windows up because of the mosquitoes and sand flies. We had a canvas bag filled with water that was tied up in front of the car to cool the water down but a can of properly chilled soft drink from a road house was always so much better, orange flavored drink was my favorite. I drank so many cans of it on that trip to Darwin; I drank to last the rest of my life. I never ever in forty plus years since had another can of such drink!

Sometimes we got off the road too late for different reasons and ran out of clean feeding bottles for our baby and I had to wash and sterilize the bottles in boiling hot water on the edge of bitumen road in the middle of the hot day whilst Rolf was waiting in the hot car trying to keep our baby cool. The heat from the hot bitumen below and the sun above was so extreme it almost cooked me alive while I was cleaning and sterilizing the bottles. I could have had the feeding bottles sterilized in chemical solution but I didn't trust it was safe for our baby. It would have been even easier if I was still breast feeding our baby but when he was only 6 months old I had to stop breast feeding and put him on the baby formula as I needed to start to take the contraceptive pills to prevent unwanted pregnancy. I didn't want to have the slightest chance of harm to our baby by breast feeding whilst I was taking the pills.

Even though I had hoped to have a large family, the reality in life didn't allow me to continue such a dream.

Some 80 kilometres of unsealed road before Port Headland was really bad it was a very slow and tiring trip. Some places of it were covered with about 80 millimetres rubble and Rolf had to drive ever so slowly not to blow the tyres on the sharp edges of the sun heated hot stones. Fortunately Rolf was a very careful and experienced driver having driven on all sorts of road conditions for his work for the drilling company.

I remember he told me about the terrible experience he had one time coming back all alone on a very hot day from a place called Poseiden at Mount Windara near Laverton in W.A. where they were drilling for nickel. He was on the road merely a bush track with very heavy corrugations; two of the tyres of the utility he was driving were blown one by one. In such heat he managed to replace the first one with the spare tyre he had with him. But when the second tyre had its wall cracked open by a sharp stick lying on the road and there were no more spare tyres. The only thing he could do was try to stuff some rags between the rubber wall and the tube of the tyre so the sharp edge of the wall didn't puncture the tube. Then, he had to drive ever so slowly 40 kilometres to 50 kilometres per hour for more than 300 kilometres all the way back to Kalgoorlie. It was such a painfully slow and nerve-wracking long trip for him but he was very lucky he made it all the way back to town safely. If he had opted to wait there in the middle of nowhere until he was able to get help he may never have survived in such heat for a number of days without any food and water.

The road conditions only worsened as we drove on. Almost all of 600 kilometres of the Great Northern Highway to Broome was not sealed. Many parts were very soft sand being so close to the Great Sandy Desert - it was indeed a very stressful slow trip to endure with an infant in such heat. Rolf had to watch ever so carefully where he was going not to get bogged in the sand as it was too far from anywhere to get help if something bad were to happen. Whilst the car was moving with all the windows down it wasn't too bad but once the car stopped for any reason the heat was just unbearable.

I don't remember much of what I saw around those troublesome roads I was too exhausted in the heat and worried about something bad might happen. Something bad did happen a few kilometers before Broome. One of the U-bolts holding the axle of the trailer had snapped. We were in a panic worried about how we were going to manage to tow it all the way to Broome. Luckily Rolf was smart to be able to work out how to fix it temporarily well enough to get us to Broome and get it repaired properly when we got there. We were lucky it did happen not too far from the town and I thought Rolf was a genius for what he did. He was quick to figure out what he had to do and managed to tow the trailer in such a condition with the heavy load we had all the way to Broome.

Knowing that Rolf was such a mechanically minded person assured me to feel safer for the rest of the journey.

In those years Australia was amidst changing from imperial to metric measurements. The currency was already changed to decimal by the time we arrived in Australia but most of the measurements were still in the imperial system. It added to problems at times for me as I was taught in metric only. Rolf had a road map of Western Australia in metric given to him from R.A.C.W.A. (The Royal Automobile Club of Western Australia) as he was a member but the Speedometer of our Holden Kingswood was still in imperial. Luckily Rolf was already pretty good at converting from imperial to metric even though he was also taught only in metric at school.

While our trailer was in the garage getting repaired we drove around Broome and looked around. I noticed many Asians on the street and I was surprised they were so dark skinned almost as dark as the many aborigines they were sitting side by side with under the scorching sun seemingly oblivious to the heat. Nevertheless seeing Asian people squatting down by the road side socializing brought me back some fond memories of how we used enjoy having a chat with neighbours sitting around like that on the little walk-ways outside our homes. Something I hadn't seen in Kalgoorlie. We learned later that those Asians were mainly pearl divers and originally came from China or Japan a very long time ago. Because they worked in the sea all their lives their skin had got so dark and some of them were inter-bred with aborigines.

We found a little water hole not far out of town, the water didn't look that clean but, it was a nice and quiet place so we thought we'd stop there for a while and rest. As we started to unpack a few things out of the car, a swarm of March flies came from nowhere and started to bite us. In terrible panic I covered our baby first to protect him and then we threw everything back in the car as fast as we could as we brushed the horrible March flies off us and quickly we drove away.

From there we went to the beach, it was a far better place. While we were relaxed and enjoying the sea breeze we saw rather a large fishing boat, which could be a pearl lugger, lying on its side on the mud on a low tide about 50 metres away from the jetty. It looked pretty much abandoned and made Rolf wonder why anyone would abandon such a boat. However when we drove past again later at high tide we saw the boat was upright and people were busy loading things into it, which made Rolf realize that the tide must be unusually very high there to be able to stand such a large boat upright again.

We picked up our trailer having had a new U-bolt fitted and we freshened ourselves up at a fuel station and topped up everything. Last before we left Broome we treated ourselves to a nice Chinese meal at a restaurant in town and avoided eating another evening by the road amongst mosquitoes. The meals were tasty and it was so nice to have it in the comfort of a room. We drove only until the sun started to lose its heat and getting a little cooler. The best thing was we didn't need to do any chores that night amongst the mosquitoes and sand flies and could go to bed early.

The road was sealed until we got to Fitzroy Crossing but just after the Fitzroy Crossing the highway had lots of storm-washed pot holes, this slowed us right down. We saw many Baobab trees, the strange looking trees with swollen fat trunks and here and there we also saw ant hills in different shapes and sizes. They were all amazing and very different to the nature of where we came from. We were yet to learn about them and not able to comprehend many things we saw, but we were enjoying very much seeing the different scenery of Australia. However different the environment where we came to live and it may have been difficult for us to adjust, fortunately we shared similar fundamental values and ethics in life. Our core behaviour was very much alike; we both had the attitude to EMBRACE our new life no matter how hard and difficult the situations were.

Each day we were getting a little closer to the life in the tropics. Although Rolf had grown up most of his life around lots of beautiful lakes, winter was extremely cold and summer was short. He had told me that there were two main reasons why he left Sweden and decided to come to Australia to live – Too much SNOW and Too much TAX in Sweden.

We saw a couple of stalls selling mangos as we were getting close to Wyndham. Neither of us ever heard of mango let alone had tasted it. It was rather expensive fruit to buy then, thirty cents each, but this intrigued us to buy one to taste. The taste was so good and we both regretted sorely that we hadn't bought some more not knowing there would be plenty more in Darwin. Late afternoon on the next day when we arrived in Darwin not only we were very pleased to see many stalls by the road selling mangoes but we were happily surprised that for only 95 cents we could buy a bucket full of mangos.

Almost 5,000 kilometers and nine long memorable days on the road later we arrived at last in Darwin. The late afternoon warm sea breeze greeted us and welcomed us. My heart was singing with joy with a huge sigh of relief at arriving there safe and well, after such a long trip with an infant. Unlike when I flew into the airport some twenty-one months earlier from Korea, arriving there after having lived in Kalgoorlie was certainly a very different experience! Everything looked so much greener and alive, I couldn't stop smiling.

We found out that ADD had booked us in a motel because the flat they had put on a contract to rent for us was not ready for us to move into. It was a brand new block of flats, three flats on the bottom floor and three flats on the top floor in a suburb called Night Cliff, on a street at a walking distance to the sea but it wasn't ready to let as yet. We disconnected our trailer, loaded with our things and stored it in the company's workshop, and we stayed at the motel for two whole weeks until the flat was ready for us to move into. It was really lovely staying in the air conditioned comfort and felt very spoilt to eat out most days.

It was a holiday to recover from the holiday!

We moved into the two bedroom brand new flat partly furnished with new furniture which was nice and modern. The common laundry had two new Simpson Wringer washing machines and was located right next to our flat which helped me to meet the people as they moved into the building. Many more new blocks of similar flats were going up right around our place. They were mostly owned by Greeks and Italians who had been living in Darwin for a long time and made lots of money from fishing or building industries. As those flats were ready to let they were filled fast with people of many different nationalities, among them there were some Asians from the British colonies like Singaporeans and Hong Kong Chinese. There were already many cafés, hotels, restaurants and grocery stores in town owned and operated by Chinese people. It was a truly multicultural society and we certainly felt we fitted in better in such dynamics of society than that of the goldfields we had just left.

Maurits turned one year old not long after we moved into the flat. I wanted to make a birthday cake for him. Last time I ever baked anything would have been at a cooking class in my high-school days. I found a recipe and tried my best to follow the instructions step-by-step and even though I had to guess some things as I didn't fully comprehend it, the sponge cake turned out great! It sure was an extra proud moment for me to celebrate our son's very first birthday with the special cake I made for him. Baking was not our way of cooking, no one I knew in Korea had an oven at home when I was growing up there, the only chance I had in baking was at the high school where we were introduced to cooking western style and was well equipped with a big oven.

As a matter of fact growing up in Korea, I don't remember having had such a thing as a birthday cake nor that I had unwrapped a present on my birthdays. My family celebrated our birthdays by having the special seaweed soup, the *Miyuck Gook* and extra nice tasty things to eat with the family. Having a cake for birthdays was not our way of life back then.

We have a party with nice food, receiving gifts from family and lots of friends when a baby is one-hundred days old, to celebrate the child having survived the danger period and to wish the child a long life. We also celebrate when the baby turns twelve months old and the next big birthday we celebrate with a party and gifts was usually not until - sixtieth birthday.

And nationally we celebrated with family and friends, every first day of the lunar calendar New Year called *Seol Nal*, and the harvest moon festival fifteenth of August by also the lunar calendar called *ChuSeok*. The most important dish for the *Seol Nal* is the rice cake soup in beef broth, called

Dduk Gook. And most gifts we received from visiting relatives or friends were fresh meat, usually beef or pork and maybe some homemade sweets, and on our harvest festival we prepared special rice cake called *Song Peon* filled with sesame seeds, beans, or chestnuts and steamed between layers of pine needles. I sure have lots of fond memories making the half moon shaped *Song Peon* with my grandma and aunties and the fond memories of picking the pine needles for it with my sister, Kyung Hee at the mountain near my home called *Nam-San*.

Rolf had to go out to places in Arnhem Land 200-300 kilometres out of Darwin and sometimes over 300 kilometres south near Katherine to repair broken down drill rigs. But I got pretty much used to Rolf being away from home with his work by then. I had a Singer sewing machine Rolf had bought for me in Kalgoorlie. One day I saw Yvonne, an English lady who lived directly upstairs from us, making her dress using pre-made patterns and I got very interested to learn from her how to use these patterns. Yvonne was about same age as I was and we both had a little son and they often played together. Her husband, Paul, was also English and was a policeman working at the local police station.

I was taught basic dress-making when I was in high-school including the basic drafting of a pattern so it was not difficult for me to learn how to alter the patterns to the style I liked and to make it fit just right for me. Soon I was able to sew most of my outfits. Sometimes I made matching outfits for all three of us in matching colours or out of the same materials. It made me feel very proud to turn up in matching outfits when we were invited out to a friend's place for a dinner party or a BBQ.

We became good friends also with a Singaporean young couple, John and Patsy who lived in the bottom floor like us. The first time we were invited to their place for dinner we were surprised to see them eating wet food with their fingers not with a spoon and it was an unexpected challenge for us both when they expected us to eat without a spoon as well. Made my stomach squirm when I saw them eating uncooked marinated meat. Nevertheless they were very nice and friendly people and we became friends with them very quickly. John was a cook working at the kitchen for Qantas airways in Darwin, his colleagues often had big BBQ parties and we were invited along. Patsy and John told me about how much they loved Korean food especially our famous pickle, *Kimchi* and made me hungrier for it, and have a go at making it, but I couldn't find the special ground chili powder even in Darwin. I tried to make it with other kind of chili powder as a substitute but the taste was never right. It's largely because I did not have any experience in making it, I needed a lot more practice I guess.

Maurits always cried badly when I took him to a barber or a hair dresser for his hair cut. So Rolf bought me a hair-cutting-kit one day in order for me to learn by practice and cut his hair at home, which turned out to be the best investment we ever made with $11. Although I never mastered the skill of a barber and as Maurits grew up gradually refused my unskilled service, I have been cutting Rolf's hair ever since. Rolf always encouraged me to do it for him, even at times when I did a bad job on him and I was sorry for him looking rather funny but he always said "It's OK, it will grow back in a couple of weeks you wouldn't know it". I dare say if the situation was reversed I wouldn't have handled it so lovingly.

Like his dad Maurits loved to go fishing. We bought a twelve foot aluminum boat as soon as we could afford it to go fishing together during the weekends. Most of the weekends we went out to the sea and caught many reef fish, snapper, whiting, parrot fish, perch and more. To freeze them we bought a 13 cubic foot (368 liters) upright deep freezer through the company called "Southland Frozen Food", the frozen food supplier who offered a good deal in supplying frozen meat and vegetables to Darwin by shipping the goods from the southern states. In the wet season when the roads were cut off to Darwin for a long period of time and there was a limited supply of fresh meat and vegetables and whatever we could buy was very expensive, it was very convenient in such times to order the frozen food that came by sea and have it delivered to the door by the company.

It was great to have the freezer big enough to freeze all the fish we caught as well. We were advised by locals not to eat too much reef fish at one time as there was a chance of contamination in the reef fish and one may get sick with ciguatera. But often we ignored what we were told as it was always nice to cook and eat the fresh catch of the day. The life style in Darwin was indeed different to the life style we had in the goldfields in many ways and the best thing about living in Darwin was that there was plenty of seafood. Going to the drive-in movie theater at night in the weekend and socializing with friends and watching movies on a big outdoor screen was also nice in Darwin. We would take 6pack of cold beer and some cold drinks. And pick up crunchy hot "fish and chips" wrapped up in newspapers from a café on the way which was an evening to look forward to. Evening sea breeze was lovely while we were watching a movie from our Kingswood station wagon with windows down.

Rolf came home from work one day with the news about an all-girl band from Korea playing at the Penthouse Nightclub in Darwin. I was so excited to hear about that the Korean band was in Darwin and couldn't wait to meet everyone in the band and looked forward to speaking Korean with someone again. I booked two seats for Saturday night one seat for myself and the other for the English friend who lived upstairs. Yvonne gladly accepted my offer to go with me and have a night to ourselves whilst our husbands stayed at home with our sons. On that Saturday morning I couldn't wait till night to meet them and I asked Rolf to take me to the hotel so I could get acquainted with them a little before the show.

Midmorning Rolf and I with our son went to the hotel and found all five Korean ladies of the band together in the dining room having a chat. I was so happy to see fellow Koreans for the first time in two years and when I heard them talking in Korean I got even more emotional. I tried to introduce myself and my family to them in Korean but my overwhelming emotion took a hold of me and was not letting me speak Korean properly. I hadn't spoken a word in Korean with anyone since I arrived in Australia, my tongue was tight, my heart was choked with emotion and I fell into an uncontrollable severe frustration, tears were running down my face whilst all the words were piled up at my throat but I couldn't speak a word in Korean properly.

My unexpected inability to speak in Korean was rather confusing not just for everyone there staring at me but also for myself. I could understand every word they were saying in Korean. They were having a discussion between themselves as to what they thought might be the reason why I couldn't speak properly and mumbling words. When I heard one of them sarcastically say in Korean "She may be from North Korea?" I was screaming in silence "Oh, No, I am not, I am from Seoul!" but they couldn't hear of-course. Another lady was looking up close and personal with our son touching his face and said in Korean "You look very cute, you look like *Go-Ba-Woo*!" A character in our childhood story we knew so well, my emotion got too much that I burst out crying and I couldn't handle it anymore, hesitated a little while not knowing what to do and I just said "Bye… and see you tonight!" in English and left.

They were very puzzled but seemed pleased to hear that I was going to come back that night to see their performance. Rolf asked me in the car what happened and he was concerned someone might have said something in Korean to upset me, I told him that I felt very emotional, so much so that my tongue was tight and I couldn't speak out in Korean even though I understood every word they were saying and wanted to respond in Korean. I told him that I surprised even myself and I hoped that I would be OK by the night when I went back.

With Yvonne I arrived at the Penthouse Night club. I was dressed in Korean costume just like when I had arrived at the Perth airport on my first day in Australia, a guide straightaway showed us to the seats in the front row as if we were special guests of the band and made us feel very welcome. The atmosphere in the room with a small stage was nice and cosy. The performance was by one on a piano, one on the drums, one on a guitar and a singer with a guitar and joined by an exotic dancer. They were very enjoyable performances. We stayed back and waited until they were ready to mingle with everyone after the show. I was by then relaxed and able to overcome my emotions to talk with them in Korean as if nothing different had ever happened that afternoon and I spoke fluent Korean without any problems. It was great to have the normal conversation with them at last.

I could tell the dancer, Linda, was a lot older than the other girls not by looks but by the way they spoke to her. Korean language has a polite form of speaking to people you respect or who are older than you thus it is easy to tell who is younger or older by listening to the conversation. Linda was most keen to get to know me and she told me that she was envious of me living in Australia. I explained to her that I hadn't met any Korean in two years since I had arrived in Australia and neither of us has any family living in Australia. Linda was sympathetic with me and could understand that I would be lonely without any family or friends living in Darwin.

The group has been working in Hong Kong before they came to Darwin with the 3 months contract. When the contract is over with the club in Darwin they had another contract with a club in Sydney to go to. Repeatedly Linda has told me that if she only could she would like to return to Australia and live in Darwin and be a friend with me. I was very touched by what she said and I have told her that it would be so nice to have her living near me in Darwin. When they left Darwin I was sad and I hoped that Linda could really come back one day.

I couldn't believe my eyes when actually Linda came back to visit us and moreover it was hard to believe what she told us, she had met a Greek man who lived in Darwin during her stay at the Penthouse and they already by then were married and were waiting for the resident visa for Linda. When the visa is granted as she has promised she would move to near us with her husband. It was unreal to see her again; she was ten years older than I was and she was from Seoul like I was but from a very different back ground. She had travelled working with the band in different parts of Asia as a dancer for a while and she had a mother who loved her and supported her in Korea.

Linda and her Greek husband, Angelo, did move to a place near us in Darwin as soon as they could. We saw each other often. Her perspective in life and her mind set was different to mine as she was a much older person and having lived a different kind of life to mine but she was very friendly to be with, she talked to me as if I was her long lost little sister and made me feel that I found an elder sister I never had. Linda was an extremely good cook as well, almost as good as my grandma's cooking which I so missed.

We visited each other often and enjoyed having meals together, mainly sharing the food we were brought up with in Korea. Sometimes it may be just hot chilies in chili sauce and steamed rice and nothing else, and it was so hot our mouths were on fire with the sweat pouring down our faces but sharing such moments with someone was great. I couldn't share such a simple enjoyment with Rolf as he was not brought up with such food and he couldn't relate to the simple enjoyments I shared with Linda.

As we became very close, Linda became controlling and behaved like a typical big sister and I didn't know how to get used to this although I didn't mind that most of the time. Sometimes, however, it was just too much for my independent spirit and we didn't get on well at all but it was not long before we were knocking on each other's doors again because we missed each other very much, just like true sisters would. We were able to talk things over and make up because we knew very well how precious our relationship was as there was no other Korean in Darwin we could share the things we shared.

It was a very difficult and sad time when Linda had the miscarriage of a baby and was hospitalized for many days in Darwin. Every day I prepared a Korean dish I knew she liked that I had once learned from her and as soon as Rolf finished work he had to drive me to the hospital to visit Linda with the food I prepared she liked to eat more than the bland hospital food. Rolf was very understanding and helped me without any complaints no matter how tired he was having worked all day in the heat.

Linda talked me into believing that women have to smoke cigarettes to look sexy and mature. Given I also used to think so in my teenage years that the boys looked more mature and sexy when they smoked cigarettes like we saw in many movies and I decided to learn to smoke. I lit a half piece of non filtered Camel cigarette Rolf had left in an ash tray before he went to work, and sucked the air in a couple of times slowly while holding a burning match in front of it; I coughed as I let one mouth full of smoke out, the taste left in my mouth was so awful it made me hesitant to have another try and in no time I felt a headache coming on as well and this led me to question myself, is it really worthwhile to smoke? I decided there and then I'd rather not smoke and take the chance of not looking sexy and mature. When I told Linda about it she told me that I would learn to enjoy the taste eventually but I have told her that I have no intention to ever try it again.

Yvonne and Paul moved away from Darwin because Paul was transferred elsewhere by the Police Force and soon a senior couple in their early 60s,

Nancy and Kingsley from Adelaide moved into the flat. Kingsley was working for The Department of Aviation and came up to Darwin to fill in for someone on holidays for six weeks. We became very close friends with them as well and they just adored our little son, Maurits. I told them about the headache I was having that morning from the experience of smoking just one puff, they burst out laughing and told me I made the right decision not to smoke ever again.

In 1972 ADD had lots of contracts with various exploration companies and their drill rigs were out busy in many places outside Darwin, to the east- Jabiru and Nabarlek in Arnhem Land, to the South- near Rum Jungle and outside Katherine.

If the place was not too far from Darwin and a safe place for me and our little son, Rolf took us with him. We went with him a few times to a place called Jabiru about 260 kilometres east of Darwin. The scenery on the way was very beautiful with lakes, waterfalls and lush vegetation, habitat for many wallabies, kangaroos, water buffalos, crocodiles and many different beautiful birds including the handsome looking birds called Jabiru, after which the town was named. Every time our little Maurits saw any animals or birds, he got very excited and loved to mimic what he heard, which made us enjoy the trip all the more.

Many years later in 1979 the area was established as the Kakadu National Park and a couple of years after that the area was inscribed on the World Heritage List and the beautiful place was protected forever. Darwin climate was mostly warm all year around with a dry season in winter and a wet season in summer, at times with very high humidity. It was a perfect place to wear the miniskirts and hot pants which happened to be in fashion in those years. I had lots of time to sew such outfits for myself when Rolf was away with work for a few days and I had extra time.

In the wet season many roads outside Darwin can be closed for a long time. Once in such a wet season Rolf had to fly out from Darwin to Jabiru in a small twin engine aircraft to repair some drill rigs. five minutes into the flight Rolf had noticed a gap as wide as a lead pencil between the engine cowling and as the plane went up higher he noticed the gap was increasing and when it increased to about 3 centimetres Rolf felt he'd better ask the pilot if it was normal. The pilot leaned over him and checked the gap and said, NO! And straight-away turned the aircraft around and contacted DCA in Darwin and let them know that they were turning back to Darwin. Rolf heard DCA ask the pilot if he needed the full emergency and the pilot said YES! As he turned the aircraft around to go back to Darwin airport Rolf saw the pilot shut down the left engine and flew with only one engine.

When they arrived back at the airport many fire engines and ambulance vehicles with flashing lights were all over the tarmac but very luckily the pilot landed the aircraft safely. If that wasn't enough, Rolf was walking around at the hangar while waiting for the aircraft to be repaired, when he accidently noticed that one of the wheels of the aircraft had a hole as big as a ten cent piece in the rubber tyre all the way into the canvas. Again he had to tell the pilot about it. The pilot then re-acted angrily at the maintenance staff at the hangar. Many hours later all the problems were fixed and finally they were able to fly Rolf safely back to Jabiru.

But given Rolf was uneasy with flying at any time it was the most terrible experience for him.

There is absolutely no doubt in my mind that without Rolf's curiosity and his well experienced mechanical mind the aircraft could easily have crashed. For sure the experience would have added to the reason why he feels so uneasy with flying.

Rolf told me about another difficult experience he had endured in the wet season in Darwin. He flew out to Jabiru in a small twin engine aircraft from Darwin and he had to fly in a helicopter from Jabiru to Nabarlek in Arnhem-land where he had to dismantle a drill rig all by himself into pieces able to be lifted, piece- by-piece, by the helicopter to be transported about fifteen minutes flying time to the top of the hill. And then using the helicopter as a crane Rolf had to completely re-assemble the drill rig before he was flown in the helicopter back to Nabarlek then back to Darwin in a twin engine aircraft.

It was indeed a very difficult job he had to do but he had managed to get it all done safely and in the same day.

Another time Rolf was working at a place not far from the ADD camp they had near Jabiru, he was cooling diamond drill bits in the water pumped from a pit of rain water. The pit was created by someone from a mining company that used a bulldozer to make a hollow in the ground but when he needed to pump more water the pump didn't want to work. So Rolf had to fix the pump, which took hours in the very hot and humid conditions but eventually he got it going again.

Only to find out later that one of the geologists had discovered a very high concentration of uranium in the area, it was a LETHAL place!

We got to know many people from different ethnic backgrounds who lived in our neighbourhood, and we were enjoying the living near the ocean and multicultural way of life in Darwin. But only after two years since we moved there, ADD asked us if we would move again, this time to another mining town, Mount Isa in Queensland – 1,650 kilometres away from Darwin.

We agreed again to move because we knew it was another opportunity for us to see more of Australia. Having done 5,000 kilometres on our last trip 1,650 kilometres didn't seem too large a distance to go and our baby had grown up to a lovely three year old who loved to go for a drive. We sold our little boat and the outboard motor because we were moving inland, far from the sea. That time most of our belongings were sent by Grace Brothers, the removal company, because what we had then was far too much for our box-trailer. Even though the company offered to fly us there and pay for all the cost to send our belongings, Rolf would rather go by our car again for the same reason - to see more of the country.

We said our farewells to many lovely friends we had, especially Linda and her husband who became like a close family. We would miss their friendship and Linda's wonderful cooking. Once again we were ready to travel a long distance in our Kingswood station wagon pulling the box-trailer behind loaded with urgent things we needed.

Heading south further away from the tropics by the hour and back to dry Spinifex country but looking forward to the change. We saw for the first time big buffalos lazing under the hot sun and every now and then hopping kangaroos caught our eyes. The road condition was very good and there were hardly any road kill on the road which made the trip more enjoyable.

Our little three year old got excited every time he spotted an animal or a bird he would shout "Mum, Dad, Look! Look!" Pointing his tiny little finger in the direction as if only he saw them, and listening to our little boy mimicking the songs and dances of the children's program he watched and learned on TV shows was very enjoyable. We stopped by the road before dark and Rolf as always parked the car facing in the direction we would be going next morning. As the night deepened the millions of stars welcomed us back on the road.

It was November 1973 in the middle of a hot summer just like the trip from Kalgoorlie to Darwin but the trip was so much more enjoyable and easier with a three year old, not having to clean baby bottles and sterilize them or having to worry about where next I could wash the nappies. Late afternoon on the second day on the road we arrived at the road house at Three-ways where the road to the east started. I overheard a conversation between a couple of people in the lady's rest room and hearing their reasons why they had left Mount Isa made me feel a little concerned to go to Mount Isa as we were beginning to head to the east toward the Queensland border.

The temperature of late afternoon was getting only hotter and uncomfortable as we drove on which reminded us of the goldfield days. We were relieved when the sun was getting low and starting to lose its intense heat. We had an early night and got up at dawn next morning and started to drive again. We were getting closer to the Queensland border in the early afternoon when all of sudden we were swarmed by millions of grasshoppers. They were so thick we couldn't see through the windscreen of our car which brought us to full stop right there in the middle of the road. We just waited and watched until all flew away taking the black sky with them. It was such a formidable scene, – something we had never seen before! I look at grasshoppers never the same again since.

As we drove past the border sign, *Welcome to Queensland*, the road condition quickly deteriorated, our car and trailer were beginning to shake badly and added to my concern that the prospect of where we were going to live was not good. We were very relieved when we arrived safely at the first township on the Queensland side called Camooweal. We saw a crowd of people gathered around and admiring an emu in a small fenced in area and we joined in the crowd for our son to see it.

We have seen a lot of emus in southern parts of Western Australia but it was the first time we saw an emu on that trip. It was a very hot afternoon. In no time we were saturated in sweat, bought some cold drinks for a relief and bite to eat at a store and topped up with petrol, and soon we were on the final stretch of the road to Mount Isa. We were anxious to get there before the ADD workshop closed for the day to be possible for us to pick up the keys for our new place to move into.

On the rain deprived sun burnt arid land cattle looked thin and often we saw hawks were scavenging from the road kill. And each time I had to teach our little son to hold his breath as we drove past the awful smell of rotting flesh. A couple of hours later on the highway of nothing much else to see, we spotted a few chimneystacks poking through between hills made us excited and sighed with relief, as we guessed that we were almost at Mount Isa at last. Sure enough we drove past a big mining industrial area of many of those chimneystacks. Soon we arrived at the township, found a newsagent in town and bought a street map of Mount Isa to find out where the ADD work shop was located and five more minutes later we arrived at there. We were very lucky we got there just before it was closed for the day.

Rolf's old boss from Kalgoorlie, Rex, saw us drive into the yard and welcomed us. We followed him to our new place five minutes drive from there. It was a two bedroom fully-furnished flat also only a walking distance away from town. It had an evaporative air conditioning system instead of ceiling fans like we had in Darwin. There were four flats in the same block but all had a separate laundry for each flat. We felt good with the new place and looked forward to starting our new life in Mount Isa. Rolf started back to work the next morning. The removal truck arrived with our gear next day and kept me very busy unpacking. Maurits was excited to have all his toys back and helped me to unpack them into his room and I was very proud of him.

Rolf went away with his work more frequently since we moved to Mount Isa. I kept myself busy sewing and started painting again not just portraits but I also tried to paint flowers, birds, landscapes and seascapes in oil on canvas as I was keeping my eyes on our little boy playing nearby me. Rolf was very happy and proud of me when I sent his parents one of my oil paintings of a beautiful tropical scene of Australia and a mosaic of a little girl's face I had made with the sea shells we collected from Esperance and Darwin. Another time I had painted a portrait of baby Dennis, one of Rolf's nephews from a photo and sent it to his brother George in Sweden.

I heard about a local art group and joined in the activities of the group of like minded people. The following year for the annual art exhibition I entered all 22 paintings I had accumulated since I arrived in Australia.

I was very proud of my paintings, so much so that I expected to win some good prizes from the competition but out of all those many paintings I had entered only one managed to get recognition of People's Choice. Soon after the exhibition two paintings were sold but I was still disappointed not getting any prizes, I thought the judge was not fair and biassed. A decade of studying art since that time I came to realize that the judge was not wrong after all, and I could see myself how much I didn't understand about art, paintings in particular, in those years.

The more I learned about art, the more I realized how little I knew and that you don't know what you don't know until you have actually learned.

However, the president of the art group, May Johnston was very impressed with my work and she was happy to recommend me to the manager of the leading fashion store called "Playtime" in Mount Isa who was looking for an artist to get a mural painted on a wall of their newly renovated store. It took me by surprise when she came to me about it and I was a little hesitant at the beginning because I had never painted a mural before in my life and it was way out of my comfort zone. However I didn't want such an opportunity to pass by and I dared to agree to do it. I got some advice what to do from May and I decided to think outside the square and have a go at painting a mural. It took me a whole week to do the mural at the down stairs area of "Playtime", where they renovated to stock "Cue" fashion for the first time.

The mural I painted there high up on the south side of the wall was a seascape painted in acrylic house paints with big brushes. I was apprehensive at the start but soon I got the hang of it, it was such fun to do and I even got paid well for the wonderful experience I had. Moreover it led me to two more commissions to paint murals. I had the pleasure of painting a mural of a sunset over an ocean on the entrance of a home in Hilary Street and I painted a rainforest scene on a wall facing an in-ground swimming-pool of a home in Alfred Street. All murals were very large and done with house acrylic paints. Awesome experiences!

The population of Mount Isa was then around twenty-five thousand and was made up of people from about 54 different nationalities as well as a lot of aboriginal people of Kalkadoon and Mitakoodis tribes. The township of Mount Isa was discovered some 50 years prior in 1923 by a prospector, John Campbell Miles, during his expedition into Northern Territory. It is a place with rich mineral deposits, copper, silver, lead and zinc. It was known then as the largest mine in the world for silver and lead and the tenth largest mine for copper and zinc. Around 5,000 people were employed in the mine alone. Being such a remote place far away from everywhere and it being a large mining town with a lot of people on shift work, the sporting culture was very strong. Unfortunately the drinking culture was also strong and it wasn't uncommon to see intoxicated people in the middle of the day.

Nevertheless it was a close knit community of many different nationalities that lived together in harmony.

Nineteen-seventy-four I was naturalized as an Australian citizen. In those years if you were living in Australia with a resident visa you had to wait at least for 4 years to be eligible to apply for citizenship. Wanting to be an Australian citizen was an inevitable progression for me, as I wished to live in Australia and wanted to have the same privileges and rights as Australian born people.

When I applied for the citizenship I requested Ann Gustavsson to be my legal name. It is pretty normal in Korean culture to call someone by just the surname to be respectable in many situations, therefore some people would call me Miss Lee by my family name which sounds more like Yi in Korean but became Lee for foreigners. Korean language being very different from English, my Korean first name, *Myung Cha* was even more difficult to pronounce or spell correctly by foreigners. A short time before I left Korea a German boss I had for a few months told me once that he would like to call me Ann since I was going overseas to live and because he could relate my personality to the well known actress of those years, Ann Margaret.

And he suggested to me to change my first name to Ann which would be a lot easier name to the foreigners. I wrote about it to Rolf and he wrote me back that he was happy to call me Ann so long as I was happy with it.

Ever since then I introduced myself to foreigners as Ann and my Korean name was only on official documents. Thus when the time came for me to apply for citizenship it seemed to me then only the right thing to make it to be legal when I had such a good opportunity. I was very young and trying to fit in the society totally different to where I came from. Nevertheless as the years passed on I do regret losing my entire Korean name as I feel my true identity, being a Korean foremost, got lost forever.

That was the very reason why some thirty years later in 2004 before I started to paint full time I created the new signature, ***agymcha***, by combining both my birth name and the Australian name, to be signed on all my art works from then on and to represent the whole of who I am.

There was a foreign commission town near my home in Itaewon in Seoul. It was a special village with high security for those foreigners who lived in Seoul permanently or for a long period of time. It was only a walking distance, 15 minutes at the most, from my home. I did tutor a little four-year old girl in speaking English. She was adopted by Mr. Pfaff a West German who was a resident at the village, and who had named her Claudia. He was married and had a wife living at his principal home in Frankfurt, West Germany, but they had no children, so they adopted the little Korean child and wanted to teach her to speak English while he was based in Seoul working.

The village was designed just like here in Australia, a bitumen road to each driveway as every household had a car or two of their own. But for us it was very different, we only had narrow walkways between the houses as no one had a private car to drive around in those years, the only things on wheels to pass through between the houses were hand driven carts or bicycles. Their life style was indeed very different to ours, I enjoyed going to the village and seeing the different ways of life the foreigners had.

The little girl, Claudia, lived with an old Korean housemaid and another Korean lady in her late 20s, whose name was Sonja and she was the overseer who managed the household as Mr. Pfaff was away a lot with his work.

Sonja spoke German pretty well but couldn't speak English. Claudia was a cute and adorable little girl who was also very smart for her age and it was my pleasure teaching her to speak English. Some months prior to my leaving Korea, Sonja left Korea for Frankfurt in West Germany to marry Mr. Pfaff's younger brother but we promised to each other to keep in touch.

Also that same year in December 1974, a terrible cyclone went through the city of Darwin; Cyclone Tracy had almost flattened the entire city on a day of all days, Christmas morning. It was a category four severe cyclone which devastated the city of Darwin and destroyed more than 80% of houses and more than 40,000 people became homeless overnight. 71 people had lost their lives and many hundreds of million dollars of damage was done.

We were very worried about our friends Linda and Angelo and all the other friends who lived there but no way could we reach any of them because all the phone lines were down. We were very surprised and glad to see Linda when she managed to come down to us with a friend they weren't yet over the shock and still traumatized. Everything that they had brought with them had shattered glass scattered through them. It reminded us all how horrible the cyclone must have been for them and what a terrible time they had endured.

It made us feel how lucky we were to have left the place a year ago. We had a lot of heavy rain in Mount Isa that week and many places were flooded and major roads to and from Mount Isa were cut. Thus we had a very short supply of fresh produce, and the supermarket shelves were bare and whatever we could get was much overpriced. But there was absolutely no comparison to what the people in Darwin had to endure. We have heard that cyclone Tracy was one of the worst natural disasters Australia ever experienced. Angelo came down a few days later and they found a place to live in Mount Isa, we were very happy to have them living near us again.

At the adjoining block from our flat lived an Australian lady in her late 60s, we called her Aunty-Jean. She was taking care of a little boy named Ben, the same age as our son, while his parents were at work. The boys enjoyed playing together and Aunty-Jean and I shared not only lots of cups of tea but also our very different cuisines. Aunty-Jean would cook me things like ox liver, beef stew, kidney pie, ox tongue and tripe, most of them I had never tasted before I met her and it was not the kind of food I liked to eat but it was good to be introduced to and in turn I would cook things like *sushi, dimsum,* fried bean starch noodles, marinated beef and some vegetable pickles and steamed rice which surprisingly she didn't seem to mind to eat any of them at all, - perhaps she too had to be polite.

Across the street from where we lived there was a big two story modern house, where a Finnish family of four lived, Pentti and Irja and their two daughters, Eija and Seija. We became very good friends with them and in no time we were introduced to a lot of their Finnish friends. In those years over 800 Finnish people lived in Mount Isa. They had a club of their own and often over the weekends they got together at the club and socialized and some weekends we went to the club with them and had very good times with them. They were very friendly people and they, being Scandinavians like Rolf, had a very similar cuisine to the cuisine Rolf was brought up with and I was very interested to learn about it.

A lot of them had been in Australia a lot longer than I but many of them didn't speak English well because they were always socializing amongst themselves and continued to speak Finnish. Most of the men spoke better English because they had to go to work with Australians. There were a handful of Swedish people who lived in Mount Isa but they were not like Fin people and didn't necessarily look for other Swedish people to be friends with. I only had met two Swedish families, one who bought a painting of mine soon after the exhibition and the other who gave me a commission to paint a portrait of his wife. It was my very first commission to paint a portrait and I was very proud to do it in black and white on silk.

Rolf was away a lot from home with his work - sometimes for many long weeks. I was very lucky to have many friends to share the interests to occupy myself and our little son was grown enough to be great company but for Rolf things were very different, not always easy for him when he was away. I remember another bad trip Rolf told me he had. One of the trips with his work, he had to go to a drilling site near Gunpowder, about 130 kilometres north of Mount Isa. He had to drive a truck to the site and drive another truck back to Mount Isa. It was a very slow trip the road being an unsealed dirt track with black soil. When he was getting close to the sealed highway, it was on dusk and getting dark, he realized the truck didn't have any lights working. So he had to stop and sleep in the truck over night covered in dust without any dinner or a blanket to keep him warm on a very cold night with a single digit temperature.

Another time he drove on another unsealed black soil dirt track in a utility which was not a 4-wheel-drive vehicle, to a drilling site somewhere between Burketown and Borroloola over 900 kilometres North West of Mount Isa near the Gulf of Carpentaria. It was in the morning on a very hot and humid summer day with a very heavy load of old engines on the back of the utility. He saw a huge dark mass of clouds rolling fast toward him. He was scared, thinking that it was going to be a bad storm soon, as he was driving a utility on such bad black soil dirt track he was worried about getting bogged and he wouldn't be able to drive to the site on time, which would mean he wouldn't have anything to eat for dinner again and he had to spend a night in such heat in the utility in the middle of nowhere. But to his amazement there was no storm and he managed to get to the site. Later he learned that it was a rare meteorological phenomenon known as a "Morning Glory" a roll of the cloud formation in high humidity and only possible to see in a few places in the world. It happened to be the one of the few places in the world where "Morning Glory" occurs.

One time Rolf had to drive a truck from Mount Isa to McArthur River in Northern Territory and drive another truck back to Mount Isa. When he was about 600 kilometres out of Mount Isa the oil light on the truck came on indicating that there was an oil issue in the engine. When he checked it he was very surprised to find that there was indeed no oil left in the engine and he couldn't believe that happened. He was all alone on the very isolated road far from everywhere, no chance of getting any help. He had a small engine amongst the load he had with him on the back of the truck, he decided to drain the oil out of the engine and used it to put into the engine of the truck. But the oil wasn't much and the truck didn't go too far before it stopped again. He couldn't do anything else but wait in very humid and hot condition for a very long time until someone drove past and stopped and offered him help. Only then he was able to send the message to ADD workshop in Mount Isa for help. He had to wait there, until help arrived late next day from Mount Isa, without anything to eat and exhausted in the heat, he had to spend another night in the truck again.

When I think about those years how terrible were the working conditions Rolf had endured clearing the heavy snow in Sweden that he got away from, couldn't have been any worse than what he had endured to survive in Australia.

But he too never looked back and did his best to cope with it all whatever challenges were thrown at him. He was a young migrant who accepted that he didn't have much choice in jobs because of his poor English and he needed a job for his family to survive. He never thought of anything else other than to apply himself to the best of his ability no matter how difficult the job was or how tough the situation he was in.

May 1975. We had been living in Mount Isa for only about eighteen months. And once again ADD asked us if we would move again, this time all the way back to Kalgoorlie, thousands of kilometers away in Western Australia where we started our life together.

We were hesitant whether we would go back there or not for a few days. Given the distance being so far, it was such a daunting task to think about driving such a long distance in our old Kingswood towing the trailer, and furthermore all the way across the Nullarbor Plain. Rolf was very well aware of how bad the road conditions of the Nullarbor Plain were as he drove across it when he moved to Kalgoorlie from Geelong in Victoria 1968.

But the more we thought about going back to Kalgoorlie, the distance seemingly got shorter and wouldn't mind going back to the sentimental place, where we started our life together and to take our son back to where he was born. Also we wouldn't mind seeing on the way the big cities in the southern states like, Sydney, Melbourne, and Adelaide and perhaps even Canberra. Another thought encouraged us to decide to go was it would be a good idea to see more of Australia before our little boy started school. Once again we found more reason to go than not to go so we decided to agree to move.

One night we were invited by Rolf's boss Rex to a big combined birthday party of his and his two friends, Marshal, a well known hotel owner in town and Don, who was a local dentist, they all shared birthdays in the same month. The party was held at Marshal's residence.

At the party when Rex's wife Mary asked me if we had decided to move back to Kalgoorlie, I told her that we would move back only if ADD were to rent a house for us not a flat. Mary was surprised to hear that from me and wasn't impressed at all not only about what I said to her but how I said to her with an attitude. It made even Rolf somewhat uncomfortable as he had no idea that I was going to demand such things from the company. But I meant what I said and I was not afraid of saying it, I thought if the company needed him to be there they should look after him better. Especially, his boss Rex who hadn't been treating Rolf as well as he deserved and I was very well aware that Rolf was putting up with him only because he needed the job and Rolf would never speak out for his rights.

Mary was in her early 50s much older than I was. Mary stared at me a little while and she winced at me as she said "We have been with the company for a long time, a lot longer than you have, but never ever have we demanded anything from the company even though there have been times we had to live in a tent let alone in a flat."

I responded with firm and controlled voice and said, "That was your life and the choices you made. Unless ADD rents a house for us to live this time we will NOT go." Rex heard about it from his wife and he came over to me totally ignoring Rolf who was sitting beside me and said to me personally that he would discuss the matter with the head office in the morning and let us know.

Next day Rolf came home for lunch break from work and was pleased to tell me that Rex informed him that ADD will rent a house and have it ready for us to move in by the time we got to Kalgoorlie. And also it was OK for him to take an annual leave for 4 weeks for the trip so we had enough time to take it easy and drive the longest distance we wished from Mount Isa to Kalgoorlie to see as much of Australia as possible on the way.

We worked out from a map the route we were planning to take, the distance added up to more than 8,000 kilometres by the time we would get to Kalgoorlie but we were planning to have a good break and rest here and there on the way.

Mount Isa was like Darwin, a friendly multicultural place, and people embraced the differences and lived in harmony; if it hadn't been for the company's wish we would not have thought about moving away so soon. However we were getting excited by the day to leave for a long holiday, looking forward to three of us spending time together every day for four weeks, and seeing many of the different parts of Australia.

Going back to Kalgoorlie was somewhat like going back home for us given it is the place where we started our life together and taking our four and half year old son back to the place where he was born and we had some good friends who still lived there. We were also looking very much forward to move into a house not a flat, with more rooms to spread out to enjoy our hobbies and a big yard for our son to play in.

Once again it was the time to say farewell to our friends, Linda and Angelo, and many other friends we had. But we weren't so sad for some reason we had in our minds the thought that there was a good possibility of returning to Mount Isa one day just like we were about to go back to Kalgoorlie no matter how far it was.

On the first day we drove past the township of Cloncurry and got off the main Highway and headed north onto the sealed but very narrow road to Normanton. There were a lot of cattle and sheep on the road as many properties along the road didn't have proper fences to keep them in; as well there were a lot of kangaroos hopping around. We had to be careful and alert also as many trucks were using the narrow road so we were driving slowly.

It was late afternoon when we were about 320 kilometres away from Mount Isa we heard a loud BANG!, the sound of collision on our car was so loud it got us all very scared, we stopped our car and rushed out in fear to find out what had happened as we didn't see a kangaroo. But it was a kangaroo that had collided with our car, it must have jumped out of the high grass beside the road. We saw a very large kangaroo hopping away. Although we heard such loud BANG, the kangaroo didn't look too badly hurt and we saw it just hopped away into the bush but the impact left a big dint on the bumper-bar of our car.

We were very lucky Rolf wasn't driving fast because the impact from such a big kangaroo would have been much worse if he had been driving faster. From then on Rolf drove extra slowly but soon we heard another THUMP, we stopped our car and rushed out again to have a look. We saw a little kangaroo knocked down and very still in the high grass nearby. We were all sad for the little kangaroo but at the same time couldn't but feel relieved to find out it didn't do too much more damage to the car. We have driven thousands of kilometers around Australia but never before collided with a kangaroo. We have learned that for some reason late afternoons to sunset and early mornings around sunrise kangaroos are most erratic in their behaviour on the road and we always had been extra vigilant for them in those hours, - we couldn't believe it happened and not once but twice!

About half an hour later we arrived at the Flinders River crossing where we expected to meet our Finnish friends who were camping there. We got there just in time to join them for a freshly caught wild Barramundi for dinner. Wild Barramundi is a most delicious fish to eat and we have been there to that same causeway of the crossing many times before to catch them. By the campfire into very late that night we shared a lovely time together. But we got up early next morning and we were back on the road again. We will miss not only the lovely friends but also the camping spot that was excellent for the barramundi fishing.

We were soon on the road to the east. The road was wider but unsealed with bad corrugation; it was very dusty and rough. About 60 kilometres later the rear exhaust pipe of the car was separated from the muffler; Rolf had to fix it at the roadside before we could drive on. Australia being such a vast land with many unsealed roads in extremely bad condition and long distances between the places where we could get any help, if Rolf was not handy mechanically, travelling by car for such a long distances would have been unthinkable.

The temperature in May was nice and comfortable by day but it was getting cooler at night, which was far more enjoyable than travelling in hot and humid November as we did on the last two long trips. 400 kilometres later, as we were getting close to the Atherton Tableland the landscape was starting to change and the sun was almost down to the other side of the hill, and we too needed the rest. We saw a running stream by the road and decided to pull over and stop for the night. We needed to get cleaned up and have something to eat before it got too dark. The camp near the running stream made all that much easier. The food prepared outdoor in simple ways is often very delicious and our dinner that night beef and vegetable stew was exceptional! That night we were clean and happy chatting away together in our makeshift cosy home of our Kingswood station wagon until we fell asleep. Next morning Rolf started the car as soon as he was awake to turn the heater on as it was freezing cold and started to drive at once. We soon arrived at the Tableland. The scenery with rolling hills and green pastures with lots of dairy cattle grazing was so beautiful and peaceful especially at dawn, it was just like some of mountainous Switzerland I saw in the movies.

It sure was absolutely breathtaking!

We arrived at Herberton soon after 8.00am. Rolf had to see someone who lived in town briefly to pass on a message for the company before we drove on. We drove past high mountains with massive clouds that looked like they have pierced through heaps of soft white sheep's wool. We saw waterfalls and huge boulders in lush rainforest. The artist in me had a big urge to paint the magnificent vista and my camera was going click, click, working fast as we drove past.

When we were close to a small village, Kuranda, near Cairns, the winding road on steep hills made the palms of my hands sweat in fear of rolling off the cliff but the view was amazing. We arrived at Cairns, a beautiful city on the east coast, close to the Barrier Reef of the South Pacific Ocean. After we treated ourselves to a nice lunch at a café and a little break we were back on the road this time on the Bruce Highway heading south. We saw more beautiful mountains with the soft white cloud mass wrapped around them and they were like back-drops of a huge stage set and kilometers and kilometers of vast land was like a huge jigsaw puzzle with many fields of banana and sugarcane plantations. Everything looked amazingly green and dazzled our eyes. It sure was a big contrast to the outback of the gray eucalyptus in the dry west. We couldn't take eyes off the lush and beautiful scenery. But as we drove further south the landscape started to change back to a drier look even though the highway stayed parallel and close to the coast line.

We drove past Townsville and Bowen on the Bruce Highway, the sun was going down fast and we found a lovely spot on the hill by the ocean to stop for the night, and planned to see the sunrise in the morning. We had been continuously nibbling on snacks while we were driving on that stretch of highway, as there were many places we could buy things to eat and drink on the way, so we weren't hungry for a big dinner, we just had more snacks. And as we were not covered in dust or sweat, we needn't worry about getting cleaned up either. The freezing cool temperature woke us up early in the morning just in time for us to be ready for the sunrise. We were all wrapped in blankets sitting inside of our Kingswood with the car engine running and had the heater turned on waiting for the sun to rise out of the ocean.

The sunrise on the east coast was truly spectacular! It was such an empowering experience I will never forget! It sure was very energizing and a sublime experience!

Soon after that we were back on the Bruce Highway travelling further south. As we were getting close to Mackay the road condition deteriorated with big potholes everywhere. Each time we drove on the potholes everything inside the car rattled and Maurits thought it was rather fun. He burst out laughing each time our heads bumped to the ceiling of the car. The weather was as funny as our mood that day with heavy rain for a minute and the next sun was shining brightly like it's been a mistake, rain and sunshine, rain and sunshine several times. Maurits couldn't help and turn it into a fun game of guessing when the rain would stop and start and we both joined in his fun game and all three of us burst out laughing together.

We would have been driving almost 3,100 kilometres since we left Mount Isa yet we hadn't even left Queensland. Australia is truly an enormous big continent. We were very fortunate to see and experience firsthand the enormity and we knew we made the right decision in driving instead of flying. We had another night by the road before we drove into Brisbane, the capital city of Queensland, as we intended to spend a full day in Brisbane and look around.

I loved the city and I am a city person at heart. At least I was in those years.

Brisbane reminded me of Seoul, in the sense that the city is built around the River, has many high-rise buildings, crowded streets with people and cars. Rolf got very frustrated driving around in the city and he complained that there were too many one-way streets, and he was bitterly complaining about Brisbane street signs which he thought were not good enough. He told me that he used to drive around much bigger cities in Europe, like Paris, without any problem. I understood his point but I couldn't help but say to him that it would also be because it had been such a long time since he had driven around the streets of such big cities.

We treated ourselves to a nice rice dish at a busy café by the street which was much nicer than the steak and mushroom pie we had for lunch at a road house on the way down. Fast food such as pies, sausage rolls, fried chips and Chiko-rolls and, if we were lucky we might be able to get cooked chicken, fish and chips or sandwiches from the road houses or small cafés by the road, but at no time were there rice dishes available. We left the busy city after we had our dinner, back on the Bruce highway south only until we found the first rest area and stopped overnight. We were woken up by loud thunder and heavy rain in the wee hours of the morning long before dawn, and started to drive as we were hoping to get to our friend Don's place in Sydney that afternoon before dark, which was around 1,000 kilometres away.

We met Don through Rolf's work while we were living in Darwin. Don had a transport business, carrying goods between Sydney and Darwin, and his service was often required by ADD. He drove one of his semi-trailers, a Mack truck, himself. Don had invited us to visit him in Sydney when we were on our way to Kalgoorlie and to stay at his home for a while. Maurits loved uncle Don and his big Mack truck. Every time he heard the loud sound of its air horn outside our place, he knew it was uncle Don's big truck, he exclaimed, "Uncle Don is here!" and rushed out to see uncle Don and his truck. Uncle Don would pick him up gladly and put him down on his seat in front of the steering wheel and let him pretend to be a truck driver, by the time Rolf and I went out to greet Don. Maurits often mimicked the sound of the horn and made up a song of his own and sang it. As neither of us had any relatives living in Australia Maurits grew up without meeting any real family, so our good friends and neighbours were his make-believe uncles and aunties. We were all very much looking forward to getting there soon and seeing Uncle Don and his Mack truck again.

It was raining heavily most of the day and the traffic was also getting heavier as we drove down south. Thirteen hours later, on dark, we arrived at Sydney. We sighed with relief when we found Don's place, in the suburb of Dural, with the help of the area map Don had drawn up for us. A big dog, a German-shepherd barked loudly at us as we drove into the beautiful property. In no time Don rushed out and welcomed us. When Maurits couldn't see uncle Don's Mack truck in his yard he impatiently asked Don where the truck was. Don promised that he would show him the big truck as soon as he got up in the morning, in day light.

We followed Don into his lovely big lounge room with a fire in fire place. As soon as Don and Rolf were settling down with beer and catching up on work I helped Maurits into the bath room and let him have a warm bath before he went to bed. I enjoyed a hot shower before I joined Rolf and Don again for a chat. Don was in the midst of going through a divorce then and was living alone but had a girl friend living somewhere else nearby.

We woke up to the delicious smell of fried bacon, tomato, eggs and toast - a breakfast Don was preparing for us all. We freshened ourselves up and enjoyed the breakfast with Don. The property was very beautiful inside and out. A large four bedroom brick home with tiled roof sitting on a gentle hill surrounded by tall and beautiful trees. It had a lovely landscaped garden, a small veggie garden and a large in-ground swimming-pool. The place was like a mini animal farm as there were a few beef cattle, horses, ducks and chooks. As well as the German-shepherd, this time wagging his tail at us instead of barking, obviously he had accepted us as the guests of his master.

I was very envious of the peaceful and beautiful place Don had and thought how wonderful it would be for us also to have a property like that someday. The third day we were there Don had to go away to deliver some gear for a company a fair distance away. He got one of his cattle put down and butchered and filled the freezer with lots of meat for us to help ourselves and left the whole property in our care with few instructions and went away. It made me believe that such a business, having to go away often for a lengthy time from home, might have been the reason his marriage had suffered and failed.

I found out Rolf had good knowledge about animal husbandry; we had the whole property under control and managed to take care of all the animals without any problems. I had to laugh sometimes watching the father and son working together and arguing who knew better what to do and how to do things. We enjoyed doing what we had to do. It was a very pleasing experience to say the least, especially for Maurits and me who hardly had any personal contacts with any animals before.

Don's place was only about 30 kilometers away from the central business district of Sydney but the traffic was so heavy, once it took us more than an hour to get to Sydney. But we had been out a few times for a drive as there was a lot to see. Once, I spotted an old traditional Korean brass table BBQ burner outside a little second-hand store near a busy street. I was very excited and had Rolf stop the car as soon as possible and went to have a closer look. It had a damaged handle but it looked OK. Given Korean cooking utensils like that were rare to see I decided to buy it. And at a large Chinese grocery store not far from there I found some grocery items I hadn't seen since I came to Australia.

When Don returned home he organized a dinner at a floating seafood restaurant on Watsons Bay with us and his girl friend. We were very happy meeting her and after we had the lovely dinner we walked around the Bay, the air was so crisp and the company was so pleasant, I felt blessed. Don took us also to a couple of parties at his friends' places who had similar trucking businesses and lived on large properties like Don. They were very humorous and listening to some of their experiences in life as semi-trailer drivers was very enjoyable.

We had such a lovely time staying at Don's place for almost two weeks and the time had come to leave. I gave Don, for a thank you gift, my oil painting I had brought with me as I knew he admired it; it was a black and white painting on silk, of a pair of doves. He was very happy to receive it. He told us that there was a good chance of his visiting us in Kalgoorlie as he was expecting a trip to Perth with work in the near future, and we farewell him with the hope that he would visit us soon.

Our next long stop was in Melbourne another 900 kilometres away by the shortest road. We knew ADD had booked us in a hotel for a week as they wanted Rolf to see how the drilling equipment was manufactured at the factory of Mindrill, which ADD was then affiliated with. We were planning to get off the main highway and drive past Canberra, the capital city of Australia, to have a look but we heard on the radio that it was snowing heavily in Canberra, so we had to give up on the idea and drove on the Hume Highway to get to Melbourne as soon as possible. It was raining heavily soon after we left Don's place and the temperature cooled down very much and pulling the trailer in such miserable weather made a slower trip. Unfortunately I don't remember seeing anything much other than heavy traffic on those roads from Brisbane to Sydney and from Sydney to Melbourne as the heavy rain kept our eyes mainly on the road for safety, and we were anxious to get to the place in daylight so it was easier to find the place we were going to.

We only managed to drive about 400 kilometres on that day and stopped overnight at a public rest area. The rain didn't stop all night and it got colder as the night set in, despite Rolf turning on the car engine a few times to heat up the car, it was still too cold to sleep. We were up early, made hot drinks before we drove on. We arrived at the ADD head office early in the afternoon. We were greeted by a couple of Rolf's bosses who we knew very well, and one of them took us to a hotel on a busy road.

Next morning Rolf went to the Mindrill factory for work from 8.00am to 5.00pm. And 9.00am every morning ADD sent a car with a driver to the hotel to take Maurits and me wherever we wanted to go, and picked us up at 4.00pm or whenever we wished to go back to the hotel. Maurits and I spent most of the days in town looking around big department stores and sightseeing. I was happy to see trams like there were in Seoul, and we had rides in them as well. It rained on and off, some days it was very cold. Seeing people in warm winter overcoats everywhere made me feel that I was indeed very far away from the hot and dusty outback, the place where people wear singlets and thongs as an outfit to survive in hot temperatures. On other days the temperature was rather warm and we would dress in cool summer outfits and still perspire just walking around in town. We had heard that Melbourne weather can be very unpredictable and certainly that was not wrong.

We were introduced to the hotel managers, a husband and wife team, by the ADD boss on the first day we arrived at the hotel. They were very kind and they let me use the hotel kitchen to cook meals for ourselves. Once they even joined us for a meal I had prepared. One night we had a wonderful meal at one of Rolf's boss's home. Other evenings we went out and had a meal at a restaurant.

Rolf had prearranged, by phone, with *"The Church of Swedish* seaman" in the suburb of Toorak in Melbourne to christen Maurits. Rolf thought we should while we had the chance. Maurits was almost four and half years old then, christened by a Swedish priest with a simple ceremony. Nevertheless we were very pleased for him and it was my first experience of such a Church service. On the way back from the church we stopped at a large Art gallery, I don't remember now what the name of the gallery was, but I was very inspired at seeing many of the wonderful art works exhibited there and it was my very first experience to visit an art gallery in Australia.

The week went past very fast and it was time to leave. The hotel managers surprised us with gifts, a couple of small antique porcelain whisky jugs and a couple of lovely metal trays, one with Fosters and the other with Victorian Bitter beer logos imprinted on them, together with many lovely swizzle sticks. They were very appreciative as we were to them, for the time we shared together.

We decided to drive via the Great Ocean Road to see the beautiful coast line of Victoria, and Rolf wanted to show us around the city of Geelong where he first arrived from Sweden. Rolf was then twenty-seven and didn't speak much English when he arrived at the immigration camp there in Geelong. Soon after he arrived there, the government officials allocated him to a job at the International Harvester as a helper for the gardener while the factory was closed for the three weeks Christmas break. It wasn't his preferred work but he took it as he didn't have many choices, not being able to speak much English. When the factory resumed after the Christmas break he was offered a job at a sheet metal section where they manufacture the harvesting machines and the farm tractors. He worked there for 16 months manufacturing the mudguards of the tractors until his home town friend, Carl, who came to Australia with him, came back to Geelong to persuade Rolf to follow him to Kalgoorlie. Carl had been working for the Diamond drilling company in Kalgoorlie and came back to Geelong to convince Rolf to go with him to work for ADD in Kalgoorlie.

Rolf was pleased to be back in Geelong again and drove around to show us a few places he had been and I was very pleased to be there to see where he'd been in the past and I thought once again how wise it was to go by road instead of flying. Had we flown to Kalgoorlie we would have missed all those wonderful experiences of seeing the places together where he had once lived.

It was amazing to realize the differences of the temperature in June in different parts of Australia; where we were in Victoria was like autumn or early spring in Seoul, yet we heard that it was snowing heavily in Canberra like mid- winter in Seoul and that it was still warm in Darwin like summer in Seoul - all 4 seasons at the same time in one country. For me it surely felt unreal! We left Geelong and continued on the Great Ocean Road to the west. The next place Rolf wanted to show us was the Great Otway National Park near the small township of Lorne. The scenery of the rain forest packed with giant tall trees, huge ferns, and many different magnificent ancient plants was fantastic, and the place was serene. The rain forest was close to the highway yet it felt like we were somewhere far away and tranquil, amazingly disconnected from the sound of the busy traffic of the highway.

We would have loved to have seen more of that place but it was a very cold day and we still had a long way ahead of us. We were back on the Great Ocean road and not long after we arrived at the famous "Twelve Apostles" in the sea just off the shore. It was late afternoon and the sun was low in the sky, and the scenery of the seaside was magnificent and breathtakingly beautiful! If it hadn't been so windy and cold we would have stayed near there overnight and would have loved to have seen the shore at dawn. But it was much too cold to stay overnight there we just took some photos instead and drove on.

We drove on until the sun was down and parked the car near the road, again facing in the direction we would be going in the morning and had some tinned food for dinner with hot drinks and had an early night. Rolf was very tired and fell asleep very quickly but Maurits and I cuddled up together and talked for a long time as we were staring at the shining stars outside, shivering in the cold night until we too fell asleep. Rolf woke up cold in the very early hours of the morning and turned the engine on to warm us up and started to drive. It was still very early morning but the road was already busy with traffic. We soon passed the border of Victoria and South Australia. There were signs at the border to welcome travellers and another sign warning against travelling interstate with fruit, vegetables and plants, as if we were about to enter another country not an another state of Australia.

We'd travelled in our Kingswood all over the country over the years, and I'd become very fond of our car. The regular beating sound of the running engine while we were on the road, hypnotized me sometimes. I'd get lost in thoughts of yesteryears and often thought about how different my life was then compared to the life I had in Korea.

Being born and growing up in the same house close to my primary-school all of my primary-school years, when I graduated from the primary-school and had the chance to choose a secondary school to go to, the only thing in my mind was to find the farthest school from my home, so that I could travel to and from the school by bus. I was envious of people who could move to different places to live and travel by bus. The farthest girl's secondary school I could find was at the other side of the mountain about 9 kilometres away by bus from my home. I went for the entrance exam and I was over the moon when I read my name in the newspaper amongst the names of those who had passed the exam.

At first, my father was very proud of me for finding the school I wanted to attend all by myself and to pass the exam as well, but we both learned later that the Soong Yi girl's secondary school was a Christian-school. Given that my father was a Buddhist he wasn't pleased at all but it was too late to go for an exam for another school in that year. I pleaded with my father to let me go ahead and attend the school with the promise that I would change to a different school for my senior years when I graduated the junior years in 3 years time, instead of wasting a whole 12 months waiting for another entrance exam. I asked for his understanding by explaining to him that even I myself didn't know the school was a Christian-school, and that the only the reason I had chosen the school was because it was the farthest school I could find, as I wanted the bus ride to and from school.

He didn't like it but he understood and gave me permission to attend the school. My father never had been educated at school and I was the first one to go on to the secondary school in all of my father's side of the family. By then my birth mother's side of the family had moved away from the area and we were hardly in touch ever since my father got remarried.

I loved the school and I enjoyed the bus ride to and from the school so far away from home, even on days I had to walk to school because I wanted to save the bus fees for other things, given I had never such a thing as pocket money. There was a walking track, a short cut through the mountain. The walk was about 4 kilometers each way but the distance felt shorter the more I walked the track. I studied very hard to thank my father and I wanted to make my father even more proud of me.

I liked being taught at the Christian-school and learning about the faith in God which was really helpful during my sad and difficult times when my step mother was sick with cancer and died. But as I had promised to my father I did change to a non Christian-school for my senior years after I graduated the junior-school. It was imperative to make my father happy and proud of me. My father and I were very happy when I passed the entrance exam and got into the high-school of our combined choice which was well known then as one of the very highly respected girl's high-school in Seoul, Su Do Girl's High-School. I was very blessed and proud to be educated in those wonderful schools.

We arrived at Adelaide late that morning. We first wanted to drop in and surprise Nancy and Kingsley who lived there, the senior friends who used to live in the flats above us in Darwin. We drove around and found their lovely home but no one was there. We went back there again after we had lunch in town but still no one was at home. We were all very disappointed. There was nothing else we could do but leave a little note in their mail box to let them know that we had tried to see them and wrote down the address of ADD in Kalgoorlie for them to reach us.

How we lived before mobile phones was indeed so very different to how we live now.

Before we left the town we went to a small grocery store and topped up our supply of food; amongst the many things I bought was a jar of very hot pickled chilies. Then we were back on the Highway number one and drove on until it was almost dark.

A bad storm came over us not long after we went to bed, bolts of lightning were flashing followed by the loud roar of thunder and the sound of heavy rain pelting down on our car was terribly loud, it made me very scared and worried if that place was safe from becoming bogged or drowned. But Rolf wasn't concerned about any of it and told me everything would be fine and he was soon snoring again. The loud noises didn't wake Maurits either and he was sleeping through it all and I was left all alone to be frightened. I put a blanket over my head not only to block away the flashes of lightning but to block out my stream of worries flashing inside of my head. I had to try very hard to fall asleep by listening to the sound of Rolf's snoring which was at times equally loud to my ears, but blocked out the scary roar of thunder.

When we woke up next morning, the place was fine as if I had just a bad dream about it all. Rolf kept the engine running with the heater on and with our portable little one burner gas stove we boiled a pot of water, enough to make hot cups of coffee for us and a hot cup of instant soup for Maurits. The traffic on the highway was getting quieter as we drove on west. Rolf reminded me again how boring the trip would be from there on with nothing much to see. We arrived at a little township of Ceduna. While we topped up with fuel for the car and a spare jerry can we had with us, the store keeper also warned us how bad the road condition of the Nullarbor Plain was, and told us that there were no roadside services.

I could tell Rolf was very concerned about towing the trailer on such a bad road and it made me apprehensive about the trip we were about to begin. Past Penong the road condition was bad, unsealed and had many pot holes which made us all very nervous and tired, Rolf had to drive very slowly and cautiously. Out of stress I started to eat the pickled hot chilies one by one out of the jar that I had bought in Adelaide.

We were only about 250 kilometres out of Ceduna the sun was beginning to shine on our windscreen, almost blinding us as we were driving straight west. We got tired and had to pull over earlier than we had planned. After we had quick meals out of tins we went to bed covered in dust from head to toe and exhausted. Before four am, we were all awake and shivering with cold. To keep us warm Rolf started to drive slowly in pitch darkness with the car heater turned on. By mid morning we managed to get to the Western Australia border. Although the nights were very cold, the middle of the days were rather warm and we had to drive with the windows down on such dusty road. Arriving at Eucla, a little road house, feeling very dirty covered in dust we saw the sign SHOWER on a van and we got excited. We saw a lady coming out of the van with a towel wrapped around her hair and I was very much looking forward to have a shower. Whilst Rolf was topping up fuel I took Maurits with me into the van to get cleaned up. I decided to have a shower first to find out if the water was warm enough for our little boy to have a shower. To my despair the water was icy cold and it felt and tasted like salt water! Still in desperation, I tried very hard to wash my hair and be quick but my dirty long hair in such cold hard water would not lather and turned into a big Hard Mess. I couldn't even put my fingers through it so I just had a very quick wash and out, and gave up on a shower for my son and just briefly washed his face and hands.

We were told that there would be no fuel stop for the next 400 kilometers to the west. We had no choice but fill up everything we had, including our water supply. The Western Australian side of the highway was sealed but still dusty and many stretches of the road were straight and boring, which seemed like a never ending road. It was a very tiring experience to travel west in the afternoon. The sun rays danced on the windscreen for a very long time and at times blinded us. Just as well there was hardly any other traffic. Rolf had warned me that one of the stretches of the highway is 147 kilometres dead-straight and that it is known as the longest straight road in the world. He also explained to us that a part of the railway runs not far from the road, Trans Australia Railway track stretches unbelievably dead-straight for 478 kilometres, deservedly known as the longest straight stretch of railway track in the world.

Nullarbor means in Latin *"No Tree"* and it was just that, there wasn't anything much to see other than gray salt bushes and the vast land was empty and very boring without trees.

There were many bad potholes covered well with soft sand and dust. Every time our car unexpectedly drove on it, our car shook badly and it was frightening. Seeing a few wrecked and abandoned cars by the road didn't help my nerves as they reminded me what could happen on that terrible road. That had me biting my nails with stress, listening to Rolf telling us about his horrible experiences of driving across there in 1968, when none of it was sealed. Rolf mentioned also about seeing wild camels in the area before so I was looking out for them but they were nowhere to be seen.

In the late afternoon we were on that longest straight stretch of the road, heading straight west with the sun on our windscreen blinding us, which made us very tired. We pulled over by the road and had an early stop and we were very pleased we were almost at the end of the stressful Nullarbor Plain. It was our last night on the road as we expected to arrive at Kalgoorlie by next morning if all went well. The pickled hot chilies had been nice for me to snack on but my stomach was starting to ache.

Mid next morning we arrived at Norseman. We went in the store and had a drink and little snack. My stomach was still sore but I was just happy knowing that we were only a short distance away from Kalgoorlie. We had driven thousands and thousands of kilometers right around Australia to get there. As we were getting closer and closer I was excited about moving into a house and the things we could do with more space. But most of all I was looking forward to having a long and hot bath!

After the epic journey, over 8,000 kilometers on the road, at last we drove into Kalgoorlie! As soon as we drove into the ADD workshop one of Rolf's old work friends, Ray who was then the new manager of the workshop, came out of the office and welcomed us back. He told us that the house the company had rented for us wasn't ready for us to move in as yet so he booked us in a motel for a couple of weeks. An air-conditioned motel to stay for a while after such a long trip was indeed very welcomed news!

We went for a drive one afternoon to the first place where we used to live to show our son where he was born, only to see the whole block was bare, it had been demolished since. I wasn't at all surprised and rather glad it was demolished, as I knew it was such a primitive dwelling and wasn't a suitable place for anyone to live. Nevertheless standing there I couldn't help but feel a little sadness thinking that from then on that precious part of our significant history could only be in our memories, and is no longer tangible.

The place ADD had rented for us was at the southern end of the main street and the house was a big four bedroom old style wooden house on stumps that had been shifted from another place to the vacant block. The land was bare without any lawn around the house. The wooden floor creaked as we walked on it but it had plenty of room, enough rooms to have a separate room even for my hobbies- painting and sewing. Not long after we arrived back in Kalgoorlie we were pleased to receive a lovely letter from Nancy and Kingsley in Adelaide, and found out that Kingsley was in hospital and Nancy was with him on the day we called at their place. They too were very sorry to have missed out on such a rare opportunity to see us again.

We prepared a veggie garden in the back-yard as soon as we could by working the soil with lots of animal manure and to water it down while the weather was still cool and comfortable. We planted seeds of lettuce, spring onion, radish, cabbage, spinach and pumpkin as well. Even though the nights were cold the days were warm enough - the perfect temperature to grow them and everything grew very quickly. Having our veggies growing in our backyard and cooking our meals with what we had grown was such a rewarding experience; it grew into my new-found passion very quickly. I was surprised with myself how much I had changed since I came to Australia.

I would never have imagined that working with animal manure was something I would do in my life let alone embracing it so much so that it grew into a passion.

Our dear friends from Seychelles Island, Georgette and Gilbert, had a lovely veggie garden at their back-yard and they were ever so kind to teach me in all aspects of gardening. They were very pleased that we came back to Kalgoorlie to live and needless to say how happy we were to live close to them again.

We enrolled Maurits at a preschool as soon as we could. The first day he started to attend the preschool Maurits didn't like to be separated from me and he was in tears and made me worried leaving him there but to my pleasant surprise he was all smiling when I picked him up and I was so relieved to find out he experienced an enjoyable day.

One of the times Maurits and I went to town, we were walking past the stores on the main street when a fat little white mouse in a show case spinning a wheel fast at a pet store caught Maurits' eye, and he was so fascinated by it and stood there mesmerized. The store keeper came out and asked Maurits if he would like to have the mouse. What a silly question it was, the answer was of course "Yes". The next question the shop keeper asked Maurits was, would he like the fat one on the wheel or a skinny one inside of the store, which was another silly question, of course he wanted the one spinning the wheel, the fat one.

I was just letting the dealings go on between the store keeper and Maurits seeing I didn't know much about mice and just paid for the fat cute one and brought it home. At first I didn't think anything of it much and I was happy for Maurits to have it for a pet and have Rolf build a better cage for it. Within a couple of weeks the fat little mouse gave us a litter of seven tiny pink little mice. We were all so fascinated by them and we watched them grow bigger by the day, and they literally grew before our eyes.

It was all good but in a few months we saw it grew fat again and soon gave birth to another litter of eight, then we had to have a serious family discussion between the son and his parents before the army of little mice would take over our lives. The parents won the debate and to the pet store keeper's amusement we took them all back to the pet store except two male ones. Maurits had already then a couple of guinea pigs and a kitten for his pets. Maurits was sensible and had come to the agreement that he had far too many pets for him to look after!

Unlike the first time we lived in Kalgoorlie, we noticed some Asian people living there. I met a Japanese lady who was of my age, married to a German, with a little boy about the same age as Maurits, and we became good friends and more interestingly they were also into growing veggies in their back-yard like we were. Having the same interest we became good friends very quickly. Another time I met a Malaysian lady who was also around my age with a little infant, and married to an Australian geologist. The Japanese friend, Chieko spoke English like I could. But the Malaysian friend, Aggie spoke fluent English with a Scottish accent as she was brought up and educated in Scotland. We often got together and shared meals and enjoyed each other's company.

Soon after we came back to Kalgoorlie ADD was bought by Mindrill and the company name changed to Mindrill but nothing else was changed. Rolf was doing the same job for the same boss. He was away a lot in the bush as usual.

I had to walk everywhere with our son not being able to drive a car and I often envied friends who could drive. But for some reason I didn't have the courage to learn to drive a car and I felt I wasn't ready for it until one morning. As soon as I told Rolf about it he tried to teach me to drive whenever he could but it often turned into an argument. He was overprotective of my safety and I argued badly with him because I felt he was treating me as if I was dumb and didn't know what I was doing. We ended up fighting so much so I had to give up learning from him and I had to go to a driving school and learn. I should have done that at the beginning as I didn't dare to fight with the instructor as I knew I had to do just as I was told.

I went for the written test and passed straight away but I had to go three times to pass the practical test. Each time I failed I had a very good reason to tell Rolf why I had failed and as usual I would tell him that it couldn't have been my entire fault. Rolf knew better, of course, and he sure teased me each time I gave an excuse for not passing - that he knew better! Nevertheless I got my driver's licence in the end and it was wonderful and all the ridiculous fights we had, was all worthwhile! I thought about what my father had said to me at the Kimpo Airport the day I left Korea that he would have taught me to drive a car if only he had known I was planning to go to Australia.

I was thinking I was lucky that it was Rolf who tried to teach me to drive and it wasn't my father I had to learn from because I couldn't imagine me arguing with my father. Nonetheless I was very excited and proud to write to my father to let him know about my huge achievement.

Rolf found an old broken-down and abandoned car in a car-yard. He bought it for $300 and towed it all the way home because he thought it would be a good first car for me if he could fix it to get it going again; a 1968 model Renault ten, a little yellow French car. The interior was of genuine leather, very well kept and still in good condition but the engine was broken down and no one in Kalgoorlie could get the parts to fix it. Rolf was smart and was able to make the parts needed himself with only another couple of hundred dollars.

How excited we were when it was all fixed and I could drive it around. Maybe it was an old car but I couldn't have been happier with a brand new Rolls-Royce! My life has never been the same ever since! Living in a place like Kalgoorlie where there wasn't much public transportation, it was such a necessity to be able to drive and have an own car. To be able to drive to wherever I wanted to go whenever I wanted was not only convenient but it also gave me the boost of confidence to take charge of my life; the sense of freedom, independence and being less dependent on others was truly wonderful!

My confidence was on the rise and my desire to have another baby grew stronger by the day and I was very happy to find out that Rolf also thought it was a very good time and a place to have another baby. Within a couple of months when the obvious symptoms of morning sickness started and confirmed the pregnancy with our second child, we were very happy and over the moon! Like the last pregnancy I was very sick for the first three months with the horrible morning sickness, but as it did last time, it was almost like turning a tap off one day, I woke up fine and I could eat anything and soon I had my energy back to normal.

One weekend, close to Christmas, we went to Coolgardie about 40km west of Kalgoorlie to visit an old gentleman whose name was Keith. We met him when we were living in Kalgoorlie the first time. He was in his 70s and a retired gold miner, who lived alone in an historical house. We enjoyed listening to his stories of life in the gold fields. It was one of those sweltering, hot summer days when we returned home in the late afternoon we found both of our two little pet mice had died in their cage; their water bowl was tipped over and lying on its side next to them. Maurits was heartbroken and cried as he buried them near our veggie garden in the back yard. We were all sorry for not securing the water bowl properly before we left.

In the following year, Maurits started primary school. It was an emotional day not just for Maurits but for me as well. I couldn't be a more proud mum on that first day. Seeing our little boy in a school uniform, all grown up and sitting in my little car and I drove him to school all by myself.

Maurits was very advanced for his age. He could already read and write all the letters of the alphabet and showed very good comprehension in a lot of things for his age of five, which made us very proud parents. The very first time he showed me the A3 paper he had drawn, in correct details of the hinges of an entrance door of a large men's ware store where we had been for shopping a couple of times. I was very proud to see how good the drawing was for his age and able to seeing things in detail and memorizing well enough to draw in correct details.

I read an article in the local newspaper about a pottery class starting soon at the TAFE College and I enrolled as I had everything around home under control, and I thought it would be a good opportunity to learn something different while Maurits was at school. Since I could drive around by myself and my spoken English was improving by the day, and the thought of going back to a class situation to learn something new excited me and up-lifted my spirit. The pottery lessons were very enjoyable but I enjoyed more speaking English with Australians I met there and learning Australian accents. I wasn't good at working on the pottery wheels as my tummy was getting bigger by the week and uncomfortable, but I made some nice things by pinch-pot method and I loved doing things in the company of others.

I must say I enjoyed being pregnant for both of my pregnancies, although with a swollen tummy it was uncomfortable to do things at times, and I also experienced some bad cramps at nights. The overall experience of pregnancy was wonderful; I felt the contentment in my life, on a journey into my womanhood.

Don from Sydney, called in on his way to Perth one day and surprised us. When he knocked on our door and said "Anyone home!" Maurits recognized his voice and ran to the door shouting "Uncle Don is here!"

We were all glad to see him again but Don was standing there, looking sad, exhausted and heartbroken without his big truck. The differential of his semi-trailer had failed on the way and he had a hard time to get to Kalgoorlie. He stayed at our place for a few days while he was sorting out the big problem. A few days later he managed to get it repaired and he was relieved to leave for Perth to deliver his load to an army place. But to our dismay he came back the same day, he was so unlucky, the semi-trailer was broken down again. This time the engine that had seized up and he had to hitch a ride back to Kalgoorlie. He was much stressed and very disappointed.

A few days later when the problem was all sorted we were all very relieved to see Don was happy again. Don is about five years older than Rolf and has a fair complexion like Rolf. He has an explosive laugh that distinguished him in a crowd and he sure loved to have a good laugh. I was glad to see him back to his old self again joking and laughing. He was pleased to see me drive a car and that I had my own car to drive around. He was happy also to see I was pregnant and congratulated us but not without his humor-ridden, explosive laughs.

One cool evening in July 1976, a beautiful baby boy, our younger son Ed was born at the same maternity ward at the Kalgoorlie Regional Hospital where his big brother was born. We had been right around Australia and had lived in different States since our elder son was born there five and half years ago. I felt unreal to have another son back at the SAME Hospital! Even the room I stayed in was the same, room number eight. It was another very long labor, as the labor pain intensified with every contraction, at times I was scared I might die and felt extremely lonely Rolf and Maurits not being there with me. But all the fear and the pain were instantly forgotten the minute our baby was in my arms and I was just overwhelmed with joy! A pure magic moment I would hold close to me forever! I remember how blessed I felt to have another son!

Rolf had already been celebrating the birth of our baby with his friends and had a few beers before he came to see us in hospital with Maurits that night, and apologized to me for being so late.

Maurits had a runny nose and a bit of temperature. But it didn't seem to worry him he was just happy to see his new-born baby brother and didn't take his eyes off the baby and touched him ever so lovingly. I put our baby in Rolf's arms for him to hold and I saw tears of joy in his eyes.

The second time around the experience was definitely different in many ways. I was more confident as I already knew what to expect and I was familiar not only with the place but with the procedure of the maternity ward. A couple of the staff remembered me and made me even more relaxed while I was there for a week. But every day I looked forward to the time when Rolf and Maurits could visit us and we were all together for a little while and I couldn't wait for the day to take our baby home.

A week later, when we drove into the driveway of our home with our new-born baby, our next door Italian neighbour looked over the fence and shouted loudly at us to welcome us home and said: "Hey Rolf, the day your wife was admitted to hospital to have the baby you told us that this time it will be a baby girl but how do you feel now you have a baby boy again?"

Rolf didn't hesitate to respond and shout, "When did I say that? I never wished for a girl because I know girls are trouble, boys are better!" and we all burst out laughing.

The house had enough rooms for each of our children to have their own room; I had prepared our baby room long before I went to hospital to have him. Not knowing whether the baby was going to be a boy or a girl I had bought all things for the baby in neutral colours, white or yellow, not pink or blue, and everything I had in the baby's room was brand new. Because whatever we had for Maurits when he was a baby, had all been thrown away as we had shifted many times from State to State. But there was still one little old quilt mostly in a pink colour that I had made with the nine embroidery squares I had done at my junior-school days. It was much loved by his big brother when he was a baby and still there in our new baby's room waiting to be loved again.

By the time I ran around doing all the daily chores around home and attended to our children's needs I was flat out to have some rest at night while baby was asleep. Writing home was always put on the backburner. Once again it's been a long time since I had heard anything from home. One morning somebody knocked on our door and when I opened the door there was a man with a telegram. It was for me from Korea. My heart sank to the floor with fear even before I started to read the message. Then I couldn't believe what I was reading. My stepmother was hit by a bus and was killed instantly on the busy road just outside my father's business in Norangjin. I couldn't believe it knowing she would have crossed that road so many times during the past ten years she lived there.

I was utterly surprised and sad, lost in thoughts, thinking about everyone back home and I felt guilty not being in touch more often. Poor mother! It was a tragedy. She was far too young to have her life taken away so soon! I remembered her big brown eyes with prominent cheek bones and she was tall and a very good looking lady with the distinct accent of the south-eastern province of Korea, which stood out in our family not only because of her accent but her extremely good looks and bright personality to go with it. How sad and empty my father would feel losing again a wife he loved. He was only fifty-one and had lost 3 wives. How unlucky can one be!

As had happened to all of us, our little brother, who was barely ten years of age, was left without a mother. My sister, Kyung Hee who is three years younger than I am, had grown up without knowing what mother's love was. Given she was barely one year old, an infant when our mother had committed suicide and had left us, it had affected her life badly. At the time of the accident she was twenty-three and was in a relationship with a man. My two other younger sisters, they too were only little when their birth mother died with cancer, they were only five and seven. They were then in their teen years and were still living at home and had endured the inevitable conflicts living with a stepmother. Nevertheless who could have guessed such a healthy person would be taken away so soon.

Although we had lost our mothers so early in our lives there has been some stability in our lives having had our grandmother living with us and growing up with her constant love and her discipline. However I had witnessed firsthand the difficulties of living with in-laws, and such tradition caused much sadness in many people's lives in Korea. My life in Australia was very lonely at the beginning not having any family on either side of our families, but I always knew how lucky we were to be left alone to live our life in peace without any interference from any of our families.

I wanted to have a good cry but I couldn't as what I read on the telegram didn't feel real, the sadness I felt was only in my thoughts! It would have been comforting for my family in Korea if I returned to be with them. But not only the predicament I was in didn't allow me to go but we simply couldn't afford the trip. However it was a wakeup call to do all I can each day and to try not to leave what I can do today for tomorrow, because tomorrow may never come. I promised myself that I would try harder to write home more often and to let them know that I love them and miss them very much.

Time went by, the gold mining in Kalgoorlie was having an economic down turn. The report of the local newspaper said that the production reached its lowest point since the Second World War. The contract drilling company like Mindrill for the mineral exploration companies didn't have much work in Kalgoorlie, and Rolf was asked once again to move elsewhere. The company wished to send us back to Mount Isa; again all expenses paid by the company and they gave us the assurance to rent a house for us, not a flat. Our friends, Georgette and Gilbert had sold their house and had already left for Perth. Many more friends were in the process of moving out of Kalgoorlie.

The best choice we had was going back to Mount Isa with the job. I loved my old French car and we didn't want to sell it. Rolf felt he was obliging the company and didn't ask the company to send our second car by a transport company; instead he worked out how to add another axle to our box-trailer to make it legal and possible to take it with us. The trailer had already done many thousands of kilometers all over the country with us, and had some rust spots but Rolf cleaned the rust out as well, and got it all ready for another long trip.

Maurits was very sad not being able to take his pets with us - his two fat guinea pigs and a cat he loved. We went to see the pet store owner to ask if he would take them. Luckily the store owner was very kind and told us to bring them around and convinced Maurits to think that they would be happier at the pet store where they have many friends. Saying goodbye to his teacher and friends at school was also a very sad thing to do for Maurits. It broke my heart to see him in tears and to take him away from all those he loved and cared for. I knew then this had to be the last time that we'd move away while our boys were little and attending school.

There were a lot of things to sort out of a big four bedroom house. A huge task, especially with an infant baby to look after. Every time we moved, there were a lot of things we gave away or threw away even though we might need them again soon. Most of the things worth keeping were packed and the removal truck took them away. But traveling with such a little baby and a child, there were a lot of things we couldn't do without every day and had to be packed at the last minute. We loaded my little car on the trailer and secured it to travel with us and filled the car with all the things we needed for travelling, to have our Kingswood space again free for us all to sleep at night.

Our baby was only three months old, October 1976, the winter was long gone and the temperature was climbing to another hot summer. Once again we were driving away from the special place where we have experienced many of the significant and wonderful first time events; the place where it all began. It is the place we started our life together, the place where we became husband and wife, the place where we became parents. It is the birth place of both our sons and it is the place also of where I got my licence to drive a car, and as well as Maurits started his school life. I felt somewhat sad leaving such a sentimental place as I knew we wouldn't be coming back for a very long time. Because we couldn't continue to be shifted around from state to state, as we must give our children stability in life.

Every day we were on the road Maurits was missing out on school so we had to take the shortest possible route to get back to Mount Isa as soon as we could, the sightseeing was secondary. It was still a very long way, about 5,000 kilometres through the Nullarbor Plain, Port Augusta in South Australia, into New South Wales Broken Hill and Bourke, into Queensland, Cunnamulla, Longreach, Winton, Boulia, Dajarra to get to Mount Isa.

It was well into afternoon by the time we were on that long and boring straight stretch of the Nullarbor. The sun was shining behind us this time not on the windscreen as we were heading straight east but we were soon feeling tired and exhausted, having got up very early that morning doing the last minute cleaning and packing before we left. We needed the rest. We camped early by the road and we were in bed as soon as we ate something we had prepared before we left, and our baby was breast fed. Our baby sleeping in a basket on the front bench seat of our Kingswood and three of us lying together right behind the seat.

We woke up to the cry of our baby in the very early hours of the next morning, still pitch dark outside. I quickly got myself ready to breast feed our baby and Rolf started to drive. Soon the rising morning sun was shining on our windscreen and danced as we continued to drive straight east. Rolf had to drive slowly and we were getting more apprehensive as we were getting closer to Eucla thinking that soon we would be on the South Australian side of the Nullabor where that bad unsealed road was. But when we got there, the road was sealed! We were so surprised but very pleased about it. The construction of the new road must have been in progress when we drove past 16 months ago but to a little south not on the same route. For some reason we missed out hearing anything about the construction of the brand new road. I guess as migrants limited in the language, we couldn't absorb all that was going on around us in those years. The new road was only just completed and opened less than three months prior and there were piles of left over materials still here and there by the road side. Not having to worry about breaking down Rolf kept up the speed to the speed limit; we drove over 1,000 kilometres on that day.

Next morning early we drove past Port Augusta and by midday we arrived at Broken Hill, a mining town in New South Wales, known as "The silver city", just past the border with South Australia. We had nice "fish and chips" at a café and bought a BBQ chook for our dinner as well. At a service station we topped up with fuel and ice before we headed off to an unsealed but shorter road to Bourke. At dusk we camped overnight by the dirt road, we chose the road knowing it was unsealed because it was a shorter distance but we didn't know how bad the condition really was. Some places were pure sandy road, very difficult to drive. We were so lucky to get through there and not get bogged with such a heavy load on the trailer. Rolf told us a story that was hard to believe. Apparently many millions of years ago there was an inland sea there, eventually the sea water dried up but the sands remained to this date. It was unbelievable that so far inland once was a sea.

The vast sun-burnt land was empty without much life of any kind; each kilometer we drove was only a relief for me.

We drove past the border into Queensland and we were just a few kilometers south of Blackall, we decided to stop for the night and drive into Blackall in the early morning. While we were topping up our water, we smelled an unusual odour and the water from the tap was very warm and steamy. We learned that it was called artesian bore water. Not just the smell but the taste of the water was unpleasant as well but that was the only water they had. We couldn't help but wonder why people would live in such a harsh and remote place permanently. However one good thing I was told was that soaking in the artesian bore water is a good remedy for aches and pains.

We drove on, past Winton and then Boulia. The road condition was getting from bad to worse. it was a narrow and uneven track and it was extremely dusty and slowed us right down. But late that afternoon, after almost 5,000 kilometers of a week long journey on the road with an infant, covered in dust from head to toe but safe and well, we were driving into Mount Isa once again. Our faithful old Kingswood towing the same box-trailer this time loaded with my little old yellow car.

We were excited and shouted in unison when we first spotted the chimney stacks of Mount Isa mines in the distance, "LOOK, there are the chimneys!" And breathed a huge sigh with relief and were happy. We went straight to the company's work shop which was then called, Boart Australia instead of ADD. We got there just before their finish time. Rolf's old boss, Rex, came out of his office and welcomed us back. Just like the time when we arrived there from Darwin. And he explained to us that the house they had rented for us was not ready for us to move into and he had organized a flat for us. And he continued to explain to us that the house we were to move in was the house he and his wife used to live in when we were in Mount Isa last time. Since they bought their own house and moved out it was rented out to someone else. But luckily Rex found out that the house was about to be vacant again and he managed to tell the owner to hold it for us as he knew we would like the house. We were very pleased to hear about it because we have been in the house before when Rex and Mary lived there and he was right, we liked the house and we were happy to wait for it.

Chapter Six

We moved into the flat and unpacked only what we needed straight away, it was good to have my car off-loaded from the trailer and emptied. The first thing we enjoyed was to have a long shower in a proper bathroom instead of a quick wash on the road. It was also so nice to have a washing machine to get through the big pile of laundry. Although we were lucky to have the hot and dry weather all the way, washing baby's nappies everyday by hand and getting them dried had been a hard chore.

The first weekend after we were back in Mount Isa, we had an invitation from our friends for a BBQ. Laurelle and Mike were organizing a big get-together party for our return and our mutual good friend Don from Sydney was also expected to arrive on that weekend. Mike worked for Boart Australia as well and we were good friends since the last time we lived in Mount Isa. We were very much looking forward to seeing them all again and to catch up.

I was in a hurry putting through the last load of nappies in the washing machine before we left for the party. The washing machine was a Simpson Wringer washing machine which I knew very well how to use as we had the exact same brand of washing machine before in Darwin, Mount Isa, and Kalgoorlie.

As I was leaning down to reach the last few nappies at the bottom of the agitator, to put them through the wringer which I had spinning at the middle of the machine, THE WRINGER CAUGHT my long hair and QUICKLY WOUND it UP!

WITH a QUICK HARD PULL, I just PULLED MY HEAD BACK! It all HAPPENED in a SPLIT-SECOND! No time to think to push the lever to release the hair as I was in shock and panic-stricken. I screamed for Rolf "HONEY Honey!"

By the time Rolf heard my scream and rushed to me, I was already knocked down on the floor. I saw the wringer thick with my black hair still spinning in the middle of the washing machine. I touched my skull as I felt a strange tremor, it was smooth but luckily it was not bleeding. My whole body was trembling in shock with so much fear that there was no chance yet to feel sadness or tears! Rolf was horrified with what he saw and helped me to sit up and hurried to take me to the hospital straight away but I told him to help me to the mirror in the bathroom first.

When I saw myself in the mirror I had the worst shock in my life and fainted on the bathroom floor.

Rolf helped me to the lounge room. While I was lying there in fear not knowing what to do and petrified, I saw our six year old son come inside from playing outside, seeing me lying on the floor with such an ugly bald head all of sudden, he was horrified and without saying a word rushed straight back out as fast as he could.

Seeing his innocent reaction in fear I felt the whole world tumbling down on me!

Rolf wrapped my head with a large scarf and insisted on taking me to the hospital. I told him I wasn't going anywhere but as I was lying there and thought about it, I was getting desperate to find out if I would ever have my hair back or not. Rolf was right; I had to go and face the reality and see a doctor.

As I was getting myself and our little children ready to go to hospital with us I was crying in fear and I couldn't stop crying. When we got to the hospital we had to wait a long time before it was my turn to see a doctor, seeing it was a Sunday. There was a minimum staff on duty and there were a lot of sick people in the waiting room. I was scared and very nervous the whole time I was there waiting and I kept touching my scarf to make sure it was securely covering all of my ugly bald head so that no one could see it.

Finally when it was my turn to see a doctor I felt like running away instead but Rolf was very loving and helped me to the doctor's office.

It was a consolation to me to see it was a senior female doctor, how embarrassed I would have been if the doctor had been a good looking young male! Rolf followed me in and explained to the doctor why I was there and helped me to take the scarf off my head. She looked at it and took her time, looked all over it with a magnifying glass and felt the scalp of my head with her hand but without saying anything at all. In total silence for all that time - the wait seemed an ETERNITY!

Rolf too couldn't wait any longer and in unison we asked "Is the hair going to grow back, Doctor?"

She responded with a silly smile on her face and an empty stare without any sign of empathy she said "Not… really … sure, at least your scalp was not hurt, it all depends on how deep the follicles were damaged I guess… only time will tell."

That was what she actually had said but I heard it as "No your hair may not grow back and I can't guarantee it will grow back." My heart was broken into a million pieces. Whilst Rolf heard what the doctor had said was, "The scalp was not hurt so there was no reason why the hair would not grow back". He was my rock and my only hope; I would have felt better if I could only go with the logic in his way of thinking. Not having any assurance from the doctor, we returned to the flat feeling even more scared and afraid that I may never have my hair back.

My tears were dripping down on my baby in my arms while I was breastfeeding him. I felt as little and vulnerable as my baby having lost all my confidence in life. What's left of my hair on one side of my forehead looked stark against the empty white scalp, it would have looked better if there was nothing left and I was completely bald, yet I couldn't allow myself to shave off what was left. Rolf had contacted Laurelle and Mike to apologize that we couldn't come to the party and told them about the bad accident. The very next morning Laurelle came around to see me. I wasn't ready to face anyone yet but I had no choice. And she was a good friend.

When she saw me with my head all wrapped up in a scarf, her instant reaction was somewhat naïve; with a big silly smile on her face she couldn't hide she apologized in a guilty voice and said "I am sorry for LAUGHING, Ann" "You will be OK, just BUY a WIG!" Still, she couldn't wipe her silly smile off her face. The way she said it sounded sarcastic to me. I wouldn't have reacted that way if the situation was reversed. I was hurt and thought that she was not such a good friend after all. For many weeks I was wondering if I should forgive her. It got me thinking about the people who were disabled or handicapped, how sensitive their feelings might be and I promised myself to be even more sympathetic toward them.

When the house was ready for us to move into I wasn't at all ready to move in the neighbourhood where many people who knew me lived nearby. And I would have preferred to stay on in the neighbourhood where no one yet knew me. But we had to move. I wasn't ready to talk about why I had to wear a scarf all the time and I tried to avoid everyone I knew as long as I could. I was nervous that I may run into people I knew every time I drove Maurits to and from school and went out shopping. Luckily many people I knew didn't yet know that we were back from Kalgoorlie, moreover wearing a scarf was in fashion during that summer and wearing an outfit with a matching scarf was very popular.

Anyway I wasn't ready to talk about it even with Linda, to whom I felt very close like a sister. By the time we returned from Kalgoorlie, while we were away from Mount Isa, Linda had brought her mother and her little daughter out from Korea and they were living with her in Mount Isa. For some reason, Linda had never before mentioned to me that she had a little daughter who was left with her mother in Korea. It was a big surprise for me to find out about it and I was dying to meet them yet I was very reluctant and delayed seeing them.

I guess I wasn't ready for their pity for me.

Any little hurt on my body, even a little bump on my toe, was first felt on my skull. And I was always very nervous to make sure my scarf was secured in place, even at night when I was in bed sleeping. Although Rolf was very caring for my feelings and made me feel at ease with how I looked, I couldn't bear the thought of Rolf unexpectedly seeing my stark white scalp in the middle of the night and scaring him. When I was alone I took my scarf off sometimes and examined if there was any sign of regrowth of my hair by feeling the scalp with my hand. Rolf's ongoing loving support and the assurance that it will grow back kept my hopes alive. Rolf was the only person who I could trust, he genuinely cared about me. I didn't write anything about it to my family in Korea, it was not something they could help me with and I didn't want to add my sadness on to them, as it wasn't long after the sudden death of my step mother.

Rolf had a lunch break from his work every day for an hour from noon to 1pm and he always came home for a hot cooked lunch if he was not away from town, unlike most Australians who were brought up eating sandwiches or something simple for lunch. We both preferred to have hot cooked meals even at lunchtime despite at times it was far too hot to eat a hot meal, let alone cook it. I have always prepared a hot lunch for us and still do to this date. Every time Rolf came home from work, he was hoping for the good news about the re-growth but for weeks then months there was no sign of it at all, and worrying about it day after day for so long I became very depressed, struggling to regain my confidence in life.

There was a day I was very depressed I thought about even ending my life.

But I just couldn't dare to abandon my little children and my husband I love very much. How selfish it was of me thinking such unthinkable thoughts and my heart cried! But not knowing whether the hair was going to grow back or not was killing me slowly inside. Christmas and the New Year passed without any of the usual celebration, barely struggling to cope with it all each day surviving one day at a time. It was really a testing time for my faith in God. Rolf being Swedish, he was born into the Lutheran faith but he didn't believe in going to church, and even though I was taught to believe in God through my junior years at the Christian school neither did I belong to any particular church.

However, a long time ago I had the profound experience of the awakening of a faith in God.

One day, unintentionally, I was standing on a small ant nest in the bush. I saw many tiny little ants crawling around my shoes and I realized, how big and enormous I was compared to them and thought about the vulnerable life of the ants hanging on the balance under and around my feet. I could have easily ended their life by stepping on them. In that very moment my belief in the existence of The Almighty God became very certain. The thought of the existence of something far greater than we are, above we humans, was an awakening moment to the meaning of faith in God, and my life has been much more meaningful since.

I have been trying hard to hold on to it.

I was in the bathroom getting ready to have a shower one morning, took my scarf off and I felt around my scalp as I had done for weeks and months.

That morning, I FELT it! And was caught by a huge surprise!

I FELT "YES!"

Some parts of my scalp were a little rough! I felt it again and again just to make sure I wasn't just dreaming but it really felt like when I touched Rolf's chin when he hadn't shaved it for a day!

I was ecstatic with joy!

So much so my legs became weak and I fell onto the bathmat below. With tears in my eyes and my both hands interlocked tightly and I yelled, "Thank you God! Thank you so VERY MUCH!"

I thanked the Almighty God for giving me another lease of life.

As I shouted loudly and thanked God again in the shower I heard my baby cry. I picked my baby up as soon as I could in my arms and I danced around stark naked until I came to my senses to feed my hungry baby, and put some clothes on myself and the scarf back on my head. The clock read 10.50am. The clock hands seemed to be moving ever so slowly that morning, waiting for Rolf to come home for lunch at noon seemed an eternity.

The minute Rolf arrived home I rushed out to the carport to see him; he could tell that I had good news even before I said anything to him, and he was instantly in tears with joy. He hugged me very tight and sighed and whispered in my ear "I have told you so" We were happy and relieved in each other's arms. I knew I would have to wait for many more months or even a year until it all grew back but it didn't matter anymore, knowing that it was starting to grow back for sure I was only happy to wait. The huge stress of not knowing and forever waiting to find out finally came to an end; the enormous stress was lifted off and instantly replaced with the joy of a brand new beginning! In no time I regained my sanity and my confidence, and had the inspiration to do the things I used to enjoy to do and embraced every minute of my new lease of life.

I finally had the courage to go around to Linda's place; my scalp still wrapped in a scarf, and met her lovely mother and her beautiful little daughter Jackie. Linda's mother was in her early sixties and Jackie was only seven. I felt very close to them straight away as if had I known them for a long time and I could even talk about my hair with them without too much stress. I often went around there to speak Korean with Linda's mother and keep her company, being with her and having the conversation in the same Seoul accent made me feel at home, as if I was with my grandmother. The meals she prepared were just like the delicious meals my grandmother used to cook as well.

I re-joined the local art group I used to be member and reconnected with like minded people, and I volunteered as an English tutor for new migrants and I was passionate about helping out the new migrants I met, in any way I could. My own English was improving much faster as I was helping the migrants and I had gained a lot of general knowledge from migrants from different countries and it further broadened my perspective of life. It was very satisfying; sharing the knowledge we had and learning from each other. Mount Isa being such a multicultural place, volunteering for English tutoring was very much appreciated.

As my days were fully occupied with many different interests, writing to my family in Korea was left behind again even though I often missed them and thought about everyone and wondered how everyone was coping with life. However it was only in my thoughts and writing to them was on the back burner, something I could do later.

One morning another telegram from home arrived at my door and devastated me once again. "Oh! No!" I murmured in disbelief and re-read it. The message I read cannot be true, it stated that my father had passed away suddenly with a hemorrhage in his brain while he was sleeping.

The devastating news made me flop down on the floor in shock and I went numb in disbelief.

I couldn't come to terms with the fact that my father, who had always been very healthy and strong, had died. I can't remember that my father was ever ill except that he suffered aches from a broken wrist every winter, since he had a bad car accident some years before. My heart was trembling but I felt no tears. I wanted to cry but I couldn't even feel sad. I felt just numb!

I was imagining how hard the last twelve months would have been for my father, since he lost his wife in the accident, it must have been very stressful for him. Although that year I myself had such stressful times, I felt extremely guilty for not getting in touch with him often and I regretted deeply that I had never given him the chance to see his precious grandsons and his son-in-law. He would have loved seeing them; I would have made him so proud given how important it was to have a son, an heir to a family in Korea in those years.

I remember how relieved and happy we all were when my brother was born. Everyone of our family waited for a long time for a baby boy to be born, as my father had six daughters from his first two marriages before he got a son from the third wife at last.

Myself and my younger sister from my mother and then, he had four more daughters from my first-stepmother before she passed away with cancer. My youngest sister was only a few weeks old when she died with a sudden infant death syndrome and the second youngest sister died about three months after my first-stepmother passed away and she was only three years old.

I will never forget the day we had the *Mudang Goot,* a shaman ritual we had in Korea to placate the angry spirits of the dead after a funeral. The shaman who happened to be a mother of one of my friends came to our place in company with musicians of a *Jang gu,* a drum like musical instrument, a cymbal, and a flute. They prepared for the ritual with some colourful paper trimmings in the room which was already set up with lots of sweets and fruits for a kind of offering to the dead, in the room where my stepmother had lain ill for many months with the cancer before she died. The shaman set up a stack of four trays and each tray was filled with a bed of rice. Apart from the top tray she added some paper cuttings of different shapes inside of each tray around the edges. Then she told me in particular to sit next to it and have a good look at each tray and how they all were layered out.

She was dressed in shaman's colorful costume with a hat and started to perform the ritual in the room. She danced a shamanic dance I have seen before. As she danced to the music her team was playing she kept on murmuring something, as if she was talking to herself. But at times her voice was shaky and shrill, everyone watching could hear from outside of the room because the double door was wide open, as if she was in the midst of having a conversation with my deceased stepmother we just had the funeral for the day before. After a little while she stopped the performance and the music stopped. She put down the top tray on the floor and she again asked me in particular, to have a good look at the tray to see if those paper shapes had moved and if I could see a big shape of a bird on the bed of rice in the tray.

Growing up in our neighbourhood I had seen such a ritual, *Mudang Goot* a few times, but I was neither superstitious nor interested in finding out about what kind of affect such ritual would have on people and I was rather skeptical about it. Furthermore that year, I was in my last year of my junior years in the Christian-school, deeply into studying the teachings of the Bible. Skeptical as I was, I was so very surprised and couldn't believe my eyes at what I saw on the tray. A lot of the paper cuttings in the second tray had actually moved about under such a heavy tray of rice, and there I saw a kind of a pattern made by indentation on the bed of the rice looking like a shape of a bird. The shaman caught my honest instant reaction and was waiting for my honest answer. I wasn't comfortable admitting to her that I had seen and I was hesitant to make a comment but nodded my head as I had to. Because I could honestly make out the shape of a bird and witnessed many of the paper shapes had actually moved about on the tray.

Then she told me to pay close attention to what she was about to tell me. Her emotion ridden expression took a strong hold of my confused emotion and she said in a low and shaky voice like a ghost if you will, "As you can see, your mother has become a stork and she is now flying free from all the pains and she is watching over all of you." I was scared and shaken and had my tears running in confusion, feeling the presence of my stepmother in the room. It felt as if my stepmother was back with us. I was sobbing, missing her even more.

The shaman put the top tray back on the stack and she danced again to the sounds of a *Jang Gu*, a cymbal and a flute until the music stopped. She removed the first and the second top trays together that time and put them down on the floor again and told all of us siblings to come in and have a look at the inside of the third tray. There were some indentations on the bed of rice in the tray and I tried hard to figure out but I couldn't see a pattern for anything I recognised but, unbelievably I could notice, many of the paper shapes had moved there as well and were mingled in different places. She looked at the tray as if she was also trying to figure out what to say to us and I was very anxious, waiting in anticipation to hear what she was going to tell us next. I was by then reasonably convinced that she knew what she was doing and she had some kind of a power to communicate with the deceased people.

The place was in total silence. Whether one is a skeptic or not, everyone was just waiting quietly to hear what she was going to say next. When she was ready she said to us siblings with a very sad and soft voice "Your mother was very sad and sorry she left you all behind and she was very worried about your youngest sister who was not well. She is going to watch over you all closely for the next few months and if she feels that you are failing to take good care of your sick little sister, she will take her away from you."

Then she raised her voice a little louder and started to repeat it in her ghost like voice for others to hear. It scared us even more and put all of us into the extreme fear of losing our dear little sister. My twelve year old sister, Kyung Hee and I comprehended straight away what she meant by it and we became so scared and burst out crying. All of our little sisters became sad watching us crying and that made them all cry with us. I couldn't handle it anymore. I picked up my youngest sister in my arms and rushed outside the room, all my sisters followed me out crying all together in each other's arms in the yard whilst the rest of the family, friends and onlookers were staring at us with pity.

I was fifteen then and Kyung Hee was twelve. My other sisters were seven, five and three. Our youngest, the three-year old, was very thin and getting weaker by the week, in our eyes there were signs of malnutrition. We got so worried and didn't know what to do to save her. We were just kids; we didn't understand why she was thin and weak. We weren't brought up to ask adults too many questions knowing that they were already fully aware of her condition. We didn't know either what they were going to do about it, or to demand them to take her to a doctor. Kyung Hee and I thought that we would save our little sister from dying of hunger if we could find the way to earn some money and buy some nice food so she could eat more than she normally would, and she would get better soon.

There was a little scrap dealer not far from our place who would give us some money if we brought him some old copper wires, used pistons or any kind of re-usable metal scraps. We could sometimes find things like copper wires exposed on the dirt road after a storm and odd pistons from my father's garage. When we got some money, we didn't tell anyone, it was a secret between Kyung Hee and me. We went to the market near our home in Itaewon after school, one of us carrying our little sister on our back and the other holding her little hand and we walked to the market to buy the things she liked to eat, as much as we could afford, and fed her.

There were days we couldn't buy much of anything nice for her to eat and we would be very sad sobbing together all the way home. No one in the family ever knew about this, not even our other two younger sisters, because we didn't want to take any chance of any adult stopping us from what we were doing. Many days I walked to school and back to save the bus fees to spend the money to buy more fruit and street food our little sister liked. But despite all the love and effort we made to help her to get well, on the third month she died. It was such a painful memory that I will never forget and I knew very well the whole matter could have been dealt with differently if she were born a son or grandson not another daughter or another granddaughter. I also knew very well my stepmother lived her married life feeling inadequate for not being able to give birth to a boy. The culture we had was old, unfair and at times really cruel.

When my father got married again, he was thirty-nine years of age; the hope of having a son, the heir for the family was well and truly alive again. Everyone in the family hoped sincerely for my father to have a son and I was glad when my father found a good looking healthy young woman for our stepmother. The week our stepmother was due to give birth was the week before I was expected to go to a weeklong school excursion to a famous holiday place by the sea, "Hae-un-dae". I had never been to the beach nor had I ever been on holidays, thus it was the trip I was very excited about and really looked forward to go.

My father was preparing to deliver the baby himself. I was told by my father to assist him and I was trying to do the things my father told me to do. But accidently I spilled boiling hot water on my thigh, and got burned while I was pouring the hot boiling water into a big container to sterilize things he needed to use for the delivery of the baby. Even though it wasn't a deep burn it was very painful and there wasn't anything we could find in the room to treat it with. I was in agony waiting and waiting into very late in the night for my stepmother to give birth. It was a long labor and the contractions went on for many hours through the night. I was in pain with the burn and very disappointed thinking that there was a chance I wouldn't be able to go to the school excursion now I have such a wound to heal. I felt cranky and became tired and fell asleep and slept through my stepmother's labor pain.

When I opened my eyes the baby's umbilical cord was already clamped and cut and my happy father was wrapping up the baby in a towel and the room was filled with a peculiar odour I'd never experienced before. My father must have been very good at delivering the baby all by himself and didn't wake me up to help him, and let me sleep through it all. The minute I saw my father's smile from ear to ear and the proud smile on mother's face I knew it was a baby boy and I was so relieved and happy for all of our family and I thanked God it was a boy.

At last a son for my parents, a brother for us, and an heir we had been waiting for so long! A baby boy, at last! No words could describe the joy we felt that night. And the baby, my precious little brother, was Absolutely Gorgeous! The joy of having the precious baby brother was so great it even subdued my terrible disappointment of missing out on the school excursion of a life time. Next morning the special rope with some dried red chilies and charcoal pieces poked through, was hung proudly outside of the gate of our home, to let the neighbours know that a baby boy was born; it would have been another plain rope without any chilies and charcoal pieces if it had been a baby girl.

Now that I am thinking of it all, life at times doesn't make any sense at all, neither of my parents had the chance of seeing their precious son grown up. My brother was barely eleven when they were taken away from this world. Life is unpredictable and unfair to take them away so soon from us. Perhaps I took it for granted that they were young and that they would always be there for me to return to. I never thought for a moment that I might lose them so early.

It can't be real! It didn't feel real! I was too far away in other parts of the world to come to terms with my father's sudden death.

I have always focused on taking good care of my own family in Australia and tried to fit into the community wherever we lived, and I always had in my mind doing right and acting responsibly was to honor my father. Visiting my home in Korea wasn't an urgent thing to do and it was something I hoped to do later when I could afford it. However I felt very sad and miserable for not have given my father a chance to have the pleasure of meeting my family. Nevertheless the chance was lost forever now and I have to live the rest of my life with the regrets. I told myself once again that I mustn't take anything for granted, or procrastinate, as it may ultimately lead to such regrets.

I worried about my poor family in Korea, left without my father and without the security of the main income. But I knew I was not able to help, we were just getting by with one wage, and we didn't have very much money saved, having lived the life we had. I felt very inadequate not being able to meet my obligation to honor my family by returning home to Korea in such a sad and difficult time. My heart was torn between wanting to go and not being able to go. Rolf understood how I felt and was very supportive and tried his best to comfort me. So did my friend Linda's family.

Linda's husband, Angelo, was running the kitchen of the Irish Club Restaurant in Mount Isa. Linda was also a keen cook and Linda's knowledge of cooking had become even better since she had watched and learned from Angelo. They often discussed opening a small seafood restaurant that Linda could run, catering for Korean style seafood cuisine with a Greek twist which would be unique in Mount Isa. There weren't any such exotic restaurants in Mount Isa in those years. Within a few months they organized themselves and opened a small BYO restaurant, seating about sixty, just off the main street in Mount Isa and called it 'Korean Seafood Restaurant' and it was an instant hit and kept them very busy.

One day when I called in to see Linda's mother she asked me if I would be able to leave my children with her for a little while and help Linda at the restaurant, especially on days like Fridays and Saturdays when they were very busy and needed extra help. Linda's mother thought that someone like me, who understood Korean as well as English, would be a big help. The restaurant was opened for business only for dinner but not for lunch, which meant my daytime schedule shouldn't be affected by it.

Even on nights when Rolf was away from home, my children would be cared for by Linda's mother. I realized it was a good opportunity for me not only to earn some money we needed but to learn to work in a restaurant. But I had huge worries about convincing Rolf. Rolf always insisted that I should be at home to take care of our children whilst they were little. He had told me several times that he hated that his mother went to work when he and his siblings were little.

But I wanted to try and to find out what it was like to work at a restaurant when I had such a good opportunity, and Linda's family were very persistent, telling me that I was needed badly there because they wanted someone who could communicate with Linda in Korean and be able to attend customers outside. When Rolf was away with work and not at home at night, I left my children with Linda's mother for a while and I went to help at the restaurant. I instantly fell in love with what Linda wanted me to do, communicating between the waitresses and Linda for the best service possible for the customers. I enjoyed the work very much and to be able to earn some money was really great! From then on no one could tell me that I shouldn't work, even Rolf. Rolf then realized my mind was made up. He didn't dare to try to stop me going to work anymore.

Linda didn't need help from me through the daytime while she was doing the preparations and she understood that I needed to do my own things during the day, therefore my usual daytime schedule was not affected by the job. I prioritized in such a way to ensure all of my regular housework was up-to-date and my family's needs were all well taken care of, so Rolf could see that there was no problem with my going to work a few evenings a week at the restaurant, and it was well within my capability. And it was a bonus that the extra income could be saved to give us more options in life.

It was a very happy day for us all when we were able to buy our first brand new colour television with the extra money saved. I had all twenty-four $50 notes spread out on my bed and took a photo of them before we went down town to pay for it. I didn't think I was ready to look for a job before, not only because I was discouraged by Rolf but I was also thinking that there weren't many good job prospects with my English still being not perfect. But having discovered what I could do for employment, not only any job but a job I would enjoy doing, it was so fantastic!

Linda was amazingly capable at cooking and running the kitchen and the restaurant was very popular. The business was doing well but Angelo was beginning to feel he needed a change and thought that such a restaurant would do even better in Darwin. He missed Darwin, the life by the sea, and Darwin was well on the way to recovery from the terrible cyclone. Despite Linda's wish to stay on he gave up the business at the Irish Club and insisted on closing down the seafood restaurant and moving back to Darwin.

When they left, I was without the job I had fallen in love with and the company of a very loving family living nearby.

It was unbearable not having the job that I enjoyed doing and not having the extra income I had become used to. I was no longer contented and decided to look for a job and thought hard about where to look for it first. A job in a hotel made sense to me. No matter where we went in Australia, there was always a hotel even in very little places where only a few people lived permanently. Thus I came to the conclusion that if I could be trained to work in a hotel I would always find work wherever I went in Australia.

On the way home after I drove Maurits to school one Monday morning I made up my mind to go down town as soon as the hotels opened for business and look for work. I got myself ready to look my best while my eighteen months old baby Ed was having his morning sleep in his cot knowing that he would be sleeping for another hour. I left the radio on to minimize the sound of disturbance and I locked the house and went for the five to seven minute drive to the hotel in the main street, which I thought was the best one of the hotels in town.

At first I went to the reception desk and said to a lady standing behind the desk, "Good Morning, I came to look for a job. Could you tell me who should I see please?"

The receptionist pointed her finger to the direction and said, "Through that door and you will find the manager's office on your left."

I said "Thank you!" and as I walked in that direction my heart was starting to pound, responding to my early fear of possible rejection. I stopped a couple of steps before the office door in the short corridor and took a big breath and exhaled and walked to the door. The top half of the door was left opened so I didn't have to knock on the door and I saw a young man and a large lady busy counting the money from tills.

The young man saw me standing at the door and said with a kind voice, "Can I help you?"

So I said, "Yes, Good morning, I came to look for a job."

And he said, "Please come in." I opened the door and went inside.

He pulled a chair for me to sit down and continued counting the rest of the money in the till. Both were continually focused on counting the money from till to till, from a pile of tills in front of them. I made a conscious effort of sitting up in good straight posture like a well brought up lady, with both my legs together to one side, and waited. A minute or so later he stopped counting money and turned the chair he was sitting on around to face me and he apologized "Sorry to have kept you waiting."

I nodded my head and smiled at him instead of saying in words that it was OK and I was preparing for the interview in my mind to give my best effort to speak as an educated person.

"My name is Shane" and he smiled back at me but he looked awkward and hesitant, not sure if he should shake hands, and waited for my response.

I responded by nodding again and instead of a handshake said "Oh, nice to meet you Shane, my name is Ann."

"Have you worked at a hotel before?"

"No, I have no experience of working in a hotel."

"If you haven't worked at a hotel before what kind of work are you looking for here?"

I could sense by his expression that he was disappointed and I didn't want him to think that I was a "no hoper", so I responded positively by saying "I have never had a proper job as yet anywhere in Australia, apart from a few months recently when I gave a hand to a friend who had a restaurant, but now I would like a job in a hotel, any job. I am a very fast learner and will do my very best to learn quickly whatever you would care to teach me."

He looked at me with a somewhat puzzled look and continued, "Are you married?"

"Yes, I am married with two children"

"How old are you?"

"I am twenty-seven and I am from South Korea and I have been here seven and half years." He stared at me somewhat lost in thoughts and I could see in his eyes that he didn't know what to make of the Korean lady before him.

Hesitantly he gave me a paper and a pen and said, "Please write down your full name and contact phone number here."

So I said, "I don't have a telephone at home yet, so I will write down my home address instead."

He looked at the paper briefly and said, "That's fine, we will contact you if any job comes up."

I left the office with a short "Thank you!" as if what he had said was fine with me but my heart was starting to thump, thump again as if that wasn't OK. It felt as if I had done something I shouldn't have. I rushed home and found my baby still soundly sleeping in his cot and I made myself a cup of coffee to calm my nerves by telling myself that at least I had made myself very clear to him that I wanted a job, any job, and that I would do my best.

When Rolf came home for lunch, I kept swallowing the words without telling him that I put my name down for hotel work. There was no need to upset him prematurely as there was no guarantee that I would get a job out of the very first interview. One thing I was sure of was that there would be many experienced hotel workers around waiting for an opportunity to be employed at a hotel as such, and an inexperienced person like me would be the last in the queue and I could be waiting for a long time or maybe never get a job there.

Two days later early on Wednesday morning, I was hanging out the washing on the clothesline in our back yard when I heard a man's voice "Excuse me, hello, do you remember me?"

I was startled by it as I wasn't expecting anyone that morning and when I turned around I saw the young man from the hotel office.

"Oh, hello, of course I remember you."

"My father is the manager of the Isa Hotel and he wants to have an interview with you, can you come in to the hotel sometime this morning?"

I couldn't believe what I had just heard. I heard it as if he'd said "You now have a job at the hotel."

"Yes, of course, I will be there as soon as the business is open and thank you so much!"

As he turned around and walked away from me to his car parked on the road outside of our home, he shouted with such a satisfied voice of mission accomplished "See Ya, Bye!"

I responded with my happy and joyous loud voice, "Thank you very much and See you soon, Bye!"

I finished pegging the washing on the line and rushed inside to my mirror in my bed room to check how I looked then without any makeup and hair not yet brushed. I was embarrassed with what I saw in the mirror. I washed my almost shoulder length hair and blow-dried it into a style and put on a little make up. The noise woke up my baby Ed a lot sooner than normal from his mid-morning sleep time and I fed him a little snack and changed his clothes. I changed my comfy house clothes to a nice conservative two piece smart outfit in navy and white and white shoes with a high wedge.

We arrived at the hotel right on 10.00am the same time as the door opened for business for the day. I went straight to the manager's office and stood at the door. As I looked in through the open top half of the door I saw a man of my father's age and the large lady I had seen last time.

I said, "Good morning, my name is Ann and I came for an interview with the manager."

The man smiled at me as he opened the door for me and said, "Oh, come in we were expecting you, take a seat." and gestured toward the same chair where I sat the last time. I sat there holding my little son, Ed, on my lap.

He introduced himself and his wife to me whilst they both were standing close in front of me. "My name is Vic and this is my wife Kerri." and he extended his hand out to me for a handshake so I shook his hand as I spoke, "Nice to meet you", in unison with him and I shook his wife's hand and said, "Nice to meet you."

And she said "Nice to meet you too." The questions and the answers in the interview were almost identical to the last one with their son, as if the whole process was a replay. The manager and the manageress stared at me for a little while as if their decision wasn't quite finalized and this made me anxious to wait to find out what it was all about.

The manager started to speak to me and said: "From Monday next week there will be a vacant position coming up at our drive-in bottle-shop. It is a full time job forty hours per week; and it is a split shift, from 10.00am to 2.00pm and 6.00pm to 10.00pm five days a week. What do you think?"

I didn't comprehend fully what he'd said, not only about the hours but what I'd have to do as a hotel bottle-shop attendant, but I was willing to try any work as long as they would give me the chance.

So I said, "I have never worked in a bottle-shop before but if you would give me the chance and teach me, I will learn fast and work hard to my best ability." They looked at each other with big smiles. They seemed both happy to hear my words and liked my attitude and they both looked satisfied to give me the chance thinking that I could be taught to do the job.

I shook hands with them again with sincere thanks while I was still sitting on the chair, with one hand holding my son, and accepted the position as a bottle-shop attendant at the hotel drive-in bottle-shop. I promised to start at 10.00am sharp on the following Monday morning. I left the office with my heart racing with a joy, sat in my car for a while to try to put it all into digestible pieces to take it all in. The first thing I thought about was the hours of the work. The hours weren't all that bad, by 10.00am Maurits would already be at school and as I would have the break between 2.00pm and 6.00pm, picking Maurits up after school was no problem either. However there was a big problem about finding a babysitter for my baby for the morning shifts and for both of my children for the evening shifts on the days when Rolf was away from home. It would be much more difficult to convince Rolf to accept me getting into the workforce if I couldn't find a good babysitter.

Some months earlier, I had met a lady in a very unusual way. That summer, 1977-78, wide legged long pants were in fashion and they were comfortable to wear. It was an easy design to make and looked nice on me, having a small waist so I had made a few in different materials and I often wore them to town. One day when I was about to go into the K-Mart store in Mount Isa, I heard a woman's voice coming from behind me, speaking abruptly "Excuse me." I turned around to see who it was but it was a person I had never met although I had seen her around often in town. She was very thin and about my height, 153 centimetres tall and dark skinned with a distinctive look, and deep dark spots on her thin face and with noticeable several gold teeth. She looked like an African Asian.

When she got my attention she continued with a smile but still in an abrupt tone of voice asked "Did you make those pants?"

She pointed her finger to the long pants I was wearing and it made me a little apprehensive not knowing what it was all about and I was impelled to answer her. In a doubtful, low voice I said "Yes, but…why are you asking?"

As she pointed her finger at my long pants again and said "I like the pants you are wearing. I have seen you wearing many different ones. You make me one and I will pay you."

I got rather scared and didn't dare to say No and I said, "They are very easy to make, I will teach you to make one if you like." I could read in her eyes that it wasn't the answer she wanted to hear.

She said "I can't read or write English. You come to my place one day and help me, I live at Leila Street." So I asked her what was her name and she told me that her name was Zainab. As I was writing her name and the address down in my notebook I told her my name was Ann and I promised her that I'd contact her, and feeling relieved I went into the store.

I found Leila Street on a local Street Directory. It was close to my place, in a side street, half way to town from my place. That was probably the reason I often saw her walking to and from the town. I thought I'd better visit her soon and help her to make the pants before I ran into her again. A few days later I went to her place. Her home had a fence with a walk-in gate secured by a latch. I looked inside the yard, hesitant to go in at first as I was afraid there may be a dog in the yard, but I didn't see any dog so I went inside and knocked on the front door of the house. I heard dogs barking from inside then and when the door was opened I was rather relieved to see a European looking man with a kind smile. A couple of dogs were with him but she was out. I introduced myself to him and explained why I'd come and told him that I would come back around the same time next day, and I did.

Zainab was from Malaysia and her long time partner Erik was from Denmark. They didn't have children but they had a back yard full of animals; a goat, and a couple of dogs, many cats, chooks and lots of pigeons. They also had lovely gardens around the house. It looked a peaceful place and the more I got to know them the better I felt they were very nice and kind people. Zainab didn't have a job but Erik was a forklift driver working for Mount Isa mine. I made her the wide legged long pants with the materials she brought to me but I didn't charge her any money for making them because I liked both of them. We became friends and have shared meals at each other's home a few times since.

I thought I had a good chance that Zainab might return me a favour for having made her pants, and babysit for my baby until I found a babysitter. Also her place was very conveniently situated as it was on the way to my home. So I drove to her place first. I was very lucky that morning as she was at home. I explained to her that I'd just found a job at the hotel and I was to start work in a few days and I was desperate to find a babysitter straight away. I pleaded with her to help me out for a few days until I found a babysitter. She was reluctant at first as she had never done babysitting for anyone before but she must have felt obliged and agreed to help me out.

I sighed with huge relief, being able to leave my baby with such a kind person and having sorted out the biggest worries I had if Rolf were to be against me taking the job. I drove home very satisfied with the outcome of my effort. As I was preparing a nice hot lunch for us, a big part of me couldn't wait to tell Rolf all about it soon enough but the other part of me felt that I needed some more time to think; in case there was anything else I had to sort before telling Rolf.

I opted to tell him all about it in the evening when he was more relaxed instead of during the short lunch break so that I'd have the chance of sorting out any short comings as it was very important to me to have his 100% support. I was pretty confident that I could convince him that I needed the job as we needed to start to save some more money for our better future. Rolf was not even aware that I went to look for work, therefore he was very surprised to hear the news that I had already found a job, not just any job, but a full time job and had already managed to organize someone we both knew to babysit for our children. Rolf couldn't deny the extra income would do us good, he didn't have the slightest case to go against me and he had no choice but to support me. I was much relieved to see Rolf was convinced and I had his full support.

After all that I still had to pinch myself if it was all real! It was that quick and easy to get a job, in a hotel in Australia! I couldn't believe my luck at finding a job, the full time job with my not so perfect English and moreover without any experience of working in the hotel. How lucky I was to get a job from the very first place I went to look for work. I didn't yet know what my job in the bottle-shop would be like but I made sure I was organized and ready to learn whatever I needed to know and was ready to give my 100% to the job.

Before the Monday I started to work, I made sure all my housework was up to date and I cooked extra meals and froze them for the busy days. I got up at dawn on the Monday morning and from then on I did the same on all my working days, as there were many chores to do before I left home to start work at 10.00am. I started the routine with watering the gardens around the house and my pot-plants. Not only did they need to be watered daily during the hot summer months but I enjoyed watering very much, it was therapeutic. Then I prepared breakfast for everyone and had it together before Rolf went to work to start at 8.00am. Making the beds, helping Maurits to get ready for school and driving him to school before 9.00am, cooking lunch and getting it ready for Rolf to heat up and eat when he came home on his lunch break, and getting my toddler Ed ready to go to Zainab's place and finally getting myself ready for work.

I had to apply the multi-tasking skills to get all jobs done on time by 9.30am to leave home and drop my toddler on the way to work at Zainab's place with his needs. I'd arrive at the hotel car park for the 10.00am start. The first time I left my little son with Zainab I was worried as I had never left him with her before but Zainab made it easier for both of us. I could just disappear without upsetting my toddler while he was busy chasing a cat in the back yard and Zainab was very good at keeping him happy away from me. I was relieved knowing that Zainab was relaxed around him.

The work in the bottle-shop was pretty easy to follow, there was an experienced lady working with me to show me what I had to do: attend to the customers who drove in to buy whatever the bottle-shop had in stock which was all kinds of beers, soft drinks, wines, spirits, bagged ice and snacks. Using the till, and then recording most of the items sold into a book to re-order as well as maintaining the shop area clean and tidy by putting away the delivered items into the right places. I had to apply my common sense and learn fast about the unfamiliar names of the things we were selling and memorize the prices and where they were kept but the routine was not hard and the bottle-shop wasn't busy during the morning shifts.

I had a lot to remember but it was manageable and I felt I was very welcomed by the people I worked with and the customers alike and felt very good with the work place. As soon as my morning shift was finished, I drove to Zainab's place to pick up my baby hoping that everything had gone well with them. As soon as my baby Ed heard my voice he ran into my arms with a big smile and shouted "Mummy Mummy!" With tears in my eyes and with overwhelming joy, I thanked Zainab most sincerely and drove home.

By then I was hungry not having had anything to eat since the very early breakfast before 7.00am that morning. I heated up the meal in the microwave oven I had prepared before I went to work, gave my baby a quick wash and after lunch little Ed and I lay down on the floor on a soft rug cuddled up to each other in our carpeted lounge room and took a short rest together. We got up to pick up Maurits from school and when we got back home, help Maurits with his home work and I cooked dinner for the family. By the time Rolf arrived home from his work soon after 5.00pm I had already bathed our baby for the night and prepared the dinner for the family and I was about ready for a quick bite to eat before I got myself ready again for work to start my evening shift at 6.00pm. Rolf would have dinner with the children a little later and put them to bed for the night.

The evening shift was a lot busier but it was good as the time went much faster. At 10.00pm I shut and locked the bottle-shop, handed in the till at the office and drove home. Rolf switched on the kettle to make me a cup of tea as soon as he heard my car drive into the car port. I was pleased to hear the kettle was on as I walked inside the kitchen door and Rolf welcomed me with a big hug and kiss and I had a quick peep at our children in their beds sleeping peacefully before I sat down for a cup of tea and a chat with Rolf. It was such a wonderful day, the first day of my employment, I had a lot to tell Rolf and we went to bed satisfied and looking forward to the better future.

I worked Mondays, Tuesdays, Wednesdays and had Thursdays off and worked Fridays, Saturdays and the bottle-shop was closed on Sundays. The split shift was perfect for me. Trying to remember all those names and prices of things we sold in a short time was not easy but what I had to do was pretty simple and enjoyable. Many of the customers were aborigines and came by a taxi and they bought mostly the cheapest wine by the flagon. The way they pronounced it, sounded to me "plagon". And it took me a while to understand their way of speaking English as I never had anything to do with them before. Most times they came intoxicated and had unpleasant body odour, I was put off a little by it but I found they were harmless people and there was no need to be scared.

Once I got everything done and organized for the day I had some free times between serving customers. The job was very simple and stress free, didn't need much thinking, I had to find something to occupy my mind not to get bored. So I used the free time to my advantage, and wrote letters to Korea or read a book, knowing that I couldn't find time for such things when I was at home where I had to run around the clock to fit in all my chores and make time for my family.

The management team was very satisfied with my work. They often complimented my efficient work and even gave me a nick name, *"Spot on"* which made me very pleased. I was also very pleased with Zainab, although she had asked me a few times if I had any luck finding another babysitter she seemed always pleased to have my baby around. She was very kind not to stress me too much with it, even though she could tell that I was not seriously looking for anyone else.

I had been working at the bottle-shop for only about three weeks when the hotel manager first asked me if I would consider working at the à la carte restaurant upstairs instead of the bottle-shop. At first I didn't take him seriously as I thought he was just saying that to let me know that he was very happy with my work. I had no interest in finding out more about it nor had I any intention to change my job so soon. But the manager was very persistent and told me that he felt I was wasted doing the work at the bottle-shop and I would be more suitable for the work in the restaurant as a hostess.

He tried his best to convince me by explaining that not only it would be better hours for me because the restaurant was opened only for dinner therefore I wouldn't need the babysitter through the daytime but also the pay was much better. Furthermore, he told me, that I wouldn't have to handle the heavy cartons of beer like I had to in the bottle-shop. He made me feel obliged to think more seriously about working in the restaurant as a lot of things he said made good sense to me as well.

I told him that I didn't know anything about cocktails and had never worked in such a classy restaurant, but he reassured me that wouldn't be any problem as he was very sure that I would learn very quickly. and he believed I was the perfect person for the job. Having such kind and overwhelming support from him, I knew I had a very good opportunity to advance my career in the hotel industry and I had nothing to lose. He gave me an absolute assurance that if there were any reasons I didn't like to work there I could come back to the job in the bottle-shop at any time. On Thursday evening that week when it was my day off from the bottle-shop I went down to the hotel just before 6.00pm; the manager was glad to take me up to the restaurant, I followed him up the stairs feeling still a little unsure if I had what it took for the position.

The manager unlocked the side door with a key and we went in. There was a lady already working inside of the restaurant. She was smartly dressed in black and white and on high heels, busy getting ready to open at 6.00pm.

She said, "Good evening!" looking toward us as if she was expecting to see us both. She looked a bit taller and younger than I was.

We both responded in unison "Good evening!"

The manager called her to introduce me to her, "Hey Robyn, come here and meet Ann" She walked toward us as fast as she could in her high heels, she had trendy styled short brown hair and had a gorgeous set of brown eyes.

The manager said, "Robyn, this is Ann and Ann, this is Robyn!"

Robyn said, "Hi Ann!"

And as we shook our hands I said, "Nice to meet you!"

The manager said to Robyn, "I want you to show Ann around the place and it will be good if you could show her what she needs to do."

"Yes, Of Course!" she seemed pleased to meet me and I was very pleased to meet her. The manager left me in her care and he was gone in a flash. At first she unlocked the main entrance French-doors and left them opened and I followed her around and met everyone in the kitchen.

Some months earlier, my Korean friend, Linda and I went around town one night just to have a look at what other restaurants there were in town before Linda opened her seafood restaurant. I remembered looking in the very same restaurant and I was impressed how classy it was. But I had never been inside of the restaurant. Standing inside, it looked and felt even classier and more beautiful. It was fully carpeted in a luxurious thick red carpet and the cream-white walls had a few beautifully framed classic Victorian style red motifs, well spaced out, to match the red carpet on the floor, and the room was laid out beautifully and furnished in the classic style.

The tablecloths were very good quality white cotton starched and pressed. The tables were set for ninety people and the settings were very formal, set with polished shining cutlery. On the tables there were folded large red napkins in *bishop's-hat* design, ash trays, and sets of salt and pepper shakers. The restaurant had a separate cocktail bar with a pre-dinner drink area and there was a big circular open char grill area inside the restaurant against the wall to the kitchen. It had swing doors on each side of the grill to the well equipped kitchen.

Robyn must have been told by the manager to write down a list of what I had to do. She unfolded an A4 paper and asked me to sit down at the bar and read. The page was full, hand written in small running writing. Some things I read were about how to do and what to do, but things weren't explained clearly to me and I wondered how on earth was I going to learn to do all them correctly. It made me feel a little intimidated and made me more conscious of my poor English.

The restaurant was starting to fill with people and there were two waitresses serving meals and about 7.00pm another waiter came in to assist Robyn, making cocktails and serving drinks to the tables. They all looked busy and I didn't want to interrupt so I remained seated on a high stool at the cocktail bar, and observed every little thing that was going on in there, for a couple of hours. A lot of things written on Robyn's list made more sense and were easier to comprehend by just watching. The ambience of the restaurant was very pleasant with soft classic music that I loved, and I felt good being amongst a lot of people dressed in their best outfits and relaxed and having a good time.

I kept my eyes focused on Robyn watching how and what she was doing and I couldn't help but notice that even though she looked pretty she was abrupt and easily flustered. She certainly wasn't communicating well with the staff on duty. It was obvious that she was either inexperienced or she lacked leadership quality. Watching her work made me realize why the manager was desperate to replace her. I could also sense Robyn was not as friendly toward me as the time passed on; she wasn't at all interested in explaining anything to me and was rather sarcastic.

I felt my competitive streak wriggling deep down inside me with rising confidence and heard my inner voice telling me to move out of my comfort zone and grab the opportunity.

I didn't want to let Robyn's sarcasm put me down.

I was sure then I wanted to be the hostess of the restaurant. Before I left the hotel that night I told the manager that I knew there were many things I had to learn fast, but I believed I could do the job and I would do my very best not to disappoint him. He told me he knew that already and he had no doubt that I could. I thanked him very much and left the hotel in high spirits!

I went home very excited and felt adrenalin pumping hard inside me. Rolf was very happy and supportive. Rolf drove around town next day during his lunch time while I was back at work at the bottle-shop and bought all the cocktail books he could find for me and bought any magazines that had any information about fine dining service. I read and studied as much as I could in three days. Zainab and Erik were happy for me as well and very supportive and promised to help me out if I needed someone to babysit for my children in the evenings, when Rolf was out of town with his work.

On the following Monday evening I went to start work at the restaurant, dressed smartly in black and white. The manager took me up and introduced me as the new hostess of the restaurant to everyone, and before he left he gave me a briefing of my duties for the night. They were;

A) Greet the customers as they arrive

B) Encourage everyone to have some pre-dinner drinks before showing them to their reserved tables

C) When customers were ready; take their drink orders from the table

D) Prepare and serve - cocktails, wines, beers, spirits, liqueurs, cognac etc.

E) Take charge of looking after final accounts of all meals and the drinks for the night

F) My last duty of the night was to shut and lock the restaurant

G) Hand in the till to the office before I left the hotel. He also mentioned that he would come back close to closing time late that night and show me how to shut and lock up.

Robyn wasn't there to help me that night, in fact I never saw her again, but a couple of waiters came in soon after I arrived to assist me. I had a fair idea that Robyn was given my old job in the bottle-shop but she didn't like it so she left. I didn't know the names of the items we sold or where everything was kept, or how to mix the drinks and how to serve properly.

I didn't even know what lemon-squash was that night let alone knowing how to mix cocktails. Rolf drank mainly beer in those years and I preferred to drink water than any soft drinks and did not yet drink anything alcoholic. So everything was new to me and I had to learn fast, very fast, not only about the drinks we served but also how to use the till, which was different to the bottle shop till.

In those years, long before computers, the credit card charge dockets were done by using a credit card imprinter and all dockets had to be manually hand written with carbon paper under it to make the copy for customer. Being taught without a calculator at school and although I was very good at adding the sums of the dockets in my head, often I used a calculator to double check to ensure the sums were correct, thus everything took a lot longer than using the computerized check outs we have now.

I was lucky that Monday night was not too busy, we served only a few of the hotel house guests and some local business people and the evening went smoothly as the entire wait-staff were only too happy to help me. The rest of the week I managed by being honest with the customers, letting them know that it was my very first job mixing drinks and, pleading with them to teach me exactly how they would like me to mix their drinks.

Soon enough, I realized that that was the best way anyway if I wanted to please the customers individually.

Not only mixing exotic cocktails but even mixing the simple drinks such as 'scotch and dry' which could be mixed in so many different ways. In fact, I discovered up to 6 different ways, as people preferred different quantities of soft drink and ice in their mix, as well customers preferred different kind of glasses for their drinks. Just learning from books by reading was not sufficient to please everyone. If you are sincere and honest to the customers, most of them were only too happy to help so they could have the drinks made and served exactly how they liked.

How right was the saying of the Korean proverb, *"Even you know the road ask as you go"*

And also learning directly from the paying customers was far more pleasant and intimate than trying to learn all things from egocentric or inexperienced co-workers, with the added disadvantage of the likelihood of disappointed customers. Moreover it was the only way to impress the co-workers how well I managed my position without them being aware of how inexperienced I was.

Customers of all different status from all walks of life became my teachers showing me how to do my job the right way to please them and I was very good at remembering their faces and what I had learned from them to individually please them. The following week, on Tuesday morning while the restaurant was shut, I went in with my little toddler son and spent many hours of my free time to reorganize the whole cocktail bar area to suit my height so that I could serve quickly. I also rearranged the wine stock and stored them to correspondent with the wine list by numbering them both.

While I was doing that I became more familiar with the items we had as well.

I took on full responsibility and applied all my common sense to improve the bar area for the efficient service, thus as the week went by the job got so much easier and quicker. The bar didn't have keg beer, only bottled beer and cans of beer were served, thus it was much easier to change things around. Luckily I had the full support from the management team for whatever changes I had made.

Mixing cocktails became easier and more fun, as I arrived there earlier to ensure that all garnishes for the drinks were prepared in advance and ready at the start of the evenings. Garnishes such as fresh lemon and orange sliced in different shapes for different cocktails, olives, maraschino cherries, cucumber skin peels, pineapple cut up into small triangles, ground nutmeg, salt, toothpicks, drinking straws, swizzle sticks, small ornamental umbrellas and of course lots of crushed ice.

It was very interesting to learn all aspects of wine from the customers who enjoyed drinking wine and I am especially grateful to a couple of Mount Isa Mine executives, who had traveled the world extensively, and who were very fussy and wanted to be served in a particular way. They taught me well in all things to do with *silver service*. In those years people in Mount Isa didn't yet drink much wine. Cold beer and spirits like scotch or Bundaberg rum were more popular than wine with men. Apart from those MIM fussy executives who liked to drink wine, people drank mostly sweet and bubbly wines, such as Star wine or Lambrusco and moselles like, BenEan moselle. Beer and spirits were popular even for ladies and sophisticated people enjoyed cocktails more than wine. I have witnessed Australians becoming more wine drinkers over the years and there is no doubt that the wine we produce in Australia is now world class.

The Copper Grill Restaurant was the most popular place during week days for business people. The executives of Mount Isa Mine and other business people in town regularly entertained their business associates, not only from interstate but also their international guests. During weekends, the restaurant was filled with locals who came out for fine dining. The restaurant was à la carte style and catered for up-market French influenced cuisine. The menu was an extensive one and from appetizers to entrees to main meals to desserts there were many fine choices. Sea food dishes such as Barramundi-mornay and Lobster-thermidor were so popular as well as many char-grilled steak dishes such as Fillet-mignon, Peppered-steak and Carpetbag-steak. Our chef, Frances was an extremely good cook and she was a lovely person to work with. So was the grill cook whose name was Pearl.

Only a few months after I started to work at the restaurant, I was still relatively new in the position, the managers were transferred and a new husband and wife team arrived to take their place and I was so worried that I may not have the support from the new managers as I had previously. Fortunately the new managers could see how confident I was in my job and liked what I was doing, they let me keep going with what I was doing and gave me support as I needed it.

As I knew my job was secured I became more passionate in making new outfits for myself to look my very best at work. I had very good reasons, not only did I want to look good at work but I enjoyed sewing for myself and loved being dressed up. Being the hostess I was allowed to wear whatever I wished, even though I loved wearing black and white I didn't have to wear a black and white uniform like the waitresses. It was not easy to find from the stores something I liked to wear and that would fit me properly, if I found anything at all, being shorter than average, every time I had to alter and shorten about 3 centimetres off the bodice of a lady's size 10.

It was much easier and quicker to alter a pattern to suit me and sew a new outfit than try to alter a bought outfit and of course when you make your own, it's unique. Being a short person, only 153 centimetres tall, wearing shoes with heels was essential for me and I liked to wear them because it made me feel good and very feminine. I preferred plain colours or classic pin stripes when I chose materials to sew and liked to wear body hugging long evening dresses or soft flowing long pants in jumpsuit style to look taller, elegant and sexy and most importantly I wanted to look uniquely exotic. All dressed up and working in air-conditioned comfort amongst happy diners didn't seem like a job most of the time and felt like I was out socializing.

It was the perfect job for me also to improve and polish my spoken English and to express and explore my creative mind in many ways, and most of all it suited my personality. I liked when the restaurant was full and busy, the busier the better. The busiest time was between 7.30pm to 9.30pm every evening and at times it was extremely busy, but my adrenalin always kicked in and I liked working at a fast pace. I felt comfortable in the crowd and I enjoyed making sure everyone was well taken care of and enjoyed the evening.

I loved the challenges of interacting with people with status and I didn't even mind sorting out the born nitpickers or downright rude, obnoxious people although at times it was way out of my comfort zone to deal with them and it was a difficult challenge and I wished I was wiser.

Nevertheless I got better at it with the daily practice. It was such a rewarding and fantastic feeling when I got those difficult souls eventually to come down to my level by consciously behaving myself in style and humility to have them behave rationally, the experiences taught me not to get intimidated by rude people and rise above them.

It was the perfect place to study human psychology in a practical way. Studying how people think and process their minds was fascinating for me and my skill at handling difficult situations - the problem solving skill - became better all the time. Those practical lessons helped me to be more confident and easier to approach people of all walks of life, which was a huge bonus on top of what I got in my pay packet at the end of each week.

I was very proud and I loved every aspect of my position as a hostess yet I had the problem letting my family in Korea know about it. In Korea in those years a woman working in a hotel as a hostess had a somewhat undignified stigma. Although the job description was not the same I knew my family would expect me to do something more prestigious. Having been brought up in Korea and yet to lose such a stigma, if I was able to speak fluent English, probably I would have looked for work in an office rather than in the hospitality line of work in a hotel. However it didn't take long at all before I overcame such a silly dilemma and embraced the opportunity with open arms.

The job was like a match made in heaven for me.

The hardest thing I encountered at the beginning, interacting with people would been understanding Australian jokes, not only because of my not so perfect spoken English but also because the basis of the jokes was different to the jokes I was used to in Korea. My permanent casual barman, Billy, was an Irishman who never ran out of jokes. It took me many weeks to figure out that many of his jokes were based on sex. Having been brought up thinking that for a woman talking in public about anything to do with sex was somewhat dirty and improper, when I finally did understand what the jokes were all about, I didn't want to respond to such jokes especially in the presence of men, as it made me feel somewhat degraded and uncomfortable. In self-respect I opted to be left out of those conversations and preferred to pretend I didn't understand the jokes because of my poor English. People who use swearwords made me feel very uncomfortable as well and it took me a few years to feel comfortable or would tolerate them.

Another thing I had to overcome in terms of cultural differences was calling people by their first name. In Korea to address an adult or the people you respect by their first name was considered to have lack of respect or being rude. Instead one was called by one's family relational position or profession. It took me a year at least to greet the customers by their first name and feel right about it. As I got to know people well, many had expressed to me that they preferred to be called by their first name, and encouraged me to overcome my reluctance.

About six months into my job we traded in our old Kingswood station wagon and took out a small personal loan for a brand new 4-wheel-drive Toyota Land Cruiser. It made us happy to have a reliable new car but I was very sad and in tears when we had to let go of our dear old Kingswood that had played such a big part in our lives for so many years. Soon after that we bought a small aluminum boat again as well and often on Sundays we went out to Lake Moondarra, about 19 kilometres out of town for fishing and socializing with friends. In the same year, for the very first time in my life, we got our home phone connected as well.

There were no other Koreans in Mount Isa since Linda had moved back to Darwin. I was the only Korean who lived in Mount Isa permanently in those years, although there was a Korean helicopter pilot mustering cattle for large stations not far from Mount Isa, who called in to see me in the restaurant when he was in town for business. There were not too many Asians living in Mount Isa at that time until a few years later. But I met a few other Asian migrants, when someone needed an English tutor and I was contacted to help them. It is fair to say that it was because I was there at the right time that I stood out in the crowd, and doing what I did for a job, quickly I was known to everyone.

One day I got a phone call from the Mount Isa base hospital and I was asked if I could come to the hospital and interpret for a Korean patient who was flown in from the Gulf, because one of his fingers was chopped by a propeller of the prawn trawler he was working on. His name was Choi and he was just a little younger than I was and understood very little English. In the past I had been contacted by the hospital to help out to interpret for a Japanese tourist who was hurt in a motorbike accident, and I was glad I was able to help out with the help of my Korean-Japanese dictionary, but it was the first time I was called in to help a Korean and needless to say I was very excited to have the chance to meet a fellow Korean.

Choi was appreciative of how I helped him and comforted him while he was hurt and lonely in the hospital for a week. When he was ready to be discharged from the hospital he told me he was planning to bring his wife from Korea, and to come back to Mount Isa and live near me as soon as he could. I told him that I would love that but I didn't expect that would ever happen. However in a few months Choi actually came back to Mount Isa with his wife who was pregnant and gave me a huge surprise. Soon there were more. After they came to Mount Isa one of his friends, Kim also gave up working on a prawn trawler and came to Mount Isa with his wife to live near us as well. All of sudden I had many Korean friends and I loved their company, I helped them every way I could, from finding a place to live to finding a job, at times standing in a queue for the Centre Link payment for them. I helped them to get a job at Transfields in Mount Isa where they worked as labourers until they were offered work at Mackay, and left Mount Isa.

One of the most joyous moments I will never forget was the time I was asked to be in the room to interpret for Choi's wife when she gave a birth to their first son. It was certainly an extraordinary and memorable experience, to witness the birth of a brand new life. Words can't describe how I felt and it brought to me the memory of the night when my father delivered my baby brother and how happy we were to have the heir of the family at last. We were all so happy with the arrival of a baby boy!

The doctor, Mark Weller, couldn't believe when I translated to him soon after the baby boy was born that Choi and his wife were going to name the baby after him, but not as Mark but as Weller. I knew they would think that Weller was his first name as in Korea the family name comes first. It sure was a joyous experience for us all to share!

After we bought the new four wheel drive and when it was a school holiday and Rolf's annual leave was due, I managed to get permission to have a couple of weeks off from work as well and we went on holiday to visit Linda's family in Darwin. We towed an old caravan we had for going on fishing trips on some long weekends so we had a mobile home with us to have somewhere to sleep for all of us and not to trouble Linda's family too much. We parked our caravan in the back yard of Linda's home, and we slept at night in our caravan and enjoyed the time with Linda's family, as well as visiting some old friends we had there. Linda and Angelo were busy running the lovely seafood restaurant there and had a nice home with a big back yard. It was really good to spend some time with them. It was lovely too to see Linda's mother who was well, and young Jackie was doing very well at school. It was also great to see the beautiful city; Darwin was getting more and more rebuilt since the bad cyclone, Tracy.

In September 1980, our landlord decided to sell the house we were living in and had it on the market. A few real estate agents often wanted to show the house to the potential buyers and I didn't like people walking through my home, especially when things were not tidy therefore these visits kept me even busier. And one morning both of our children, then nine years and four years old woke up very sick with tonsillitis. When I got back from seeing a doctor early that morning with my children, there was a salesman from an agent waiting in my yard with some people, to have a look through the house and as it happened to be such a morning, none of our beds were made.

I was extremely annoyed they came around that early and without letting me know, but I realized that the salesman couldn't reach me by phone that morning as we were out early at the hospital. I was obliged to let them through. The experience compelled me to ask myself why I was in such a predicament. My pride was hurt and I was very unhappy that I didn't have a choice but to let other people invade my privacy.

The issue of owning our own home became my utmost priority to think about that day. I made up my mind to look into seriously all things possible to buy our own house and prevent such a degrading experience in the future.

I had discussed with Rolf in the past about saving money to buy a house but Rolf was not keen on buying a house in Mount Isa, and he wished not to be tied up at such an isolated and remote place so far away from everything. He wished to move away from Mount Isa before we committed to buying our own house.

But I knew it could be many years before we could move away from Mount Isa whilst we both had good jobs. I was indeed very stirred up that morning and I made up my mind to go ahead and look into buying one anyway, at least I wanted to find out what sort of possibilities I had. I had to wait for a few days, until our children got over the tonsillitis, and were well again and just kept thinking hard about all aspects of how to go about buying a house. First of all I needed to find out, if the company Rolf was working for would still give us the cheque fortnightly for the rent, had we bought our own house. I needed to find out a few things myself before I discussed anything further with Rolf.

As soon as our children were better, one morning, I dressed myself ready to impress and after I dropped Maurits off at school, I headed straight to see Rolf's boss, Rex at the company's workshop on the other side of town.

I walked in his office with our little Ed and said, "Good morning!"

Rex was surprised to see us, "Oh, Good morning, Ann, good to see you, what can I do for you?"

I came straight to the point and said, "Hello Rex, we are thinking about buying our own house and I need to know if we buy one, would the company still continue to give us the rent cheques?"

He looked even more surprised and said, "I see. You are not planning to buy the house you are living in now, are you?"

"No, not at this stage, we haven't found one to buy as yet but I need your answer first."

"I don't know, Ann, I have to consult the matter with the head office in Melbourne before I can give you the answer, and I will let you know this afternoon."

"Thanks Rex. I will wait for your call. Bye." I left the office with some dissatisfaction not having the answer straightaway, and I began to wonder why he didn't telephone the head office immediately for me, instead of leaving it to do it later. I didn't like it. My brain was ticking fast in search of the solution as to how I could persuade the company to continue to give us the rent cheques.

By the time I arrived home I figured it all out. I picked up the phone as soon as I went inside, dialed Rex's office number and my heart was racing faster than the sound of the ring tone and I was ready to fire my words.

Rex finally answered the phone "Hello, Rex speaking." His voice had a *short of breath* sound as if he seemed to have rushed to answer the phone.

"Hello Rex, this is Ann. You know what, Rex, you don't need to phone the head office, we will buy a house and rent it out and we will remain living in this house, therefore more or less nothing would be any different to how it is now." I made sure that he got the message that under no circumstances would I accept the refusal from the company.

He said, "Ah haaaah, you are right Ann, in that case there is no need to consult with the head office, you will get the cheques so go ahead." He spoke to me lovingly as if he was speaking to a naughty daughter he loves.

"Thanks Rex. Bye." I put the phone down feeling very satisfied about securing the cheques and proud how I have conducted myself over the matter. I just hoped that Rex had assumed Rolf was in this with me, and didn't bother to mention about my visit to Rolf, as Rolf had no idea about it.

I was very much aware that Rolf didn't like Rex as a boss. I did what I did because I Knew I could handle Rex better over the matter. Nevertheless Rolf would not be pleased to hear firsthand from his boss about my visit, and would want to know why I didn't bother to discuss it with him and had sneaked around to see his boss without telling him. When Rolf came home for lunch I could tell that, as I had hoped, Rex hadn't mentioned anything to him. I broke the news to him gently about my sneaky behaviour of that morning and I managed to convince him that I was very serious about buying a house whether he agreed with me or not.

Next I needed to find out from our Bank if there was any possibility for us to buy a house. Soon after lunch I phoned Westpac Bank where we had a saving account and I made an appointment to see one of their loan officers that afternoon. When I arrived there the branch manager himself was waiting for me. I knew him well as he was one of our regular customers at the restaurant. He welcomed me into his office.

"Hi Ann, how are you? So I've heard that you are looking into buying a house, let's have a look!"

He made me feel at ease talking with him. "Yes, please and I am hoping that we can."

We had then about $8,000 cash in our saving account. He asked me, "What sort of price range of house are you looking into buying?"

I said, "I have no clear idea as yet but the house we are renting at the moment is for sale and I found out that the asking price was $29,000 and I will be happy if we can afford to buy something like it. A three-bedroom modern brick home with an established garden in a nice area close to Sunset State primary school where our elder son goes." "And I must not forget to tell you that other than the money we saved, I also found out this morning from my husband's boss that the rent cheques we have been receiving every fortnight from the company will not stop, even if we buy our own house."

"Oh, that is very good news. In that case I don't think you have any problem but let me see, give me a few minutes Ann."

My heart was starting to fill with an overwhelming joy that was hard to contain – an unreal feeling of the possibility that we were able to buy our house. I was waiting in anticipation for the final verdict while he was working out the sums in some kind of method with a calculator.

He beamed at me to match my equally lit up face and said, "You know what? Ann, you can buy a house today if you want to, go ahead and have a good look around." I couldn't believe what I had just heard. He also looked pleased to tell me that, and continued, "You would be able to handle the repayments very comfortably having the pays from you and your husband's job as well as the rent cheques. You can look for a house up to $30,000 without any problem."

"Oh! Really? I can't wait to tell my husband, thank you so much. We will start to look around straight away."

He handed me a little pile of papers he'd been working the sums on and said, "Show these to your husband so he can have a look, and I hope to see you soon, Ann."

"Yes, I will, and thank you very much again! See you soon," bye!"

How easy was that? I never thought that I could turn the situation as big as that around completely in a few days!

The thought of buying our own house was only in the distant future and was not tangible until that afternoon! The joy was too much for me to contain alone when I returned home, and I couldn't wait to tell Rolf. I phoned him at work to let him know about my visit to the bank. He was very surprised and I could sense in his voice that he was somewhat disappointed to hear that I already had been to the bank to discuss such matters without him; nevertheless he agreed with me that it was very good news.

It was great knowing that our next move would be into our very own house, not to another rental place! But we had to find the house we liked before the house we were living in was sold. We looked around with a few agents whenever we could for the next two weeks but we couldn't find any house we liked more than the house we were living in. Because we knew our place well, there wouldn't be any hidden bad surprises and we didn't have to go through the headache and hard work of moving out and moving in, if we could buy the house we were living in.

So we decided to look into buying our place instead of looking around any further and we had to buy it quickly before we lost it to someone else. I went to see the land lady, who lived down the same street and I suggested to her to take the house off the market because we were seriously interested in buying it. I told her that my bank manager already had approved the loan and I offered her $27,500 for it, knowing that she didn't have to pay the sale commission to the agent if she sold it to us privately. She got back to me the next day and told me that she would sell it to us for $28,000 but I took the chance and insisted to her that my offer was still $27,500. Later that afternoon she phoned me and told me that she would take the offer.

October 6 1980, after about 4 years when we had rented the house, it became ours - our very first house!

We didn't have to move out or move in! I felt a huge sense of achievement to sign our names on the dotted lines and that never again would it be determined by others where we lived.

I have learned another huge lesson that anything is possible to achieve and it all starts with wanting to achieve.

Living with a man who was very uncomfortable in getting into any kind of debt or taking any risk, it was inevitable that I had to go around him - it was my way to get things done to improve our living standard. Rolf was a good man to let me take over the management of our finances from then on.

January 1981, our elder son Maurits started grade six in the primary school and our younger son Ed started preschool. At work we had a new manager again and the new manager and the manageress were very young and didn't have the maturity or experience to run such a hotel. They were from a big city and wanted to change many things to suit them, without getting to know the characteristics of the outback mining community, and created many problems that separated workers instead of having them working together. They only lasted ten months before they were sacked and I was very relieved when they were gone. The next managers, a husband and wife team, were also from a big city but they were a little older and knew what they were going to do to improve the business, and had the skills to make people work together in harmony again.

They were very friendly with me and it was good to learn from them some new things like how to prepare the charge accounts better, and set up the new system for Mount Isa Mine as they were the most important clients for our restaurant. They had a little three year old daughter, Julia, and often on Sundays I invited her to my place to play with our boys. They looked forward to Julia's visit on Sundays. At the beginning Julia didn't like to eat anything other than steak and sausages with mashed potato or fried chips with gravy, anything green other than peas was not edible for her but within a few months she developed the taste and loved the food we ate, and looked forward to coming to our place on Sundays, not just to play with my boys but she looked very much forward to what I would cook for them.

The restaurant was getting more and more popular and it was the perfect place to get well connected with people from all walks of life, not only the locals but also the interstate and overseas guests staying at the hotel. I had even the pleasure of meeting famous movie stars like, Robert Vaughn, Graham Kennedy, Leonard Teale, and Helen Morse while they were shooting a film produced by Jill Robb around Mount Isa. The working title of the film was called "The Alcheringa Stone" but later called "Silent Reach" – a 1983 TV mini-series. The whole production team had dinner at our restaurant for the duration of shooting the film. I hardly ever heard of any of them as we hadn't seen many movies in Australia, and didn't know how famous they were until they were booked into the hotel. As soon as they were booked in they were the main subject of talk for days and weeks in the hotel, even I couldn't wait to meet such celebrities.

It was a pleasure serving them and they enjoyed our warm country hospitality. Before they left all twenty-six of them had written a short thank you note, each personally to me, signed with their autographs, all on the back of one of our menus which I was very pleased to keep. I will never forget, Graham Kennedy took his shoes off every time he was in the restaurant and walked around in his socks as if he was in his own lounge room at home, and how he never ceased to amaze everyone with his ever so witty and clever words. Just having him in the room was enough to put a smile on everyone's face.

I also have met many sales representatives from different businesses and got to know them well. Especially Lutz, a rep from Taubmans Paints, I had the great opportunity to buy some house paints for my house at bargain prices directly from him. The house we bought was a besser block home built in about 1972 and it was time that the outside of the house was repainted. The job felt like it was a daunting task, especially as I hadn't done any house painting before, and also knowing that I had to do it mostly by myself, because Rolf had to be at work most days. But I had been thinking about doing it ever since we bought it, given that I had the good opportunity to buy the paints directly from Lutz, so I made up my mind to have a go at it.

I learned from Lutz and our Finnish friend Pentti, who was a part time house painter as his second job. I learned well from them what I needed to do to prepare, and all the hints on how to do the job well. I scrubbed and cleaned the outside of the whole house and prepared it properly to my best ability, and painted the under coat once and the top coat twice, in cream with dark olive green trimmings. I had worked very hard, day after day, for many weeks to prepare and to paint whilst I was still going to work at nights. It was back-breaking hard work and I became very run down and exhausted in the end but it was worthwhile! The place looked so fresh and new and I was very satisfied and proud when it was all done, knowing that I was able to do most of it myself with a little help from Rolf.

A brand new ten pin bowling centre was built very near our home, owned and operated by our close friends, Des and Lauriet. The competition games were in full swing. I became very interested in the games as it was a game I could play indoors in the air conditioned comfort, a good place for socializing with friends old and new. With a few friends we formed a team and joined in the league to play every Thursday morning. We named our team "Peppers". I was a beginner and, having said that, I never got much better in the three years I played but I enjoyed the social aspects of it very much and made a few very good friends - close friends to this date for over 30 years.

1982 was another significant year for us. Maurits started year seven, the last year of the primary school and Ed started the first year of primary. Ed was excited to go to school with his big brother. Having such a big age gap between them I often noticed Ed looked up to his big brother and tried hard to be close to him. But more often than not Ed was far too little for Maurits to play with. Seeing both of them in the same school uniform and Maurits holding his little brother's hand and taking him into the school yard was a very proud and pleasing moment for me to see as their mother.

My life was full on, with many things I had to do and things I wanted to do and the way we lived was improving in every sense. We were even able to phone overseas and speak with our families who had the phone on at home and could receive their calls since we had our home phone connected. Although we didn't call that often as the international call was not easy to make and it was expensive, it was so great when we did call and hear their voices.

I was very well aware of the difficult life my family was enduring, since my father had passed away. My younger sisters were struggling to support my grandmother and our little brother with their small wages. I had thought about bringing our brother out to live with us and helping him to get educated here in Australia. However when I enquired about it a few years earlier, I was told not even to think about it by the immigration office, until at least we had our own house, and could prove to the Australian government that we could afford to support him. Thus, I was concerned more and more about the future of our little brother who was in his early teens and having some teenage issues. The responsibility of giving him a good education was overwhelming for Myung Hee who was twenty-six years old and was in a relationship with a boy friend but had to take care of our grandma, our youngest sister Myung Sook as well as our brother. One day she phoned me and pleaded for my help.

By then, my full sister Kyung Hee was already married with two little children and lived in isolation and was not in touch with anyone in the family. I discussed the situation with Rolf and Rolf didn't hesitate a minute to agree with me, and to look into it again to find the way to bring my brother out to us. Since we had bought our house we were hoping that we had a good chance. But, even then, there were many other obstacles to go through. It was a very long and slow process. I was so worried that he might do something silly, waiting in suspense for so long for his fate because I heard from Myung Hee that he kept on disappearing from home. My friend Frances wanted to help me find out if I was only chasing an impossible dream, and even organized a meeting with a fortune teller. The meeting with the fortune teller was taken at Frances' place.

The fortune teller, Molly, who was an Irish lady, brought some dried tea leaves for us all to have a cup of tea. My friends Frances, Dianne and Flo had prepared lots of tasty little sweets to have with our tea. After I finished my tea Molly told me to put the empty cup upside down on its saucer and she spun it gently once and stood it up right back on the saucer. She looked at the cup seriously for a half minute or so and said to me, "Have a good look at the edge of the cup."

I had a look at it but I couldn't see anything but some wet tea leaves stuck on it, I asked, "What am I supposed to see?"

She replied, "Can't you see a big plane?" Hearing that not just me, all of us got the goose bumps, we all looked at each other in amazement. It was like *hit the nail on the head*. She was exactly on track with what we were after. I could then almost see the shape of a plane made up from the wet tea leaves on the edge of the cup. We looked at each other in disbelief and we had locked our eyes and our ears on Molly, - she said, "In the near future someone you've been waiting for a long time will come from far away by a jumbo plane." It almost blew us away. It was like as if someone had told her to say it.

And she was right as well, within a few days we received the letter confirming that his visa was granted.

Then the National party MP, for the division of Kennedy, Bob Katter Senior, took on my case personally even though it was a very unusual case. He helped us in every way he could to get him the visa. We couldn't have done it without his kindness. He was a gentleman who was very down to earth and kind, and we were very blessed to have had his assistance.

Chapter Seven

August 12 1982. The plane arrived at Mount Isa with my little brother whom I hadn't seen for over twelve and half years, since he was three years old. All of us and Choi's family were at Mount Isa Airport waiting in anticipation of his arrival. My heart was pounding hard with the joy of seeing him. The image of my three year old gorgeous little brother I so missed was in my head and wondered what he would look like now? The airport being small, we could see the plane landing right in front of us. A tall and thin handsome young fifteen-year-old Asian man stood out amongst many Anglo Saxon Caucasians getting off the plane and walking toward us, I rushed toward him as I called his name loudly and waved my hand profusely. When we got close to each other I gave him a big bear hug, tears in my eyes with the overwhelming joy, but his hug for me wasn't the same and rather awkwardly he pushed me away and he gave me a bow instead and greeted me in the Korean way.

I could sense that he was rather embarrassed by the hug, only then I realized that he was not used to hugging in public and it was only the beginning of the many challenges that lay ahead of us, because we have lived apart for more than a decade. There were many challenges to overcome to re-adjust and to fill in the huge gaps made by those many empty years. Nevertheless I was overwhelmed with the joy of seeing him again and relieved that he arrived safely. The initial greeting was somewhat awkward and nothing like how I expected. Nevertheless the introduction was behind us and driving home with him in our car I felt unreal that actually he was here by my side.

My mind pondered, would I be mature enough at my age of thirty-two to bring up a teenager who is almost sixteen years old, whilst I think of him still as the brother who was once no older than three - a little brother I so loved. Having the language and cultural barriers, would I be able to keep my family all happy in harmony. Would I be the big sister he was hoping for and most of all I wondered what kind of person he became and what influence he will have on our boys and our lives. I reminded myself that I had taken on the huge task, out of my depth and it was all up to me to lead him and all of us into a better future.

Our house had only three bedrooms so I made the space for another bed in Maurits' room. Maurits was eleven and given only the four years of age gap between them, they would be more like friends rather than an uncle and a nephew. It would also help him to learn to speak English faster from Maurits. I had arranged enrolment with the state high-school in Mount Isa for him to start school from grade eight even though he was much older for the grade, because of his poor English. He attended the last semester of grade eight that year and as I had requested, the school provided extra English classes for him.

He really stood out wherever he went, looking very exotic, tall and handsome, with lots of charisma - he was an instant hit - and loved by all especially the female students and teachers alike! At home I continued to endeavor to speak in English with him whether he understood or not and I spoke Korean with him only when it was very necessary, as I knew that was the only way he would learn English quickly and adjust to the Australian way of life. It was not easy for me to get into his wavelength of thinking, given I was much older and he was a teenager. In fact, we were more or less like strangers to each other. He appeared to be somewhat disappointed about the place where he came to live but I knew it would pass with time as I had been there; my experiences of my early life in Australia were a lot worse.

I was in the room cleaning, and the smell of tobacco led me to find a couple of used cigarettes in his room, hidden amongst his belongings on a shelf and soon enough I could also tell he was already into alcoholic beverages. My heart sank and I became very worried about how was I going to make him understand that he had to stop the bad habits, and I couldn't help but be stressed about the inevitable bad influence he'd have on our boys. I tried to reproach him in Korean with an imperative tone of voice like my father reproached us when we did something wrong, and tried to correct him and to coax him out of the bad habits, but to reproach him in Korean didn't feel right for me so I ended up reproaching him in English like I would my boys.

I was upset finding out his bad habits, but I was more hurt inside seeing the sadness on his face while I was reproaching him, the look on his face that he disliked being reproached by me and the predicament he was in, being restricted and not able to live life as he pleased. Although we were brother and sister we were brought up in very different times and circumstances. Whilst my love for him was cemented in my heart long ago, and I loved him ever since, his love for me was merely one of imaginary thought, and not real as he was only three years old when I left Korea, and he had grown up all his life since without having any personal interaction with me. I was no more than a stranger to him.

For sure I wanted to take good care of him and wanted to make him feel very welcomed in our home, but having said that I wouldn't want to let him behave disrespectfully to us and become a bad influence on our boys. Juggling all those emotions was a mammoth task for me. Rolf was very much aware that I rather wanted to reproach him myself, so he willingly stood aside and let me correct him my way, to avoid the chance of hurting my feelings whenever he was upset with him. As a matter of fact Rolf was used to step aside and let me handle most disciplinary actions, as I have never let him even raise his voice to our boys.

When our boys were small, I once saw Rolf was very upset about something Maurits had done, and to my dismay he took his belt out of his trousers ready to smack him, and I got so scared I told him there and then if he ever threatened our children in such way again, I would leave him for good. I said it with such a tone of voice that Rolf knew I really meant it. That was the first and the last time that Rolf did that and ever since then he left most corrective measures for disciplinary action for our children to me to handle. But Rolf was always supportive whenever I needed advice or help from him.

I must admit though there were many times, as our children grew older, that I wished Rolf was tougher on them and I regretted that I took it all on my shoulders.

I treated my brother as if he was another son. Rolf loved him the very best way he could and our boys adored him. Nevertheless it was inevitable our peaceful lives were suddenly disrupted since he came to live with us, and he was not the only one having a hard time to adjust to the changes.

Rolf built an extension, the full length of our house at the back and paved the floor to create a lovely outdoor entertainment area. It was very nice. It kept the house cooler from the hot afternoon sun and gave me a perfect place to display my pot plant collection. Soon my passion for growing plants became serious, Rolf had to build me a green house as well, a lovely 1.5 metre wide x 3.5 metre long x 2.5 metre high in size at one side of the back yard, next to a brick BBQ he had built some time earlier.

The hot summer was closing in; at times it was unbearably hot with high humidity, which added on more difficulties for my brother to get used to. We had the evaporative air conditioning system built in the house but it didn't cool the house down much at all on the days when humidity was high, and rather than cooling added more humidity which made the house unbearably uncomfortable.

Christmas in Mount Isa was far away from the Christmas we had in Korea, not in the sense of the distance but of the differences in culture, the way in which we celebrated Christmas, but most of all the difference in the temperature. Wherever I had lived in Australia, Christmas was always hot, even though I have been living here for such long time I still have difficulties getting into the mood of the festive season. However our first Christmas together turned out great and we had a lovely time together. Every one of us was slowly adjusting to the changes and beginning to feel comfortable living with one another.

The following year Maurits started the first year in high-school, in grade eight and my brother in grade nine in the same high-school. It was an overwhelming joy for me seeing them side by side riding bicycles to school. My brother handled the command of English surprisingly well, and it wasn't long after he started grade nine, when I got the written message from the headmaster of the high-school, to say that the special arrangement for him to learn English was no longer necessary, as he was coping so well already. I was in tears reading the letter and I was very proud of him for doing so well at school.

Our little Ed went up to grade two and not only did he miss not having his big brother at school but he was also affected at home, since his uncle had moved into his brother's room. The Sundays were the best days for him because Julia would come and play with him. It was a sad day for both of them when Julia's parents were transferred to another town and she left with her parents. But then it was fortunate that our next door neighbour Davina had her grandson Jordy move in with her; he was a little boy a year younger than Ed. And Jordy and Ed soon became good friends.

I became used to working for new bosses and it didn't concern me too much anymore working under new management. Soon after the new boss came I took a couple of weeks off from work while the school break was on, and all of us went on holiday to Mission Beach, 1,200 kilometres away from Mount Isa. Our friends, Pentti and his wife Irja, had a new home getting built by the ocean for their retirement, and very kindly offered us to go there and stay for a holiday. It was a very long 14 hour drive and my brother wasn't used to such a long trip, and he was bored at times but the rest of us were excited to be going on holiday together, and looked forward to the holiday at the beach.

It was such a fantastic opportunity to have such a place to ourselves, a four bedroom brand new home by the sea. There was a big snooker table in the lounge room and being a home of Finnish people, it had even an indoor sauna room. It was an absolutely beautiful place surrounded by the World Heritage listed rain forest on one side and the Great Barrier Reef on the other, and beautiful Dunk Island offshore. We caught some fish at the beach, made some sand castles, played ball games, picked some coconuts and went for long walks along the beach, a 14-kilometres long pristine golden beach it was. The sunrises were different every morning but all magnificent and every hour of the day the scenery of the sea side was changing by the light and just wonderful to see!

We had an amazing close-up experience with a big Cassowary and her chicks, native to the area. We saw also many hand woven cane baskets in the stalls everywhere, the baskets made with cane from the forest and I was very drawn to them. I couldn't resist, when we saw vines in the forest by the road that looked very much like that cane, we stopped our car by the road to pull some down to weave the baskets, however it was very tough to handle and hard on hands to work with. My brother was the only one strong enough and had enough interest to have a try at weaving. He was also a leader at climbing up high to get coconuts from the tall coconut trees. The holiday was wonderful and we all had a great time.

Before we left I bought some of the beautiful baskets, locally made, and also took with us the ones my brother was able to weave which had made me very happy and proud. We loaded them all on the roof rack of our Toyota Land Cruiser together with many coconuts we collected, and drove into Townsville on the way home for a little break and shopping. The 14-hours-long-trip back home wasn't boring at all as we were all busy talking about the good times we had. When we were home I was telling everyone what a wonderful holiday we had and explained about weaving our own baskets out of the vines from the forest only to find out that it was an illegal thing to have done. I sighed with relief at how lucky we were not to have been caught while we were at the side of the road pulling the vines from the forest! It was a wakeup call for all of us to know that there were laws to protect the natural forest in Australia. None of us was aware of such laws yet and I couldn't help but feel embarrassed about it.

I had been driving my old Renault ten for about eight years and I would have driven it forever if I could. I liked the fact that it was one of a kind in town, very old and very French and everyone knew it was me driving it. Unfortunately it reached the stage where there was no way we could get it fixed again, and I had to replace it. One evening a well respected business man in town and owner of a car sales yard came in to have dinner at the restaurant. Having guessed that my old car was no longer roadworthy and dangerous to drive, he jokingly said to me that he may have to let the air out of my tyres, or he would do something bad to force me to come to his sales yard and buy a new car, to replace the old bomb.

We replaced it in the end but not with a new car, with another second hand small sedan, a very common Japanese car a Datsun 120Y. Still I was attached to my Renault; I didn't have the heart to take it to the dump and kept it in our back yard for many more months. Until, to my surprise, somebody who had the same old broken down Renault, knocked on my door and asked if he could buy it to use it to repair his. Even then I was sad to let it go but I decided to do so, but not before I had my photo taken with my beloved old car.

My grandma passed away that year after a short illness, my last telephone call with my grandmother was a very sad one to remember. We hadn't shared a decent conversation in all those years since I left Korea, for several reasons; we didn't have a phone connected at home for many years, it was hard to be connected at times, as well as the international call being expensive, the calls we made were always very short and very few and far between. Therefore grandma had some difficulties recognizing my voice. She no longer had the patience to try to understand me and she would pass the phone back to my sister whilst I was hanging on to hear more of her voice. This made me feel abandoned and I was in tears as I was missing her very much.

I found out some time later that one of the reasons it took so long for my brother to come to me was, that my grandmother was heartbroken, and didn't want to let go of her precious grandson because she may never see him again, as I had never returned for all those years.

My grandmother lost her husband whilst her children were small; we've heard that it's an extremely rare case but our grandfather died of choking from hiccups. Since then my grandmother as a young widow left the farming land with her little children and moved up to Seoul, the big city where she didn't know anyone, midst of the HORRIBLE and long years of Japanese Colonial Rules occupied Korea. She had to work very hard mainly doing laundry by hand for others in all seasons just to put food on the table for her children.

She was then in her 80s and it would have been very hard for her to see her grandson go. I missed her badly and I am indebted to my grandma for my upbringing, as no doubt she was the one who had mostly prepared me and shaped me to be the person I am today.

Rolf took his long service leave from work and built for himself a besser block work shed, 5.5 metre wide x 7.2 metre long x 2.5 metre high, step by step from the drawing stage to the finish all by himself, with the council approval. Soon after he finished building his shed he built also a boat trailer in the shed for the 4 metre aluminum boat he had, mostly with used-drill-rods he had from work. I was very proud at how good he was at building anything at all he put his mind to.

Rolf thought about changing the job he had had for 16 long years, and I was hoping that he would do so because we needed to give ourselves more stability in life instead of being moved from State to State by the company. One of his old work mates, Bob, who was very well aware of the situation, one day phoned Rolf to tell him that there was an opportunity for him to get a job in the electricity board. Rolf knew about the job advertised in the paper but he didn't think he was qualified for it and didn't look any further. But Bob was working there and knew the job was suitable for someone like Rolf and encouraged him to apply for it. Bob was right, Rolf got the job and he was most pleased to walk away from Rex.

At first he was working as a just mechanic, but soon he was put in charge of maintenance of the generators in all the generation stations in the small towns around Mount Isa: Cloncurry, Julia Creek, Dajarra, Duchess, Boulia, Camooweal, Normanton, and Burketown. He still had to work away from home at times but the working conditions were much better, and he liked the people he was working for and felt comfortable with his responsibilities.

By the time my brother finished grade ten, he was already eighteen years old, three years older than most of his classmates. When he had an opportunity to get an apprenticeship in the electrical trade with Mount Isa Mine, understandably he opted to take the opportunity to start the apprenticeship instead of continuing high school. He was excited about getting the trade and looked forward to becoming independent. We were very pleased for him when he was accepted by Mount Isa mine and he started the apprenticeship with them. He got his licence to drive a car and he moved out as soon as he was able to look after himself, and he put his bicycle to rest and bought a second hand Ford LTD sedan as soon as he was able to borrow a small loan from a bank.

Living in a remote mining town very far away from universities, it was a trend for boys in Mount Isa when they graduated secondary school, to opt to take on an apprenticeship in those years. There was a very good chance of getting an apprenticeship with a big company like Mount Isa Mine, relatively speaking only a few boys went away to university in the city. And as there was no available public transportation in Mount Isa, apart from taxies; it was of paramount necessity to obtain a driver's licence as soon as possible and having one's own car.

The house was empty without him but he wasn't far away, and it was nice to have a relative living nearby for the first time in our lives. We enjoyed visiting him whenever we could, most of all I was proud to see him all grown up into an independent adult.

That winter during the school break, we took a couple of weeks off from work and went on holiday with our boys back to Mission Beach again, and that time we towed our little aluminum boat behind our Toyota all the way, as we wanted to go four kilometers off shore and explore Dunk Island. Although it was winter time and the beach was a cool place to be, there were a lot of holiday makers around, staying at a caravan park or a hostel nearby. A lot of them were back packers from Europe; our winter cool breeze didn't seem to worry them. Whilst we were all wrapped up in warm clothes, they were in summer clothes. Our Finish friends let us to go to their new place by the beach again – it had been two years since we were there last. We missed not having my brother with us that time but he was a grown-up young man and had his own interests. We had to re-adjust to the changes after more than two and half years of living with him.

We celebrated Ed's birthday at Mission Beach on the next day we arrived and he was only happy to blow out all nine bright candles on his birthday cake. We took the boat across to Dunk Island and spent most of the day lazing around the Island sightseeing and satisfied our curiosity as to what it was like there. It was a lovely place to visit. Going out there in our little boat was easy but coming back was rather scary as the little boat was rocking badly in the current. Whilst the boys thought it was fun I was petrified that it might tip us over because I didn't know how to swim. I was relieved when we made it to the shore and got off the boat safe at last.

Another time we visited Mena Creek Falls, a 40 minute drive by car. There was an authentic Spanish castle nearby a big water fall, built by Spanish immigrants in the 1930s, surrounded by lush tropical rain forest with many different magnificent tropical plants. It was a great experience to walk through such an old castle and soak up the history of yesteryears and the unique ambience of the place. Another day we drove all the way to Cairns and back just to enjoy the wonderful scenery of that area. Every day we were at Mission Beach, no matter how cool it was, every morning I walked on the beach to catch the sun rising from the ocean - it empowered my soul and my being!

When I returned to work from that holiday I decided to reduce my working days to give myself more time with my family and to fit in other things I enjoyed and would like to do. Thursday was always extra busy as I played tenpin bowling in the league in the morning so I asked my boss if I could have Thursday evenings off permanently and he agreed. It was great to work just five evenings and have the extra evening free and have family time at home.

A friend of mine who had a hair dressing salon, was going to be involved in the Hair Show, together with two other hairsalons in town, for a charity event that year and asked me if I would like to be one of the models to represent her salon, and I was to help her out with the making of the costumes for her models.

I was a little hesitant at the beginning because I had never done either modeling or making any costumes for any kind of shows before, but although it was a way out of my comfort zone, the more I thought about it the more I was intrigued and Caroline was very encouraging. I dared to agree to do it in the end, and it was great that I did, as it turned out to be the most fun experience I ever had. Doing something I had never done before gave me the opportunity to think outside of the square. It was truly a memorable experience!

We decided to make the outfits for the six models to go on the stage with me in quick and simple but effective designs, out of different grades of industrial garbage bin bags, in orange, black, white and green colours. We made kimonos, body hugging one piece long dresses in Spanish style with lots of frills, by using strong sticky tape and applying long hand stitches for the gatherings on heavy bags, and machine stitches for lighter bags. The whole idea of the outfits came about very spontaneously but it worked out wonderfully well!

Caroline and her team of hairdressers created more than thirty different hair styles including mine and the six stunning models in my team looked just fantastic. The hairdos - coloured, woven, foiled, pinned, feathered, braided, curled, straightened and decorated with flowers, shiny foils and feathers, somewhat outrageous yet fabulous creations! My thick hair was then a little longer than shoulder length and was woven into a mat on three sides of my head with many chopsticks and I, being the leader of the team for our segment on the stage, wanted to wear something different from the other models and I wore my Korean national costume and someone loaned me a set of 5 centimetres long false-nails to wear, adding more interest.

The girls walked on the stage with a large paper parasol each and I with a mega size foldable hand fan. I led the team onto the stage in authentic Japanese tight steps to a Chinese tune, ding-dong-dong....none of us knew what the song was all about, but it didn't matter given the show was about the newest hair style creations, and an ensemble to create the overall oriental theme. The models of my team looked fantastic in those outfits made with garbage bags with the fabulous hair styles; they followed me out two by two onto the stage to represent one of the segments of the Capricorn Hair Salon, the salon owned by Caroline. The charity show attracted many local people; the Civic-centre was completely packed. It was an awesome experience to hear the roar of the spontaneous applause from the audience for every step we made on the stage. Not just our hearts were filled with excitement but the atmosphere of the huge hall, packed with people applauding was so wonderful!

It was all in all a wonderful experience, working together as a team for a good cause. All six models including myself were career minded people and we were all busy working different hours on different days of the week, it was therefore very difficult to find the time free to get together to rehearse. Two days before the show we finally got together, after the final fittings of the outfits, in the back yard at our place to rehearse our stage presentation. My little Ed had to be the DJ to press the button of our portable audio cassette player to turn it on and off to play the Chinese song for us to practice walking to the music, again and again.

It's hard to believe that 30 years have passed since that performance. In those 30 years the VHS video tape and the Audio cassette which were fabulous inventions in those days became a thing of the past, it seemed like it was the dinosaur age given we now are living with the technology of an internet dominated world. But when I re-play and watch the tape, I feel as if it was only yesterday and seeing myself on a big stage still makes me feel somewhat apprehensive.

The Mount Isa hotel, the Argent hotel and the Tavern, all three places in Mount Isa were owned by the Carlton & United Breweries, the CUB of Australia until the major shares were taken over by Elders IXL in 1983. Elders was interested in buying a British Brewery and had a plan to raise the funds they needed. The strategy was to sell off the non-profitable parts of the various hotels they had in Australia; thus in 1985, all three premises in Mount Isa were on the market. Since then the everyday operation of the hotel wasn't the same anymore. Stocks we needed didn't arrive on time to keep up with the standard we used to have. As the months progressed the uncertainties brought out more and more of the negative behavior of most people who worked there. We lost our head Chef, Frances, as she had a good opportunity to lease the kitchen of another hotel in town. The situation became even worse and was beyond my ability to improve; therefore the thought of finding another job was getting stronger on my mind.

One evening a Chinese gentleman came in for dinner and told me about a dilemma he was facing and asked me if I could help him. I had heard of him but I'd never met him before. His English wasn't very good and his accent was not easy to understand. His name was Freddie and he was the owner of a Chinese restaurant in town; it had been operated successfully as a Café for "take away only" Chinese meals, for a number of years. But recently it had been expanded and upgraded to a liquor licensed restaurant. Since then it seemed he was facing ongoing problems with running the restaurant, as he had a dilemma not having much knowledge about beverages and also because of the language and cultural barrier. Communicating with the people working for him, who were not Chinese, was very difficult for him.

Although I was in the midst of thinking seriously about leaving my beloved job in the hotel, working for a small Chinese restaurant didn't appeal to me at the beginning. Nonetheless I felt honored that he came to me for help and every time he came back to tell me more about the problems somewhere deep down inside me the thought of helping him was growing stronger. The more I thought about it, the more I liked the idea of taking charge of the beverage side of the small restaurant and learning to manage it became more appealing to me. I went to the Chinese restaurant on my nights off from the hotel just to find out what it would be like to work there, and to observe how it was running. I discovered there were things I could do for him to make a difference to the business. When I gave him advice he was very appreciative. From then on the thought of how to run the Chinese restaurant consumed every hour of my days and I had sleepless nights thinking about it. Already my heart was focused on how to improve the Chinese restaurant. I became obsessed thinking about all aspects of running the business and my heartfelt urge to help the fellow Asian to succeed. I told Freddie that I was prepared to leave my job at the hotel for him and that I would do my very best to manage the beverage side of the operation and take care of all accounts for him, but managing the kitchen was his responsibility.

I told him also that I was willing to work for him - a minimum 40 hours a week - as long as he offered me a good salary with 4 weeks annual leave. He agreed with my conditions and offered me a salary I couldn't refuse. Next step was to give my resignation to the hotel, by then I was very excited about the new opportunity and I was ready to move on without any regrets. I explained to the manager, John, about the fact that I was offered a good opportunity to run a small business and pleaded for his kind understanding.

The manager was surprised and sorry that I was leaving the job I enjoyed very much, but he understood the situation in the hotel and accepted my resignation, given the hotel was on the market and no one including himself, knew how long the uncertain situation would continue. John was the sixth manager in eight plus years I had worked there and not only he but everyone else who worked there, knew how much I loved my job and understood that I had good reasons to leave. Before I left I was assured that I could come back to the hotel management team if there was anything I could learn from them to do my new job well.

I knew it would be inevitable that I would call on them as I had to learn from the beginning, how to deal with lots of business people at a totally different level to what I had been used to.

Dealing with different business people at a professional level, at times, was somewhat out of my comfort zone mainly due to lack of experience, but knowing I put myself in there I tried to rise to the challenges, I had to learn properly and succeed. I had to apply all my people skills and most importantly be truthful with the people I was dealing with, and asked to learn as much as I could about the business. Consciously I tried to treat people in the way I would like to be treated.

I went to see my old boss, John, at the hotel a couple of times to get some advice on account keeping and buying the beverage stocks we needed from the wholesalers, and to learn how to price them to sell them at a profit. If he wasn't sure of something he was very kind to put me on to someone who knew better. I had to figure out the best way to order the right amount of stock for the turn over, and to store them efficiently in the limited space we had. I asked Rolf to build a set of large metal wine racks to store the cork-sealed wine bottles we had in those years, in the right way and set them up in Freddie's home in a place where the temperature was most consistent. I created a simple wine list to suit the Chinese cuisine we served and taught all the wait-staff to serve them the correct way that I knew. Every aspect of my duties was all a very exhilarating experience. I learned most things from my own mistakes, but quickly, and worked hard to be better because I was very interested in what I was doing.

Of course throughout those eight plus years I had worked at the classy à-la-carte hotel restaurant in town as the hostess, I had earned a good reputation and already had very good connections with many of the influential people in town, which was a huge help. As a Korean person working closely with the Chinese boss and the few Chinese men he had working for him in the kitchen, it was somewhat like working for a family business.

Although I didn't understand any Chinese, there were many similarities, not just in our looks but in the way we were brought up in Asia, and that made us feel close. I found out that Freddie's wife was an Australian born Chinese. She went back to live with her parents in Sydney and took their little son with her after they had a huge disagreement about upgrading the take away café into a licensed restaurant. It was imperative for Freddie to succeed with the expansion to win his family back and I wanted to help him to get there rather sooner than later.

I got my brother to work for me some nights during the weekends as an extra casual barman. It was good for him to earn some extra money as a first year apprentice wage wasn't much and it was a good opportunity for him to broaden his connection with people, and improve his people skills. As I expected, not only his good looks but his charismatic personality was much appreciated by everyone.

Having lost my parents so suddenly and never having the chance for our sons to meet their grandparents, I didn't want the same thing to happen with Rolf's parents. I wanted, as soon as possible, to take my family to Sweden to meet them. By then our home loan was reduced almost to nothing as we had paid extra with a small lump sum Rolf received from his final pay when he changed jobs, and as well I had made the extra payments every fortnight, as much as we could afford.

By September the following year I was due for my annual leave from my new job so I planned for all of us to visit Sweden to meet Rolf's family. However in the meantime we heard the exciting news from Sweden that some of our relatives were coming to visit us on New Year's Eve that year. It was such wonderful news for us all, to be able to meet some of the family before we were to go to Sweden, and I couldn't wait to meet them. Rolf's youngest brother, George, and two grown-up children of one of Rolf's sisters, Benny and Maylie, were coming. Rolf hadn't seen them in almost 20 years since he left Sweden in 1966!

It was almost the end of the year, and with Christmas becoming closer, the restaurant was extra busy, packed with people almost every night. I loved it. The atmosphere of the restaurant full of happy diners enriched my spirits and fuelled my soul. I became busier at home as well to prepare for our relatives, and managing the restaurant required 24/7 attention, even on days off there was always something to care for and needless to say that managing the household wasn't any different. I had to be extra organized at home as well as for the restaurant, prior to the family's arrival because neither of us could take any time off from our work whilst they were here. I made sure I was well prepared to be able to relax as much as I could with our family guests and have the business run smoothly as well.

Chapter Eight

The last day of 1985 we were at Mount Isa airport saturated in perspiration, but excited, waiting for our relatives to arrive. The first time in almost 20 years Rolf was about to see his youngest brother George he so missed and his grownup nephew Benny and niece Maylie, getting off the plane.

Rolf had tears in his eyes with joy when they landed from the plane and this made me tearful watching the happy re-union as well.

It was wonderful that all three of our Swedish relatives spoke good English and the boys were glad to meet their Swedish uncle and cousins for the first time, and being able to communicate in English made them feel closer straight away. Because of the huge barrier of the language as well as the culture, the experience we had on the day my brother arrived wasn't the same. Having said that I must point out that no one could ever have guessed then that he could command English in such a short time, and adjust to the Australian way-of-life so quickly. He was there with us to welcome our relatives and I was a very proud sister to introduce him to them.

For a long time I have envied friends when they had family re-unions and I dreamed about having such life for us one day too, and at last, the dream came true! It was for sure a very significant moment of our lives to have relatives visiting us for the first time and what was more significant, was knowing that only in 9 months time, we too would be able to afford to travel overseas to visit our family.

We woke up on New Year's Day with the relatives around us. The year 1986 was indeed a Happy New Year for us all.

The three weeks they were here was during the school holidays but Rolf and I had to go to work as usual. However we tried to fit in as many different activities as we could together and when we could, whilst Rolf and I were at work most of the days in the week, our dear friends, Pentti(The Finnish friend) as well as Erik (The Danish friend) were shift workers in the mine, and were very kind to entertain our visitors as much as they could, when they were free, driving them around for sightseeing and more.

We went out together to Lake Moondarra during the weekends with our boat for a swim in the lake, and had a BBQ at the park near the lake with our friends, eating big steaks and drinking beer, which they loved very much, and this was always fun and enjoyable. Many nights we talked into the early hours of the mornings and we had to go to work very tired from lack of sleep, and some nights we went out for late night discos at the hotels and clubs and danced into the early hours as well. Our relatives couldn't believe how cheap the alcoholic beverages were in Australia. "One dollar Disco" was on in many hotels and clubs in Mount Isa that January. One could buy a glass of alcoholic beverage for just one dollar at whatever club or hotel where you could disco dance to loud music, which was very popular amongst the young ones.

Benny and Maylie were young, in their early 20s and loved the nightlife in Mount Isa and went out with my brother and soaked up the Australian way of life as often as they could, and people here loved meeting Swedish people.

They told us that where they live in Sweden they had to pay around $8 dollars for the first drink in similar places because they had to pay for the cover charge which usually came with a plate of snacks, and from the second drink on they would pay around $5 for a glass of alcoholic beverages. They told us that even the price of meat in Sweden was much more expensive than what we paid here. Our guests couldn't believe how big the size of the steaks we ate here.

They not only loved the taste of our beer and the steaks we cooked but also they loved our laidback- *It's alright mate!* – The easy going mentality. I was surprised to find out that unlike Rolf they enjoyed eating spicy food and pasta dishes, and they seemed to have embraced the new cuisines as they were introduced to them in the past. They liked my hot chili sauce, the mixture I made of extra hot chili sauce, soy sauce and sesame oil which

I put on most of my meals since I couldn't cook anything with chilies because Rolf couldn't eat them. They were easy to cook for and it was such a pleasure cooking for them. I made sure I prepared the meals for everyone before I went to work each shift. Little things we shared together such as that they were able to enjoy the same spicy food or pasta dishes made us bond more quickly. I must admit I missed such simple company for all those years given Rolf not only did not like to eat anything spicy but also he didn't like any pasta or noodle dishes.

Maylie was looking forward to getting a good suntan from Australia before she returned to Sweden. However one day Rolf drove to Lake Julius with a car full of people and took our boat to have a ride on the lake which was less than 70 kilometres away from Mount Isa. The road condition was terribly bad and he had to drive in very low gear most of the way, it took almost two hours to get there. Maylie was wearing a sleeveless top over her bikini and sitting in the back seat with car windows down, as it was a very hot day and the car didn't have an air conditioner, the sunrays were so severe her exposed tender, fair skin was blistered, and she learned fast in a very painful way how intense the Australian sun was.

Another thing that was important to them was seeing kangaroos. We had driven around the bush near Mount Isa many times and they had been out in the bush with our friends but strangely they didn't see any at all. As it was getting close to the end of their holiday in Australia, I had to do something about it and I was lucky to find a person who had an injured kangaroo in captivity while it recovered, and he allowed us to visit. The kangaroo was tame enough for them to feed some bread by hand and it was good to have the opportunity to take some photos of them with the kangaroo.

The three weeks had passed very quickly and it was time for them to leave but they were very excited about our forthcoming visit to Sweden in September that same year. I was more certain about the trip to take my family to Sweden since I had met them and I wanted to meet the rest of the relatives as soon as possible, especially Rolf's parents.

The counting of the days had already begun in my heart as they flew away and left us with the fun memories of the good time we had shared.

Early in the year Freddie bought a house and was ready to move into it. His wife and son returned to him and they tried to restart their life together. Having been born and educated in Australia Freddie's wife spoke fluent English with an Australian accent, and I had clearly noticed that she had a very different outlook on life and different values from her husband, who was born and brought up with strong Chinese values.

There were ongoing problems in many things in their private life and it started to have an effect on the operation of the business. I talked his wife into doing what I do, to take over from me while I would be on holiday later in the year. I thought it would be ideal for them to run it together and I had in mind to go back to working in the hotel or club when I returned from our holiday. At first they both could see my point and reluctantly but agreed to try yet, neither of them seemed to trust one another.

After a few months of trying, his wife couldn't take it anymore; she left again, back to Sydney with their child. Freddie was left with stronger grudges against his wife for the fact that she abandoned him each time he needed her most and he felt his wife didn't respect him as she should. Many times they argued about trivial matters and neither of them had any intention to compromise. It was obvious that his wife didn't share some of the strong Chinese values he had and Freddie tended to ignore his wife's opinion even though at times she had good valid points.

Our sixteenth wedding anniversary day, April 1986, was an extra special day to remember. It was the day I went to the bank to pay the final payment of our home loan and could say we owned our home outright and we were debt free. Walking out of the bank that day my steps were lighter than a feather I could have been blown away in the wind. From there I walked straight into a travel agent nearby and booked the return flights to Sweden for the four of us to travel in September, and paid the deposits!

It felt so GREAT! It felt like I had the POWER to Move Any Mountain, it sure was a very energizing experience.

I booked the flights to stop at Frankfurt in West-Germany on the way over and I looked forward to seeing Sonja again after the 17 years we hadn't seen each other, and looked forward also to meeting her husband and son. I hoped to see Claudia again as well, the little four year old girl I taught to speak English in 1969 and hadn't seen since. I was excited thinking of it all and I had to pinch myself that it was real and Not a Dream - we owned our home outright and we were totally Debt Free! What's more our flight to Sweden was booked and our seats were secured! We sure had good reasons to celebrate. I was then thirty-six and Rolf just turned forty-seven.

That night, I couldn't wait to finish work and go home to celebrate with Rolf our extra special wedding anniversary. Although I don't normally enjoy bubbly wine I bought a bottle of chilled champagne to celebrate in style, and Every Bubble we sipped went down in Happiness!

I needed to find someone to do my duties while I was on holiday so we advertised the position and I chose a young Pilipino lady who appeared to be polite and seemed to be the best person to get on with Freddie. Freddie didn't appreciate her at the beginning but she was proven very capable for the job and honest and most of all she understood Freddie's psychology. She got on well with everyone who worked there as well. As the weeks and then months went by I became more and more organized and ready for our epic trip to Sweden and I was getting very excited, but no one in the family was as excited as I was. Perhaps they, being males, did not show their emotion as much?

I didn't realize then but I know now that Rolf had never liked flying, and he was getting rather apprehensive as the days were getting closer. Never having been overseas, our boys didn't comprehend what to expect from such a trip. They would have been happy just the same if we were going on holiday to a place in Australia. In fact, Ed asked me if he could instead go to the cattle station nearby, where he had been a couple of times during other school holidays with his friend, Jordy, whose mother was the station cook there and Ed liked to ride a horse there. Maurits wasn't overly excited to go because there had been a few airline mishaps reported on TV news. But I couldn't wait to travel overseas especially to meet all of Rolf's family in Sweden and to get to know them better, and I couldn't wait to experience different things in life and seeing different parts of the world.

I was counting the days and hours.

One Sunday morning about 2.00am someone knocked on our door and woke me up. It was someone we knew, who used to live in our neighbourhood, had come to tell us about the accident he saw on the road, as he was sure it was my brother's car that was involved, and he saw a few people were taken away in the ambulance. My heart sank to the floor and I became very frightened and worried and woke Rolf up. We hurried to the hospital, praying to God that nobody was badly injured. We were so very relieved to find my brother in one piece with only a few minor scratches on his face. As we had expected he was much shaken and was in shock, but we couldn't help but ask lots of questions at once.

After he finished work at the restaurant he went out to a night club as he often did on Saturday nights. After he had a few beers he decided to give a lift to a few very intoxicated friends on his way home and he was distracted by them having fun in the back seat of his car, and he lost his concentration and his car hit the guard rail and rolled over a couple of times. The car was a write-off. It was an amazing miracle that he escaped with only a few scratches, but some of his friends were injured internally and it was not yet known how badly, as they were being examined by the doctors.

I thanked God that no one was killed. My brother was very frightened and he wanted to wait in the hospital for his friends but there wasn't anything we could do to help the situation. We left the hospital and drove to the accident site and saw under the street light the guardrail on the bend of the road was badly damaged and with shattered glass everywhere, but we couldn't see the car as it was already taken away. It was right outside the primary school where Ed goes. It gave me the shivers thinking about how terrible it would have been if it had been day time when school children were there.

My brother was still paying the loan for his car at that time and the insurance wouldn't cover the accident because his blood alcohol was over the limit. He received a big fine, lost his licence and had no car. He was back on a push-bike to and from work and had to learn to cope with the consequences. We sure hoped that he had learned a lesson and would be wiser. He was extremely lucky no one was killed or badly injured and it was a guardrail that he hit and not another car full of people. At the age of nineteen and going on twenty, it surely was a huge wake-up call for him.

We took one week either side of the two weeks school break in September from work to have the four weeks holiday together. We were relieved when our dear friends, Pentti and Irja offered to move into our home and look after the place for us while we were on holiday. It was very reassuring that our pets and plants would be well cared for while we were gone. By then they already had sold their big house in Mount Isa and they were renting a house while they were getting ready to retire from the work force and move to their beautiful home at Mission Beach.

Pentti and Irja drove us to the airport and promised they would pick us up when we returned. We were blessed to have such nice people for friends. As soon as we boarded the plane, our boys were excited and their inquisitive minds soon got the better of them. They looked around, with huge interest, everywhere they could inside of the plane. Seeing our boys showing no hint of fear of flying took me back to my memories of my childhood when I was about five or six years old.

Although by then the wars had been over for many years in Korea and the country was on the way to recovery, having lived through so many wars, our parents were still very cautious and had encouraged us always to run inside quickly whenever we heard the loud sound of a plane flying over. We were taught to be frightened of planes flying in the sky as they might strike at us, thus when I heard any plane flying over us I instantly panicked, and I would hurry whoever I was playing with at the time, and made them run with me quickly by saying "Let's run to the house fast, hurry!" Once we were inside the gate of our house we would put our hands on our ears and look up at the sky with fear until we couldn't see the plane any more. Fortunately we had grown out of such fears as we grew older and the country, as a whole, has slowly recovered from those terrible wars.

Our first stop of the trip was at Darwin. When we arrived at the Darwin airport Linda's daughter, Jackie was there waiting to pick us up. We were very glad to see her again, we hadn't seen Jackie for over seven years, and she had grown up to a beautiful young lady. It was just a quick visit to say hello and good-bye as we only had about two hours of spare time before boarding our next flight to Singapore that afternoon, but we would have more time on the way back and looked forward catching up with them then.

When we arrived at Singapore airport that night, it was just like having woken up from a dream and arriving at a new planet. The place was lit up brightly and glittering. Our next flight to Frankfurt, West Germany was not until the next day late in the evening so we were looking forward to spending the next twenty-four hours there. While we were waiting at the airport to collect our suitcases, I heard an announcement in Korean on the loud speaker very unexpectedly and I became a little disorientated, for a second, I was back in Kimpo airport in Seoul instead. I felt the emotion given it was the first time I had ever heard an announcement in Korean, in more than sixteen years and it made me ponder how good it would be to really return home to Seoul!

We found a guide who was holding up a board with our names on it. It was the guide from the Boulevard Hotel where we were booked to stay until our next flight. We walked past people who were coming and going, hugging, shouting names, saying hellos, waving hands and saying good-byes. Adding to the excitement were the loud noises of trolleys loaded with heavy suitcases being dragged on the pavements, the atmosphere there that night was great and being there with my family was wonderful. We followed the guide and got onto the large hotel bus. The seats were soon filled with very happy travellers and the bus drove through the roads brightly lit up with thousands of colourful neon lights and street lights, rows and rows of the golden cane palms planted alongside the roads. My eyes were fixed on the outside enjoying the beautiful night scenery of that place while the driver was busy telling us about the history on a loud speaker.

The Boulevard Hotel was very nice, it sure impressed all of us, luxurious chandeliers hung high caught our eyes and all internal balconies and staircases were decorated with hundreds of pots of beautiful orchids in full bloom in many colours. We left our boys to settle in their room and rest and after freshening up Rolf and I went down to the lounge bar and we celebrated with a nice drink for our well earned first family overseas trip. We rose early next morning as we didn't want to miss the first scheduled lift to town. Before we got on the bus we had our breakfast in a lovely decorated dining room. Chefs in their uniforms were on hand only too happy to please us with our choice of food.

Literally we could shop till we dropped in Singapore! There were many good bargains especially of electronic goods and they made shopping an enjoyable experience for the travellers. The good system was well in place between the hotels and the stores to lure the travellers into as many shops as possible, by providing such regular lifts to and from the places by bus. Double Decker Buses were there as well as I had seen in the Hong Kong streets but they looked, for some reason, out of place even though I knew Singapore was also one of the Commonwealth countries. I pondered what it would be like to have them in our streets in Australia.

We were tempted to look around at more shops but our suitcases were already full to the limit. We went out again after a little break to have some lunch. Having lived in rain-deprived places for many years I couldn't help but notice the storm drain system they had in every street we walked past, and judging by the size of the storm drains I could guess they must get plenty of rain, and couldn't help but feel envious. We went into one of the restaurants on our way back to the hotel to have lunch.

It happened to be a Mexican restaurant; we all agreed that it would be fun trying something we hadn't had. We didn't fully understand the names of the meals written on the menu of the Mexican cuisine as we had never been in a Mexican restaurant before, so we randomly chose four dishes and told them not to make it too spicy. It took ages before the meals were served and when they did arrive they came out one dish at a time, the meals looked interesting and smelled good. My meal came out last and was a hot pot with a lid on it.

I was looking forward to the lunch and curious to find out what my meal was like, I quickly opened the lid. The smell was nice, like a hot curry, but sitting in hot steamy reddish-brown thick gravy was just a large fish head with a set of big goggle-eyes staring right at me. I slammed the lid back on! Visually, it was horrible, so much so that I felt queasy! Although while I was growing up and was taught to eat every part of a fish, including the head, it was a long time ago. Since I arrived in Australia it didn't matter where I lived, I have been cooking only the fillets of the fish without the heads; more often than not fish sold in the stores in Mount Isa were fillets not a whole fish. My family saw my reaction when I opened the lid and heard how I described what I saw in the pot, everyone lost their appetite as well and no one wanted to carry on eating their meal anymore;

without eating much at all we just paid and walked out there somewhat disappointed and still hungry.

We boarded a Qantas 747 jet late that night, our boys and I were seated in a non smoking area and unfortunately Rolf had to sit away from us in a smoking area as he was a heavy smoker in those years. Four-hundred plus passengers were sorted and seated and we were ready for the long over 14-hour journey to Frankfurt, Germany. The first stop was Bangkok in Thailand, some passengers got off and some new ones came on board and we were there about an hour before we flew off again. Light refreshments were served soon after and the stewardesses tried to sell some duty free goods before they dimmed the lights for the night for sleep. Whilst Ed seemed bored and a little restless he went back and forward to the toilet a few times before he was tired enough to fall asleep Maurits looked ever so relaxed and enjoyed the in-house movies. A few rows back, I saw Rolf had his eyes closed and relaxed and I too by then was relaxed and ready for sleep.

We were travelling west against the clock and when we woke up it was to the smell and the cling-clang noises of the stewardesses preparing our breakfast. We must have been flying nonstop through the night, about twelve hours. Soon after breakfast the plane was descending toward Athens in Greece to refuel, and the change of the air pressure was so great whilst descending, we felt the weird sensation of our ears popping. I had to show our boys to move our mouth as if we were chewing a chewing gum with our mouth opened to ease the pressure on our ears.

When we landed at the airport it would have been nice to get out of the plane and stretch our legs a little but unfortunately we were not allowed for some safety reasons. And whilst we remained seated, three Greek senior women rushed in, and gave the plane a quick clean up and took all the rubbish out with them. We remained inside the plane for more than an hour while the plane was refueled and refreshed before it was finally ready to take off again. About 3 hours later local time, around 10.00am, we arrived at the Frankfurt airport in West-Germany.

We were expecting to meet Sonja at the airport and I was getting excited to see her again. It had been almost 17 years since we saw each other. I wondered how she would look now and if she could recognize me after all those years. My steps were getting faster as I walked on and my eyes wandered around looking for her. As soon as we went out to the arrival lounge I saw, at a little distance, Sonja was standing with her husband whom I was about to meet for the first time.

It was unmistakable! She hadn't changed a bit! Her hair style was the same and even her stance was as I remembered it. I waved to her, and they walked toward us but in doubtful slow steps and when she was close enough to tell it was definitely me, I saw her hurry her husband to walk faster to meet us. It was great to see her again! Sonja and I hugged and very gladly introduced each other's family. Sonja's husband, Rudy spoke fluent English and it was lovely to meet him. Our next flight to Stockholm in Sweden was at 5.00pm local time that afternoon; we had about four hours to spare. Sonja was a florist and Rudy was a bank manager and they both took time off from work that day and drove to the airport to meet us. I got into Sonja's car and all the boys into Rudy's car and we were all heading for their home about thirty minutes away from the airport.

When we got in the car Sonja and I held each other's hands and squeezed in happiness, and for a moment we just looked at each other without a word as we both had to switch our thinking mode back to speak in Korean, as neither of us had spoken much Korean for many years. Sonja couldn't communicate in English and I couldn't in German, but it didn't take too long before we were talking away in Korean although at times we weren't sure if we spoke correctly or not, and I had to be careful to speak to her in polite form as she was much older than I was - about 7 years.

She stopped by a store to buy a few things she needed as she insisted she would cook something nice for lunch for us even though I had explained to her that we weren't hungry at all and I'd much rather prefer us to relax over a cup of tea and biscuits instead. The store was unreal; it was packed with many different varieties of sausages hung all over the place as well as on many trays in the refrigerated display shelves. As I clicked on my camera in amazement Sonja was happy to explain to people in the store that I was from Australia and I was amazed how many different sausages were there. That made the storekeepers very happy and they put on big smiles for me.

It felt like I walked in a sausage world. And it was rather special seeing there, in the store in Frankfurt, the little red Frankfurt sausages my children used to love to eat when they were small.

Rudy and the boys arrived at home before us, and whilst they were having refreshments, Sonja and I prepared lunch together as we talked nonstop to catch up. We sure had a lot to talk about. I heard about Claudia who was then twenty-two and pregnant with her first child and she lived out of town, and Mr. Pfaff got divorced from his German wife since we had met and was remarried to a Korean woman as well.

Each time when we realized one of us had said a wrong word or used a word in the wrong context in Korean we looked at each other and couldn't help but burst out laughing in disbelief for the silly mistakes we made in our mother language. We met their son Boris when he returned home from school; he was about the same age as Maurits. Boys got on well without too much problem with the language as Boris spoke reasonably good English.

After lunch we all went out, again in two different cars, all the boys in one and girls in the other. Rudy was very proud to show us around the city, especially some of the old buildings that weren't affected by both World Wars and explained to us how they were built to last. The streetscapes with such old buildings looked so rich with history and there were outdoor seating arrangements everywhere possible - outside of cafes in open spaces by the roads and many people were socializing under the warm afternoon sun. I had noticed also that most cafés didn't have curtains or blinds to let as much sun in as they could, to keep warm. It was quite the opposite in Mount Isa given we had to block the sun away as much as possible to keep cooler and to protect our things from the scorching heat of the sun.

Soon we had to go back to the airport, Sonja was driving following her husband Rudy's car, but because of the heavy traffic we ended up a distance behind. I trusted Sonja would know how to get to the airport. But while we were travelling on the express way Sonja told me in her stressful voice that she was distracted by our conversation and somehow she was in the wrong lane, and that she had no choice but to exit the express way and then follow the signs back to the airport. We both were very stressed by it as we might miss the flight.

That was a decade before we had our mobile phones. The only mobile phones we saw in those years were on the movies like 007 and it was then a mere fantasy item for most people. There was no way we could inform the boys about what had happened. I was stressed, not only because all our travel documents were with me in my handbag but also, if we weren't on that flight it would make Rolf's relatives who would have driven 300 kilometres to Stockholm to pick us up worried sick not knowing what had happened to us. We had no way to contact them either. I got Sonja even more stressed when I told her how imperative it was that we get to the airport on time.

We had to Talk Less and Pay More Attention to the Road.

We finally arrived at the airport. We ran inside and found the boys. What a relief it was for us all! As we told the boys the story why we were so close to missing the flight Sonja and I sighed with huge relief. We thanked Sonja and Rudy for their warm hospitality and we gave each other bear-hug good-byes.

On board the Scandinavian airline, we were greeted in Swedish by the stewardesses and the plane was full of people in winter outfits speaking Scandinavian languages. The atmosphere felt foreign straightaway. Having said that though, I was happy for Rolf being surrounded by people from his homeland for the first time in such a long time, and I asked him how he felt to be amongst them, seeing that Rolf has never been a person to express much of his feelings. He just said, "It's Okay." That was all!

When we arrived at the Arlanda airport in Stockholm, Rolf's brother George and nephew Benny who had visited us earlier that year, were waiting for us with Benny's mother, Ing-Marie, one of Rolf's younger sisters. We were all excited to see them there. I was very happy to meet Ing-Marie although we didn't speak the same language her smile made me feel very welcome and I felt close to her. It was unreal, to be with the relatives so far away from home on the other side of the world.

We got into two different cars again; Rolf and I with our little Ed in George's car and Maurits in his Cousin Benny's car with his aunty Ing-Marie and we travelled further -300 kilometres to Karlskoga - where most of Rolf's relatives live. Soon it was dark and we couldn't see much. Ed fell fast asleep and I kept on dosing on and off whilst listening to Rolf and George. George was speaking to Rolf in Swedish but more often than not Rolf was speaking to George in English. It was past 11.00pm when we arrived at George's home but many of the relatives were still waiting for us, and came rushing out in the cold air to welcome us.

We were all hurried inside of the house and the minute the entrance door was closed behind us the cold air was instantly well blocked out, and we felt a huge difference in the temperature inside. A few steps inside the house, the life size photos of us hanging on a few walls surprised us all, and I couldn't miss noticing the candle lit dining table, all set up beautifully with a large cake in the middle. We felt so welcome and we appreciated the effort they had gone to, to welcome us.

We met everyone in the room and were seated around the table together to have the cake. But again I was surprised, it wasn't a cake as I thought, it was a giant sized sandwich I'd never ever seen before and it was filled with many layers of all things sandwich, prawn, ham, cheese, lettuce, tomato and more and delicious. It was the most delectable sandwich I ever eaten! I knew Swedish sandwiches were well known to be delightful and it certainly was right.

Next morning when I came downstairs, Rolf was already up busy talking with George and George's wife, Mayly. George worked at a local sawmill and Mayly was on sick leave from her work to recuperate, and they were both in their early 40s, a little older than I was, and they have a son, Dennis, eighteen and daughter, Mariette, eleven. Except Mayly everyone spoke English well. We were informed that we were going to visit Rolf's parents soon after breakfast and I couldn't wait to meet them at last.

Growing up in Korea I saw firsthand how difficult it was to live with the in-laws. As a matter of fact, I didn't hesitate to leave Korea when I had the opportunity to get away from such an old Korean tradition, and eliminate any chance of marrying an eldest son who has to live with his parents and take care of his unmarried siblings. Nevertheless I did miss very much living near relatives, especially the grandparents of our boys. I always felt for our boys were growing up missing out on all interaction with relatives, especially the not having a relationship with their grandparents. Not only the distance isolated them but the language barrier of both sides of the family made communication almost impossible. Therefore I was very much looking forward to meeting them all and to share some lovely family time together while we were in Sweden.

We drove past thick pine forests and there on the hill stood a small, red two-story log house. We were told it was built in the early 1700s, more than 280 years ago. Even though I had heard all about it from Rolf before, being there at last and standing in such a property felt surreal and it was as if I'd walked into an old history book or a movie. As soon as Rolf's parents heard George's car drove in they rushed out to meet us. Rolf was emotional seeing his parents for the first time in 20 years and so were his parents at seeing their eldest son finally came home after all those years and meeting us for the first time. We hugged and hugged again in happiness. Although we didn't need any introductions, we had so much to say to one another, but we couldn't because of the language barrier between us.

But the hugs told a thousand words.

The property was called "*Skinnarbo*". It was a large acreage property. There were a cellar, a barn, a strawberry garden and a few sheds dotted around the property and nearby the house there was a small well for the water supply. The place was so serene we could hear the lovely sound of water running nearby in the little creek that ran through the property, it was mesmerizing.

As we followed them inside of the house, a very old Saint-Bernard dog walked out very slowly and straight away got the full attention of our boys, and the delicious smell of cooking from an old wood-burning stove made us feel very welcome. As I followed Rolf into the lounge room the large oil painting on the wall caught my eyes straightaway and delightfully surprised me. It was the seascape I'd painted for them on request from Rolf, and sent to them about 12 years earlier, and there were more. There hung also was the mosaic I had made for them, a mosaic of a little girl's face made with many seashells we had gathered whenever we went to the seaside. Amongst many photos of the family displayed there was a photo of our family. It made me feel so at home and I thought about how much they would have been longing for this day to come, and had missed us all.

Words can't describe how special it was to have a meal with Rolf's parents for the first time and the slow cooked beef dish in a woodstove had the sauce with a rich flavour, served with vegetables and hard Swedish bread was indeed very delicious. After we had the lovely lunch and whilst Rolf was busy catching up with his parents in Swedish and the children were occupied with the Saint-Bernard dog, Lufsan, my body clock reminded me that it was the time for a nap. I went into the lounge room to have a little rest on a sofa. Rolf's mum followed me in and put a blanket on me and tucked me in to keep me warm, it was so nice to feel her love. It sure was a very rare and Special Moment for me.

I woke up to the sound of an accordion playing and went back out to the kitchen and saw everyone was sitting around the table, entertained by Rolf's father singing in his croaky voice what seemed be an old song, as he played his accordion. I didn't have any clue what the song was about so just as our boys did, I sat there and tried to take in all the treasured moments. Rolf explained to us that his father used to enjoy playing his accordion for barn dances in his younger days. When everyone's hay stock for the cattle in their ban was all used up through the winter and the barn was empty in summer time, people often used the empty space for dances. The barn dances would go on at property after property throughout most of the summer.

The winter prior to our arriving there, Rolf's mother had a bad fall and had gone through numerous operations but hadn't yet recovered her speech and she wasn't talking much at all. But her expressions said it all how pleased she was to have us around. We were having a lovely time when George returned to pick us up. George went to his home after he dropped us off at their parent's home and had been busy helping his wife Mayly organizing a big family get together for us at his home that evening, and had returned to pick us up. Rolf's other siblings and their families were expected to come. Rolf is the eldest of the siblings and he was the only person who had left Karlskoga, everyone else still lived in town. George and Mayly's house was a large place, it was originally two units and they opened it up into one big house with many bedrooms and there were attics as well as the basement space, where their wood heating system and the laundry were. It was a lovely spacious and homely place to stay.

All the adults sat around one table and all the young ones around the other. It was really good to see our boys having a lovely time amongst many of their cousins. We ate, drank and talked the night away. It was great that many spoke very good English. A few smoked cigarettes like Rolf did and many used snuff on their gums - a blackish substance, smokeless tobacco, made from pulverized tobacco leaves. Next morning George and Mayly took us to their annual market fair some kilometers away from town. The market was very crowded with people in trench coats which reminded me of the busy market place in Seoul in autumn, and made me home sick when I saw a stall selling homemade pickled gherkins; they looked delicious and made my mouth water imagining having crunchy gherkins with steamed rice and hot chili sauce. There were many stalls of their traditional handcrafts, interesting to learn about some of their traditions but they were rather expensive to buy. Average prices of most things were dearer than Australia. The beer was not an exception in that year 1986; a carton of twenty-four, 450ml-500ml cans of beer was $60 Australian whilst in Australia a carton of twenty-four, 375ml cans of beer was only $14.50.

By the way, I was very impressed with how well their legislation against drinking and driving was enforced.

I was told that when caught the penalty for drinking and driving was very severe. The fines were calculated by the offender's daily earnings, and what's left after what the government official calculated the basic necessity for the keep for a day, was calculated into units no matter how much you earned. Therefore the richer you were, you paid a higher fine. All offenders must work a minimum for one month in a police guarded government forest camp and whilst living in a camp they had to work hard to pay their keep, cutting down trees as well as keeping the camp running and on top of that the offender lost his licence to drive for two years. People gave the camp a nickname and it was commonly called "Director's Club", and it's a club they rather would not join.

Therefore people were extremely disciplined about it. Nobody touched alcohol until the weekends when they didn't need to go to work next day thus they looked forward to Friday after work and Saturdays to relax and enjoy alcoholic drinks. Sunday morning came and no one drank alcoholic beverages to be ready for work on Monday. Unlike in Mount Isa where it was not unusual to see people drink and drive at any day of the week in those years, even though everyone knew there was a law against it, but the law wasn't much enforced at all.

Thank goodness, eventually we caught up with the discipline here in Australia as well, but not until a decade later. As I had heard the meat price was a lot dearer in Sweden; 1 kg rib fillet of beef was only $6 - $7 in Mount Isa whereas in Sweden they had to pay around $30 Australian for the same cuts of beef. I found they ate more of the processed meat like sausages than we did. Moreover we got there in such a bad time, not long after the Chernobyl nuclear explosion in April that year, and of course the food processed before the explosion became safer to eat not knowing the effect from the contamination after the explosion.

The explosion released large quantities of radioactive particles into the atmosphere in many parts of Europe. Sweden was one of the countries badly affected by it. Because of the catastrophic disaster we couldn't pick and enjoy the wild berries and mushrooms in season nor eat any of the freshly caught fish. There are many beautiful lakes around Karlskoga with many lovely fish to catch but too much mercury was found in the lakes since the explosion so it took away the joy of eating fish from those lakes as well.

They were yet to find out what kind of health risks there were for people if the polluted foods in the wild were consumed in large quantities. Five months into the study nothing was clear, people were very cautious and worried about what was safe to eat and how much they could eat each day. It was heartbreaking to be there at such a time and to experience firsthand what it was like to live there so soon after such an explosion and it made us feel concerned about the future health of all those people who were living there, especially our relatives.

Another significant event in Karlskoga that year was the celebration of their 400 years of history. Karlskoga was established in July 1586. First their Lutheran church was built and to this date, all their census records of births and deaths as well as records of marriages are kept at that church. Karlskoga is located in central Sweden in the warmer part of Sweden called Varmland around many beautiful lakes. It was the place where Alfred Nobel of the "Nobel Prize" spent most of the summers in his later years, at his manor house called *"Bjorkborn"*, which came with the ironworks factory he'd bought which manufactured gun shells and cannons. He owned Bofors. The factory was huge and it was an industry which produced chemicals and gun powder.

One of Rolf's uncles had worked there when Rolf was a child and in later years Rolf himself worked there about three and half years. As a matter of fact it was the last job Rolf had before he left Sweden to come to Australia. He worked and studied to become a supervisor there. Rolf's brother, Sivert, who was working for Bofors then gave Rolf and I a special tour of the factory. It was an interesting place but seeing many of the industrial robots were occupied doing the work instead of people, making guns and big cannons, was beyond my comprehension. It would have been a more interesting place for a young man like Maurits to visit but he wasn't allowed in as he was under 18 years of age.

George took us to the local sawmill where he and many of our relatives were employed and gave us a tour as well. It was a big sawmill and all of us were excited seeing the complex in full operation. We were surprised to hear that about 20% of workers didn't come to work on that day, and that was pretty normal as they will still get paid 90% of their normal pay for the day anyway. In those years Sweden was leading the world with their good social security and health systems, but what I heard on that day made me wonder if it was sustainable as I couldn't help but think that the system would encourage the workers to be lazy.

The temperature was getting lower as the days went by and the apple tree in George's yard lost all its leaves since we arrived there and many mornings the strawberry garden was covered in severe frost and that made people speculate about the winter closing in early.

One day we were invited to Erling's home, one of Rolf's old friends. Some of his close friends together put on a lovely smorgasbord party for us. It was lovely to meet Rolf's friends and their families and to hear some of the fun memories of their younger days together. Most of them couldn't speak English so I had to depend on Rolf to translate for me and it was difficult to express my emotion at the same moments with them. But I was able to guess a lot by their expressions, the gestures and the laughter as they were reminiscing about their mischievous younger days, especially the fun times they had shared with Rolf.

It was a special occasion for us all and I enjoyed very much being amongst them. The smorgasbord was full of homemade tasty food. It was the first time that I tasted horse meat and elk meat. The pieces I had tasted looked like silverside. Rolf reminded me of the story about the world great depression when everything was in short supply and rationed, people had to learn to survive with whatever meat they could get to eat.

Someone had invited a professional singer for the party. Someone playing an accordion suddenly appeared from outside and surprised us while we were having our meals, walking into the room singing as he played his accordion. The whole room went so silent you could hear a pin drop and by looking at everyone's faces in deep emotion I sensed it took them all into a sentimental journey of sad times. Many more songs were continually sung by him and I imagined they were their favorite old songs. Even though I didn't understand what the songs were about and I didn't want to disturb Rolf to translate for me, just being there and witnessing their friendship gave me immense pleasure and I was glad that we were there.

After the singer left we all went downstairs to the basement and saw the children having their fun in a media room playing different games. Erling set up a projector and a screen and showed us the photos he took on his movie camera in November 1966 on the last day, when Rolf and his friend Carl were getting ready to leave Karlskoga for Australia. It was a treat for me and our boys to see the photos of Rolf on such a special day and I tried to capture some of the images on my camera while the projector was running only to find out later that it was in vain, because I didn't turn off the flash of my camera. I was very disappointed. Yet I never thought of asking for a copy of it either, I guess I didn't comprehend that it was possible to make a copy.

The family took us one day for a drive to a place called Kristinehamn, about 25 kilometres away from Karlskoga, where the largest lake in Sweden,

'Lake Vanern' is. The lake is 75 kilometres wide and 140 kilometres long and I was told that it is the third largest lake in all of Europe. Near the lake shore there was a 15 metre-tall free standing concrete sculpture made by the famous Pablo Picasso of his wife, Jacqueline. The free standing large sculpture looked ever so weird and out of place and it was unreal to see the work of such a famous person unprotected in a wide open space.

Nonetheless it added an out of the ordinary interest to the lake's tranquil picturesque scenery.

Also there nearby the lake was a large wooden dance floor. How unusual it was to see a large wooden floor all by itself in the open air. It had me imagine about a lot of people getting together there in summertime, having a wonderful time in their traditional costumes, dancing to the tune of someone playing the accordion and many birds in nature would join in and sing their chorus for them. The floor didn't seem in the wrong place after all!

One morning Mayly and I, just the two of us, went out to town. She doesn't speak English and I don't speak Swedish, we knew it would be a challenge to communicate but more fun, we thought. She took me at first to the town Lutheran church where the census records are kept.

It was the most beautiful church I ever walked into!

The large pipe organ looked awesome and the art works of the ceiling were magnificent and took my breath away. No one was inside but us and the place was so serene that I felt the presence of sanctities in the room. From there we went to town and we had a look around some craft shops. At one of the stores we met a potter making pottery and I liked some of his work. I bought a pair of little doves, a ball shaped vase and a candle holder all in the same matching motives and glazes. I liked the uniqueness of their design and they were small enough to put in my suitcase.

It was getting close to lunch time when we walked past the Chinese restaurant nearby. We looked at each other and nodded our heads and smiled in agreement, we went in for lunch. We placed our order with some difficulties however we were pleased when we got our meals, it was beef in black bean sauce with rice exactly what I had in my mind that I had ordered. But I was a little surprised with the Chinese meal served for

Mayly which was with potatoes not with rice. But then I realized Mayly must have ordered it with potato. Once again Mayly read my mind and could guess what I was thinking and she pointed her finger on her potatoes and laughed so I nodded my head in agreement as I laughed as well. Mayly told the owner (a Chinese man) that I was from down under, all the way from Australia and I worked at a Chinese restaurant in Australia. He was very pleased to hear and shook my hand and he took us upstairs to show us where everything was set up beautifully for the evening meals.

Mayly and I got by sharing more laughs than words to communicate but we got by. Anyway it was a very pleasant experience; we both had a fun day out together.

Our boys had a wonderful day at the indoor ice skating rink one day. They've been on the roller skates before, but it was the first time for them to try ice skating. They fell down more than they were up nonetheless they had a wonderful time and Rolf and I enjoyed very much watching our boys having a great time with their uncles and cousins.

We visited Rolf's parents again and had a whole day with them. Whilst *farmor* (grandma in Swedish) prepared lunch for us *farfar* (granddad in Swedish) was excited to show us around the property. At first he took the farm tractor out and insisted that Rolf take the boys for a tractor ride and the boys loved every minute of it. *Farfar* was very happy watching his son and grandchildren having the ride on his tractor. He hugged me tight with joy and kept on talking to me in Swedish, seemingly it didn't matter to him whether I understood or not and I could only have a guess that he was telling me about Rolf's childhood. His joyous laughter said it all. It would have been so nice if I could have understood exactly what he was saying as I would have loved to hear all about Rolf's childhood from him.

When the boys were off the tractor *farfar* took us here and there around the farm to show us where Rolf's belongings were kept. All kinds of tools, some century old antique books Rolf had bought from auctions as well as Rolf's car - a 1956 Renault Dauphine - he'd left behind twenty years ago, was still in the shed as if he'd parked it there yesterday. Walking around where he was brought up and seeing Rolf's belongings I got very emotional. Once again, the thought of how much Rolf's parents would have missed him and would have longed for his return for all those years they have been holding on to them.

After we had the delicious meal *farmor* prepared for us, *farfar* played the accordion for us. Poor old Lufsan, the Saint-Bernard dog, tried his best to join us in the fun but with his failing eyesight and arthritic legs he got tired very quickly and had to opt out and rest. The boys were learning to play the accordion from *farfar* when George came back to pick us up. We were to go with George and Mayly to Mayly's mother's place for her sixtieth birthday party that evening.

Rolf told me that he had his own property right next to his parents' property which he sold before he came to Australia. The property was called *"Spinnarbo"* and it was a slightly smaller acreage but had a similar old log house. We hoped to have a look at the property together but we were told that there was a sign at the property *"Don't want to be disturbed"* and that disappointed us all.

We called in at a flower shop on the way to Mayly's mum's place and bought a pot of beautiful chrysanthemum in full bloom to take with us.

When we arrived at the unit we were greeted at the door personally by Mayly's mother. She was wearing a large beautiful headband made of intertwined fresh flowers, and we followed her into the room where many more fresh flowers filled the air with their rich scent. Not just us but everyone else brought fresh flowers for a gift, to the point that it was rather strange not seeing any other kind of gifts for the birthday, just pots of beautiful flowers. There were about a dozen people in the room and we sat around a table for a meal. It was a formal sit down dinner and rather rigid. It was a very cold night and perhaps the cold temperature outside contributed such an ambience. I guess, not understanding the language wasn't much help either.

After dinner I expected there would be the birthday cake with candles for her to blow out and for us to sing together the "Happy Birthday" song for her but there wasn't any of that either. But they took a lot of happy photos together around the table had all the beautiful flowers which people had brought as a gift. It sure wasn't a sixtieth birthday party we were used to in Australia with a cake and candles and it wasn't a sixtieth birthday celebration like I had seen in Korea, with lots of family and friends and food prepared for days in advance. Nevertheless I enjoyed meeting Mayly's mother and her relations and the experience of the different ways of life, which added to my list of many interesting discoveries of life in Sweden. It sure was very different to the life I was brought up in Korea, as well as the life I have become accustomed to in Australia.

Being there in Sweden for a few weeks and able to observe how they live I have gained a better understanding of who Rolf is and where he was coming from. I found out many things just by having meals with them. The table manner Rolf was brought up by was so different to mine. In Korea, meals were served in such a way that we help ourselves to eat from many shared dishes, by everyone using their own chopsticks or spoons. But in Sweden every shared dish had its own serving spoons or tongs and everyone must use them to help a portion onto their plate. Which I must agree, it is definitely a more hygienic way. But having been brought up in Korea with our chop sticks or spoon not only do we feed ourselves but we feed other members of our family, and that was pretty normal, I couldn't help but miss the joy of that kind of intimacy.

Moreover Rolf was brought up not to speak with a mouth full of food and was discouraged from talking while having meals with family, as well as at school while he was eating lunch provided by the school canteen. Whilst my family in Korea always talked while we were having meals together and speaking with a mouth full wasn't a big deal. The meal time was a happy time we enjoyed talking and laughing and we fussed around each other, to share food and we were noisy sometimes to express how much we enjoyed and appreciated the taste of the food as we ate.

When we started to live together the first thing I had to change was to eat in silence to please Rolf. Eating quietly and chewing food with my mouth closed, that I didn't mind to learn but I wished Rolf would share more conversation while we were having meals. Not only did I miss the food I was brought up with but also the enjoyment of the way we had our meals. Needless to say overcoming such differences and adjusting to each other was not easy at the start, and we couldn't always see things eye to eye. But visiting Sweden helped me to understand immensely where he was coming from and to accept who he is. There are certainly the good and the bad in each of our cultures and no culture is better than the other, just different!

A half glass of water is half full to somebody whilst the glass is half empty to someone else; it doesn't differentiate which person is positive or negative, I rather like to think that if one sees it as half empty and has the desire to fill the rest, he or she may become empowered and strive to turn negatives into positives and succeed in filling the rest. If one sees it as it as half full and is satisfied and doesn't have the urge to fill the rest, it may turn positive into negative and become lazy. It is only the differences in opinion, just a paradigm not wrong or right because wrong can be right to someone else and vice versa. Whether we liked it or not it was vital that we had to learn to respect the differences in our cultures and whilst it wasn't always easy, both of us had to learn to compromise because we love each other and wanted to live together.

Forty-four years on now we are still on the same journey, learning to compromise!

We were invited to Rolf's youngest sister, Anne-Lill's home for dinner one day and we had an opportunity to have a tour as well, of a huge waste treatment centre nearby. It was a large complex but we saw only very few people at work on duty as most operations were computerized. "Waste-to-Energy" is their main concept and was focused on waste disposal with energy recovery by incineration of household waste and animal waste converted into energy. We were told that a 17 metre high furnace expands 0.5 metre by the heat during its full operation. The heat from it was transferred to the water, forming steam, which in turn drives a turbine to generate electricity and the remaining energy was transferred to the district heating system for hundreds of villas in town. It also supplied the steam to the industries like the Bjorkborns industrial zone in Karlskoga.

I was really impressed how advanced the refuse disposal and waste management system was in Karlskoga, a small town in Sweden seemingly led the world. Every household was already allocated two wheelie bins in 1986 and people were well informed and educated to separate the recyclable materials from everyday household waste. For someone like me from a place like Mount Isa, an out back country town in Australia, it was an eye opening experience. In those years in Mount Isa we hadn't yet seen such things as wheelie bins, we still had the old metal or plastic garbage bins without wheels. All waste and refuse went in the same bin and was collected by the manually handled council's garbage truck twice a week and dumped on an open tip and the rubbish was buried as the pile got too big. Whatever we couldn't fit in the bin or if it was too much between the collections days, we were allowed to take extra to the tip ourselves and dump it in the piles. We didn't see the wheelie bins until we moved down to the Coast 15 years later in 2001.

We enjoyed visiting Anne-Lill's lovely home where she lived with her little son, Steffan and enjoyed talking with her as she spoke English well. The homemade blueberry pie she made for our dessert was delicious. It was my first time to taste blue berry pie and it became instantly one of my favourite desserts.

Rolf's friend, Erling, took us for a drive one day to their summer house by the lake. We drove south along the beautiful shore of the famous "Lake Vanern". There is always something restful about a lake side. The scenery was very peaceful and beautiful with the striking rich red and yellow hues of autumn leaves and with crisp and fresh air. When we arrived at the summer house it started to rain softly and it became colder and made us all rush to go inside.

It was hard for me to believe that such a lovely place was left unattended for weeks and months; we were told that they were there only a few times a year. The house was fully furnished with comfy furniture and all household necessities were in place ready to stay. There was no fence or gate to unlock and not another house to be seen nearby. A little boat outside by the lake completed the perfect serene and peaceful atmosphere - a good subject for a painting - I must say. I couldn't help but feel envious of such a standard of living.

One weekend we were invited to Sivert and Monica's place for lunch and we had a lovely time with their family, their four children. Their sons Mats and Lars were a little older than our boys and their daughters, Lena and Åsa were about the same age. Monica made a Lovely warm potato salad but with a twist, the potato salad tasted like fried rice without rice and it was delicious. Monica did understand English more than she spoke and everyone else could speak English, we had a lovely time together.

Back at George's place one morning we were talking about me cutting Rolf's hair for all those years and when George's eighteen year old son Dennis wished me to cut his hair, our fifteen year old son Maurits thought he was very brave letting me do that. But no way would I say "No" to such a chance given Rolf and Ed were the only clients (VICTIM in Maurits's words) I had. By looking at the photo of it in the album now, Dennis didn't look all that relaxed getting his hair cut by me. But considering it all, I remember how pleased we both were about how it turned out. I must admit though that Dennis wouldn't have complained even if he had not been pleased with my work. By the way, Maurits was relieved and happy to vacuum the hair fallen on the floor for us.

Ing-Marie organized her mother-in-law to come over to her place and show us how to make sausages one afternoon. She was ninety years old, a tiny little lady, but active for her age and was only happy to demonstrate her skill of many years of making sausages for us. A mixture of minced pork meat, boiled potato and chopped up greens and herbs with lots of black pepper and salt all went together through the sausage making machine then into the pig's intestine, and then twisted and tied up into the sizes of the sausages they wanted. Needless to say I was very excited to see for the very first time how sausages were made. The taste of the sausages boiled was very delicious, it was to die for!

Every year, before the Chernobyl explosion, they enjoyed preserving their abundant seasonal harvests. When in season there were plenty of wild berries such as blue berries, lingonberries, cloudberries, raspberries, rowanberries and elderberries as well as the mushrooms. They made mostly jams and cordials with many different wild berries they picked whilst with many different wild mushrooms they picked they fried them in butter and froze them. I knew how enjoyable and rewarding these chores were as I too have fun memories of picking wild vegetables from the field or the mountain near where I grew up. I grew up in the era when the sauces of all kinds and vegetable pickles we needed were made at home, many different kimchis or any pickles in just salt or with vinegar. As well as made all our own soy sauces, chili sauce and bean paste sauce and stored them in large clay urns. Unfortunately that is now becoming a thing of the past in Korea as the life style has evolved; given these days all those things are readily available in the shops and can be bought in small quantities as needed all year around. I was envious of how abundant they were still in the nature around where they live, for them to carry on such rewarding traditions to this date.

It was so unfortunate that we went to Sweden in that year though, as it turned out to be the worst year because of the obvious reason, the bad effects of the Chernobyl nuclear explosion. When we saw the lovely mushrooms called, Kantarell growing in the wild nearby George's home they only harvested a small amount to cook for us to taste, which was delicious, it was very unfortunate just to look and not able to enjoy them as much as we would like to.

The days passed quickly and our holidays in Sweden were almost over. Rolf's siblings decided to have a nice studio photo taken while Rolf was there, for a gift for *farfar* as his seventieth birthday was coming up in December that year, which was a lovely idea. We got our special family photo taken at the studio as well to commemorate the occasion. Posed before the studio camera, three brothers at the back and two sisters in the front and they looked unmistakably siblings with good likenesses between them. I must say, they all looked handsome, especially Rolf of course!

Another smorgasbord of delicious food was prepared for our farewell at George and Mayly's place. The relatives started to arrive and we were excited to be with them all together again, and when just about everyone had arrived we had a huge surprise. One of Rolf's old friends, Henry, the German friend I had met in 1970 in Kalgoorlie, walked in with his wife and children. Henry had been married to a Malaysian lady since he left Australia in 1972 and they went to Sweden to live, about 80 kilometres away from Karlskoga, George and Mayly had invited them especially to surprise us.

It was so lovely to see Henry again and to meet, his wife, Nora and children Roxana and Winfred, at last after all those years we had been writing to each other at Christmas time and keeping in touch. The party was also to celebrate my upcoming thirty-seventh birthday in a few days. I was given a large fresh flower band to wear on my head just like the one I had admired on Mayly's mum who had worn it on her sixtieth birthday. Amongst many lovely things I received as gifts from everyone, was a card that played lovely music as I opened it. It was the most joyous surprise I ever received and the child in me put me in tears. We ate, drank and danced. And everyone was merry, it didn't matter whether we spoke English or Swedish we had no problem getting along and partied on, it was the most enjoyable night for us all to remember for a long time to come.

Grandparents came to see us to say good-bye the day before we left. It was very emotional for me to say good-bye to them knowing that it could be the last time we'd see them. They would love to come and visit us but they were afraid of flying and it would be a long time before we could save enough money to travel back there again. As we hugged for the last time I wished the clock could pause for a while and let us be together a little longer, not able to express my love in their words made me extremely sad. Their hugs were loving and very tight, the king size wave of sadness lashed on my heart and tears ran on my face. We were comforted by George and Mayly who promised us that they were planning to come and visit us in Australia in two and half years time to celebrate Rolf's fiftieth birthday with us.

As we were driven away from Karlskoga to the airport in Stockholm I was thinking about the lovely times we had shared, and I couldn't help thinking how lovely it would be for me to go home to Korea and spend some time with my family and friends as well. I wondered how everyone was, and the faces and the names of the people I love entered into my thoughts one by one, and the more I thought about them the more I missed them. It became so clear to me that my next priority was to visit my family in Korea and I must look into it closely as soon as I returned home to Mount Isa. Just having my mind made up I was already excited and couldn't wait to get home.

We arrived at the Arlanda airport in Stockholm just in time for lunch. George and Mayly, Benny and Ing-Marie and all of us had lunch at a café before we said our farewells to each other. We were all very excited about their plan to visit us in three years time, in 1989, to celebrate Rolf's fiftieth birthday and said our farewells in happiness as we had much to look forward to, their next visit.

The atmosphere inside of the Scandinavian Airline DC Ten felt no longer foreign and rather familiar having lived there a few weeks. Soon we arrived at Heathrow airport in London. The airport was huge we had to take a bus to the Qantas terminal. Our next flight to Singapore wasn't until three hours later, but we decided to stay in the airport and look around the stores and just relax in the airport lounge. We had some drinks and watched people of all colors, shapes and outfits coming and going which kept us entertained. It was the first time for us to be there but it didn't feel strange or foreign as most people spoke English we felt comfortable. We communicated freely in English and the place felt just like somewhere in Australia.

On board a Qantas Boeing 747, all four of us were seated side by side in the smoking area as we had made the choice not to be separated from Rolf again, and were ready for the long fourteen plus hour flight to Singapore. Soon it started to roll onto the runway as my thoughts began to ponder how my brother was coping with everything at home in Mount Isa. Our cat Moki, our budgerigars in the cage and I thought about how hard it would have been for Pentti and Irja to keep up with the watering of my large collection of pot plants and our garden, as the hot summer was fast closing in. I thought about our front garden full with over-grown Bougainvilleas having missed the pruning in autumn and dreaded the job needing to be done when I get back. The thorns on them were always very nasty to handle.

As we were travelling east we had to adjust the time forward, about seven hours later the plane stopped at Bahrain to refuel. We were allowed to shop at the duty free stores inside of the airport but there were a lot of airport guards with batons on their waist belts and holding guns and made us feel very intimidated. We were very glad when the plane left that place and we felt safe. Last time I saw anyone in uniform with a baton on their waist belts and guns in their hands was when I was growing up at Itaewon, at each entrance gate of the USA military base in Seoul. But they weren't scary at all, they were kind to us with chewing gum in their mouths they smiled and waved their hands to us when we walked past on the road, on the way to the nearest public children's play ground that we had then, where I often took my little sisters and cousins with me to play there when it was school holidays.

The close to 2 kilometres walk to the playground was always fun for all but coming back after many hours of playing was a different story. Everyone was tired and without fail my youngest sister didn't want to walk back all the way so I had to carry her on my back for a big part of the way home. At the same time I had to try, to the best of my ability, to keep everyone happy and safe from the traffic on the road, and we had to make a few stops on the way to stretch my aching back and their tired legs.

It was such a long time ago and a very distant memory now, I feel as if I was remembering someone else's story.

But those experiences were my own and I guess they were the building blocks that had helped to shape who I am today.

Side by side as we were sitting in the plane watching in-house movies and being well looked after by the ever so friendly stewardesses, the plane finally arrived at the Changi International airport in Singapore. It was, at the local time, 8.00pm. Not only the clock had to be adjusted forward but in less than one day the season had changed from the cold late autumn in the West to the hot summer in the East. From people who had their heavy winter overcoat on their arms instead of wearing it, to the people in singlets and shorts wearing thongs, which stood out to us in the crowd and put smiles on our face as we knew they were fellow Australians.

We had little more than two hours to wait for the next flight to Darwin. Maurits and Ed seemed to enjoy the facilities in the airport, checking out the place, looking around the stores and enjoying the rides on escalators repeatedly, whilst Rolf and I relaxed with a cup of coffee at a café and enjoyed a chat.

Around 11.00pm, the plane we boarded was taking off into the night sky leaving the sublime scenery below! The city sparkled like one huge store full of jewels.

I couldn't help but feel blessed to see and experience so many wonderful things in life and sharing those magical moments with my husband and our sons indeed was very special for me!

I thanked God with all my heart.

Everyone dozed off for a while and as the plane descended, arriving at Darwin airport we woke up. It was around 4.00am local time. As soon as the plane landed, while all the passengers remained seated in the plane, it was sprayed to avoid exotic pests and diseases entering the country and to protect the agriculture in Australia. However it certainly was not a pleasant experience for us passengers.

When we walked inside the airport, the old floor-standing giant fans were still working overtime in vain, and brought me the memory of the day I arrived there for the first time - what felt like a life time ago! The city was mostly rebuilt and repaired since the horrible Cyclone Tracy in 1974, but 12 years on the airport passenger terminals were yet to be improved. I, as a naturalized citizen of this wonderful country, couldn't help but feel rather embarrassed by it for the foreign visitors standing in the queue with me.

We freshened up ourselves in the public rest room and we took a taxi to Linda's place as we had promised to see them, knowing that we would arrive in Darwin very early in the morning. But when we got to their home no one was there and we found out that they still went to the airport to pick us up, regardless that I had told them that we would take a taxi when we arrived back from Europe. It was obvious we missed each other on the road. They returned and were relieved to see us waiting at home. We had a lovely time catching up with them, as always, Linda's family could never do enough for us.

Mid afternoon we were on our last flight of the trip - home to Mount Isa. It didn't matter whether we were returning home by road or by air the chimney stacks of Mount Isa Mines stood out in the barren landscape, and spotting them in the distance made us always feel welcome, arriving home safely after a long trip and always it was a long trip. The place was a True Oasis in the outback!

We were glad to see Pentti and Irja who were waiting for us at the airport. We were driven to our home by them in two cars, given we had the four suitcases. As soon as we got home, the boys in unison called out for our cat, "Moky!" "Moky!" He appeared quickly out of nowhere, "Miaow!" "Miaow!" Together the boys caressed him in happiness. Everything looked well and watered! We found out that Irja had already prepared the dinner for everyone. It was good to just relax and settle in over the delicious dinner Irja had prepared and catch up about our time away from one another. We were blessed indeed to have such lovely caring friends. After they left, we took our little Ed to his bed as he had fallen asleep on the lounge next to Moky. It was good to talk with my brother on the phone; he was at nearly the end of its second year of his apprenticeship.

I was also very pleased to find out that Mary had coped well with her duties at the restaurant, just as I had instructed her, and Freddie didn't have anything to complain about. Although working for the Chinese restaurant was interesting and I learned a lot about the behind-the-scenes of how the small business was run, and all in all it's been a good experience for me. Deep down inside I missed working in the hotel environment. Freddie could sense how I felt and he was extra nice to keep me there, but while I was away on holiday for 4 weeks he had accumulated people who came to the restaurant for free meals - people like policemen, lawyers, bank managers or managers of different businesses, the wealthy and the well known people in town. The restaurant was full with such people and although it looked very busy the figures in the account books told a different story and showed the business was going into the red. Yet Freddie couldn't stop and kept on giving free meals too often to those who took advantage of his silly generosity.

There was another Chinese restaurant nearby in town much bigger which had been operating a lot longer and doing well. Something had happened some time ago between the Chinese workers of the two restaurants and Freddie wasn't happy. He had become obsessed and adopted the bad habit of driving around every night between 8.00pm and 8.30pm to check and literally count the parked cars outside the restaurants, and compared what he found. He was overly excited and happy when his restaurant had more people and if they had more his ego was badly bruised.

At the beginning I took his behavior as reasonable and understandable. But as it got worse, the restaurant was filled with many customers for free meals, and the good customers who felt uncomfortable with Freddie's overwhelming generosity stopped coming to the restaurant. I became very annoyed with him especially when he continued with such a silly behavior, and to the point not being able to pay the bills on time. As unsatisfied as I was, it was against my pride, and it was very hard for me to welcome back those people who came in and expected to have free meals.

Freddie had also a very bad habit of helping himself and spending the money out of the till, without leaving the note in the till, as though it didn't matter to him as he was the owner of the business. Each time I had trouble balancing the till I became more frustrated. I made him sit with our accountant to make him see where his unprofessional behavior and bad obsession was leading to, and reproached him to be more sensible, but all in vain. As a fellow Asian I was frustrated and unhappy to witness his somewhat silly generosity, which was not appreciated right way and was abused by those who rather looked down on him for being an Asian, and selfishly took advantage of his weakness.

He was good for a little while but didn't last long as some people were very cunning to make Freddie feel as though he was very popular with them, in order to take Freddie's weakness to their advantage and not to pay at all for the meals they had, or to get an extremely good discount. Over the next 12 months or so I had resigned from my position four times over the matter and tried to get away from working there. It was pointless and I failed each time because he made me feel very important and needed for his business, and he apologized sincerely and promised he would change. I therefore felt bad to walk away while the business wasn't making good money and the feeling of failure that I had not succeeded in what I set out to do, make me to go back and try harder to help. But in the end I had to give up, as it was starting to affect my health and impair my dignity. To help myself to walk away and not to go back again, I decided, first of all, to find myself another job before I gave my resignation.

I phoned my friend, Frances who used to be the chef at the "Copper Grill restaurant" and who then had the lease of the kitchen of an another hotel in town, the Overlander Hotel. When I explained to her that I was looking for work and why I was planning to leave the job I had, she gave me a job straightaway as the hostess of her restaurant for four nights a week, exactly as I asked for. Even though I told her that I would be away for a month in Korea for a holiday in a few weeks time, she told me that I could start to work for her straight away. A huge weight lifted off my shoulders and ultimately I was able to give the final resignation to Freddie and walk away from there.

The job at the Overlander was easy and working with the group of people I already mostly knew well, it didn't feel like a new job. Not having the stress and having the extra time on my hands again, I was able to go back to the things I used to enjoy doing but didn't have time to do, like playing ten-pin bowling. One morning I went into the bowling centre to play the game and I was very surprised to find out that Freddie had left a gift there for me. I felt the frustration of not knowing what to do with him again and decided not to accept gifts anymore, and returned it to him unopened. Freddie was so disappointed but he finally came to the realization that he couldn't lure me back to work for him anymore.

Rolf decided to build a hobby room for me right next to his work shed and he built a larger room, 7.2 metres x 8.5 metres x 2.5 metres again with besser blocks, but that time he built it, little by little, after work and in the weekends. He worked very hard for months to get it finished. The room was large and a useful space for all members of our family and we were all very proud of him.

Raking up the dried and fallen leaves from the trees we had in our yard reminded me of autumn time in Seoul and made me feel homesick all the more and remembering the old Korean proverb *"Ten Years can change a mountain or river"*, I imagined the place and the people would be very different but I was hanging onto the memories I had and counting the days.

One morning I was having a cup of tea with my neighbour, Davina, who lived next door to us and I was happy to tell her the news that I had booked the flights to go to Korea in September, and how much I was looking forward to visit my home in Korea for the first time in seventeen and half years. I told her also that I would be going there just with our little Ed without Rolf and Maurits as Rolf was not keen to fly and it would be nice for him to stay at home with Maurits preparing for the final High School exams. Davina was very happy for me and told me that she had never ever been overseas and she was envious of me going. Without giving any thought I said to her "Why don't you come with us?" But she didn't respond to what I said and seemed preoccupied and wasn't quite with the conversation, so I changed the subject to talk about other things.

Early next morning I heard Davina's loud voice calling my name over the fence as if something was urgent and I came out in a hurry to see her. She was excited and had such a happy grin on her face and said "Good-morning Ann! Is it Really OK for me to go with you to Korea?" I wasn't expecting to hear that as I hadn't yet given a serious thought about going to Korea with her, but I couldn't say anything else but "Of Course!" Even though I had no idea how my family would receive even myself or my son after all those years when I hadn't seen them, let alone an Australian friend they had never even heard of. However not to disappoint her I went with Davina to the travel agent and helped her to book her flights to go with us. Going with her being set concrete, in a way, I was looking forward to having her company but at the same time I couldn't help but feel a little apprehensive, not knowing the full situation in Korea.

One thing I knew for sure was that without a doubt it would be a very emotional trip for me to see my family and friends for the first time after all those years, and I would be too busy catching up with them we would not have much time for such things like sightseeing on the trip. I had to warn her about it and also I told her that I was concerned about the fact that she might get bored, not being able to join in the conversations, because of the language barrier. It was one of the reasons why I didn't push the issue to Rolf to go with me in first place. Another thing was that I had never been anywhere with Davina before, and I didn't have the slightest idea how she would handle not only the language barrier but the inevitable culture shock, never having been out of Australia before.

Davina is about eight years older than I am, she is a fair dinkum Australian lady born and brought up in Australia. She and her husband worked and lived in out-back Australia on cattle stations for a long time before they moved into town. She was at the time working as a casual cook at another Hotel in town. She booked the flights to Korea to go with me in a more or less spur of the moment, without asking her boss first if she could have time off to go on holiday.

Her boss was not pleased to hear about her going away on holiday at short notice, and her boss didn't like where Davina was going for the holiday. Her boss asked "Why would you go on holiday to such a dangerous country like Korea and not go to a place like Singapore or Hong Kong? Haven't you seen the TV news and read the newspapers recently about the terrible riots and the university students' demonstrations in Korea?" Her comments made Davina somewhat concerned about it. She came around early next morning to tell me that although she had told her boss that she trusted me and that I wouldn't go there with my little son if there was any danger, she wanted to hear from me if there was a risk that she should be really concerned about. It was a year before the "88 Seoul Summer Olympics" and leading up to the Olympics there had been a lot more riots and demonstrations than usual, but it didn't worry me at all and I didn't hesitate to tell her so.

In August that year Mount Isa hosted the annual Rodeo, the largest in the Southern Hemisphere - a weeklong festival that starts with the "Mardi Gras" procession on Friday night, led by the Irish Pipe Band. It is the one night of the year everyone in Mount Isa gets together on the streets in town in their cowboy and cowgirl outfits to join in the festive mood. It is a visual spectacular; there are many colourful floats, displays and performances to be enjoyed by all. Although the whole town was in a festive mood, unlike any other year my mind was not with it at all, and I was preoccupied with thoughts of our upcoming trip to Korea in a few weeks time.

It has been such a long road for us to get financially established to be able to visit our families overseas, and I was happy to inform everyone that I was coming home for a visit at last and I was coming with our little son Ed and a neighbour, who was a middleaged Australian lady. They were very excited and happy with the news and replied to me that many of them were coming out to meet us at the airport. I received a reply also from a friend Kyung Hae and she mentioned the name Chi Nam, one of our friends who would be coming out with to meet us at the airport. I remembered the name so well but no matter how hard I tried I couldn't put a face to the name. I did not forget any of the faces of the photographs I had in my photo album I brought with me when I left Korea, but I had forgotten many faces of people of whom I didn't have a photo even though the names were still very familiar.

I cooked a lot of extra meals and froze them for Maurits and Rolf and took care of whatever I could to make things easier for them while I was gone for 4 weeks as they were not used to cooking or doing the house work. Growing up in Korea in a large family soon after the war when the country was still in poverty recovering from the war, adults of our family, grandma or mum or aunties always prepared all the meals for the family, not we children, to avoid not cooking properly and spoiling the dinner for everyone as we didn't have much to cook with.

As the oldest child I was allowed to help clean up but never once was I left to cook for the whole family. Therefore as a mother and a wife doing all the housework for my family was pretty natural for me, and I always took all the housework such as cooking, washing, ironing, cleaning and shopping as my responsibilities, whether I went to work full time or not. Instead of teaching them how to do each job and delegate some of the jobs to help me out. It took me many decades, long after our children had grown up and became adults; to come to the realization that it would have been wiser to teach them to do things by themselves to be more independent, instead of doing everything for them.

Chapter Nine

The plane had only started to roll on the runway in Mount Isa airport, but my thoughts were already at the Kimpo airport in Seoul. My heart started to throb with the joy of meeting my family and friends waiting for me there. I thought of their faces, names and the places I had been in Korea.

The chain of thoughts was interrupted when I heard the announcement that we were about to land at the Brisbane airport, and it made me think about meeting the wife of the President of "Korean Society" in Brisbane at the airport, whom I had never met. She was kind to invite Ed and me for the dinner that evening and that she would even come to the airport to meet me. We were booked in a motel near the Brisbane airport overnight as our flight to Singapore was to leave early next morning. Davina also took the chance and arranged to have dinner with a friend she hadn't seen for a while, that evening.

Having lived for a long time in a place where the chance of meeting a Korean was very few and far between, I always was happy to meeting fellow Koreans. But as the years went by and I was adjusting more and more to the Australian way of life and thinking more like an Australian. Not only my command of speaking Korean became poorer but also I forgot many of the Korean ways of life. Therefore I became a little apprehensive meeting fellow Koreans who might criticize me.

As soon as I came to the arrival lounge she recognized me first by seeing Davina and Ed who were walking out with me, and greeted me with the complement that I looked a lot younger than she had thought and made me feel at ease meeting her. She left the airport as we got on the bus sent by our motel with the promise that she would send her husband to pick us up from the motel in the evening to take us to their home for dinner and I was very much looking forward to it. It was good we had the time to get refreshed before we were picked up by her husband to go to their place.

Everything was all lit up which made us feel welcome and as soon as we went inside, the rich smell of different kimchis and food cooked with bean paste (miso) and more that I so missed made my mouth water. Although I had been exposed to many different cuisines having worked at different restaurants for many years, and I was always interested in cooking, my ability at cooking Korean food was not outstanding. I have tried to cook Korean dishes from time to time as the ingredients were available to me, but the taste of food I cooked never was as good as I remembered. The food they prepared that night was authentic Korean and very delicious, exactly how I remembered. It was good also that they had two little boys for Ed to play with and they played well together.

After dinner a few of their Korean friends came around to join us for the evening. I noticed everyone brought some fruit with them and that reminded me of the long forgotten Korean way of life, which was so different to the Australian way of life I had become accustomed to. I have never ever seen anyone visiting friends late in the evening with fruit in Australia. We would have taken some alcoholic beverages with us given it was past dinner time, and this made me realize it was only the taste of what was to come when I arrived in Korea.

I was informed that night by the President that there were around a thousand families from Korea living in the Brisbane area and more and more were arriving each day, and I was amazed to hear that there would be a lot more in Sydney and other large cities.

A couple of ladies expressed to me that they were envious of my ability of speaking English, so I suggested to them that they should try to speak English when they were together, as they were then, instead of always speaking Korean. One of the men got offended by it and rather got angry with me and told me that I will be disliked by many when I go to Korea because of my poor command of Korean. Even though I agreed with what he said I didn't like how he said it, given that he had never met me before and didn't know anything about me.

What would he know; he has not lived the life I have lived?

Ever since I came to live in Australia, I have always conducted my life with dignity, never lost the pride that I was Korean born, and tried to be the rôle model in all aspects of life. The same time, living in Australia I always believed that we must strive to speak English well and adjust to the Australian way of life.

I felt he was unfair and narrow minded judging me harshly, as if I deliberately chose to speak Korean poorly.

Most of them had been in Australia for about 5 years yet their English was very poor, being married to Koreans and speaking Korean every day and interacting with mostly other Koreans in the community. It would be hard for someone like him to understand what it was like to live the life I have lived. I chose to ignore him and tried to enjoy the company of others. Thank goodness the children were having fun together, the language barrier did not seem to worry them at all nothing else mattered, although they had met for the first time.

I returned to the motel feeling a little hurt, however all in all the evening was enjoyable and somewhat helpful to prepare myself to face what was to come when I arrived in Korea, and I only hoped my family and friends in Korea would be more understanding. I felt much better after I talked about the visit to someone like Davina, an open minded person and I was glad that she was with me on the trip.

Back to Brisbane airport next morning and on board Singapore airline. The whole crew was ever so friendly and the service was second to none. The plane stopped a little while at Sydney airport, and as more people boarded we could feel the cooler air come in with them, and noticeably a lot of them were Asians. As the plane lifted off the runway, "Mummy, mummy, look! Look! There is the Opera House!" Ed exclaimed in delight and Davina and I too were excited to see the icon of Australia from high above. The scenery from above was indeed so very beautiful! It was amazing flying through the fairy floss like clouds and I thanked Almighty God for giving me the blessings and I prayed for his guidance in every step for our safe journey. From one beautiful place to another we arrived at the Changi airport that evening, all was lit up beautifully like a bright wonderland. Ed was very happy, felt at home given he was there only a year before and he guided us around as if he knew all about the place.

It was raining softly when we came outside the airport, the wet pavements glared in the many colours reflected from the bright neon lights everywhere, and people hurried to stay away from the rain. The atmosphere reminded me of a rainy night outside a movie theater in Seoul, the large crowd came out together after the movie in the rain and everyone rushed to catch a bus home. We too were running after our guide from Orchard Hotel where we were booked in for the overnight stay, and boarded the bus quickly to stay dry from the rain. 4.00am next morning we woke up to get ready for the early flight to Seoul. The bus we were on stopped at every hotel to pick up the people for the same flight. To my surprise most people got on the bus were not just any Asians, they were Koreans. Listening to people speaking Korean all around me was rather unreal and it was obvious that I had lived in isolation from it for far too many years.

The Korean people seated behind us were talking about something funny and made me look back and smile. One of them noticed that I was travelling with Davina and asked me if I was also a Korean so I gladly answered "Yes, and I am going home for the first time in seventeen and a half years." The woman looked rather surprised to hear that and told me that she was coming back from visiting her daughter who lives in Sydney and they visit each other almost every year. I couldn't help but feel envious of their mother and daughter relationship and thought about how lovely it would be to have a mother waiting for me somewhere.

Such a fundamental pleasure in life I never had experienced and I will never have a chance to experience, yet it was something I couldn't stop longing for.

We were all dropped off at the Changi airport, it was a Sunday morning at 7.30am but the airport was already crowded with people coming and going, pushing the trolleys loaded with their suitcases, and no matter how many times I heard it before, the frequent announcement in Korean on the loud speaker never failed to make my heart race faster.

This time we boarded a Korean airline; soon I would be returning to Kimpo airport and hoped to join some of the missing links of seventeen and half years that had passed. As I was getting closer I became more and more emotional with the sad thought that even though I am returning home, I will never see my father, grandmother and my stepmother again. The feeling of sadness in my heart kept growing knowing that they would not be there. Davina could sense how I was feeling and left me in peace without a word, but the man sitting next to me broke the silence and introduced himself to me. He was a Taiwanese computer salesman who had just been to Sydney and Melbourne and was returning home to Taipei; his English was very fluent, with an American accent and the conversation with him interested me and I was able to snap away from the sadness. The delicious food we were served, I knew the taste so well, lifted my spirit as well and it was good to see Davina and Ed also like the taste of Korean food. I said good bye to the Taiwanese man, who got off at the Taipei airport - I didn't even know his name.

The plane stopped at the Taipei airport for a little over an hour and we decided to have a look around the duty free shops. Davina was excited and exclaimed that everything was so cheap and she would have bought everything she saw if I hadn't stopped her. I had told her about the big markets we have in Seoul and advised her to slow down on her impulse shopping. While we were sitting at the lounge waiting to be called to board the plane, we met a couple of Australian ladies, a mother and a daughter from Perth.

Meeting Australians in such a place was rather nice and being able to share a conversation in familiar English made us feel close straight away. The older woman told us that her daughter had adopted a little girl from Korea two years ago and they were very happy with the outcome, and they were going back to Seoul this time to pick up a little boy who they decided to adopt and they praised how good Korean people were to deal with, and I was pleased to hear that with Davina. We heard the announcement to board the plane and exchanged our contact phone numbers in Seoul with them, hoping to have another chance to see each other again while all of us were in Seoul.

No words could describe the emotion I was going through as the plane was descending toward the Kimpo airport. My eyes were fixed on the window in search of the place I'd left behind, but all had changed so much and was nothing like I remembered. I thought about the day I walked away from the airport, how naïve and audacious I was leaving everyone behind without any tears. But it was indeed very different how I felt now, returning home all grown up after having lived all those years in isolation.

I asked the airport security personnel checking my suitcase with a friendly smile, "What are you checking for, I came home for the first time in almost eighteen years, do you really need to?" He looked at me with a smile of implying "Is that so?" He carried on his duty as he had to but his mind was not quite with it and asked me in an envious tone of voice "How do you feel to be back after all those years?"

I answered him with a smile from the bottom of my heart "It's surreal, like a dream!"

He smiled back at me with the look of he had a lot more to ask me, but he knew he had work to carry on and he bowed to me and just said "I hope you will have a very memorable stay!"

His kindness and politeness made me feel very welcome and I responded to him like I would normally in English "Thank you!"

As I followed my little son out, who was happily pushing the trolley loaded with our suitcases, I was thinking I don't bow anymore like I used to. The conception of bowing courteously as I was brought up seemed to have left from my brain a long time ago and didn't happen naturally with me anymore. It was obvious I was becoming a stranger in my own country and I was apprehensive at what it might bring.

As we were walking out to the arrival lounge the thought of running into someone I used to know gave me a little thrill. I looked at everyone around me, and soon I heard my youngest sister calling me "*On-ni* (elder sister)!" I saw my relatives in the crowd waving hands at me; the overwhelming emotion filled up my throat and made my heart beat very fast and brought tears to my eyes. I first saw my youngest sister, Myung Sook, she was only ten years old when I left home but she was in her late twenties then. Luckily she had been sending me her recent photos. She stood out in the crowd in a red long-shirt she wore over the white jeans on that day, and I saw her busy waving her hand at me and heard her repeatedly calling me with a big smile on her face *"On-ni!" "On-ni!"* I waved back at her as I shouted "Hi, Myung Sook!" in Korean of course. We hurried into each other's arms and hugged.

Over her shoulder I saw a very short and overweight lady holding a child in each hand. The little girl looked remarkably like my full sister Kyung Hee when she was that small and the young boy looked a lot like the man standing next to them. But their mother looked so different to the seventeen year old sister I had left behind. I had not seen a photo of her or had a chance to talk with her a very long time, not having her contact phone number. She was standing in silence with tears running down her face. In a doubtful voice I called her name "Kyung Hee?" She nodded her head and we hugged each other tight and we burst out crying. She introduced her husband and their two children to me, seven year old daughter Ki Hee and ten year old son Sang Pil. It was very emotional to finally meet her family. My emotion was running so high it didn't even occur to me to introduce Davina and Ed to anyone.

One of my father's sisters, my father's only brother and his wife, and one of my father's cousins were there as well. It was so good to be amongst my relatives again. Once I had a moment away from my relatives I saw my dear friend Kyung Hae. The friend I have kept in touch with all those years and standing nearby waiting for her turn to welcome us was the other friend, Chi Nam, Kyung Hae had mentioned in the letter.

Looking right at Chi Nam yet I couldn't put the face to the name I remembered so well and wondered if I too had changed so much and become unrecognizable. Nevertheless all three of us were happy in each other's arms. I saw Davina was busy taking photos for us and only then did I come to my senses, to introduce her and Ed to my relatives and friends. It was no problem introducing Davina and Ed to them but introducing my family to Davina without being able to use their first name and just by their relational position to me, in Korean style was not only difficult for me but I felt awkward to Davina. I told Davina that I'd explain the reason why I stumbled with the introductions later and thanked her for her patience and understanding. I guess not having many opportunities like that in the past didn't help. Kyung Hae explained to me that the Canadian Embassy where she was working was just around the block from the New KukJe hotel where we were booked, and she gave me the contact number to call her as soon as I could before she left the airport with Chi Nam.

My uncle suggested we should also make a move as he was concerned about Davina and we should check into our hotel to rest. My father's cousin had a car and came to give us a lift to our hotel in the city. I remembered his name but I hardly recognized him. I met him only once when I was about fifteen and he was about twelve when I visited the rice farm where he lived with his parents. I was closer to one of his older brothers who was a few years older than I, and worked for a couple of years for my father in Seoul, although there were two more of his married older brothers who lived in Seoul on and off near us. As I was walking alongside my relatives out to the car-park and talking with them, I felt for a moment as if I was a little girl again. The air outside was moist and pleasant to breathe. I could tell it hasn't been long since a shower of rain had passed and I saw the sun was low in the autumn sky, about to display a spectacular sunset.

My father's cousin was driving the car without saying anything much. I guessed, perhaps he had to concentrate; Seoul being one of the largest cities in the world with a population which then surpassed 10 million, the traffic was absolutely mind boggling! In silence I kept myself busy looking out trying to take it all in as the memories of yesteryears were rewinding in my mind. I could recognize very little as everything had changed so much. There used to be empty fields either side of the long stretch of road before the airport, without any buildings only a few large billboards. But both side of the road had been built up with many high-rise buildings, hustled and bustled with people and cars.

Huge changes indeed, not only to the place but also to the living standards. I thought about the time when I visited the country of my father's home town, Hong Sung, 110 kilometres south of Seoul in 1964. My first train ride to the place was also to where my father's cousins were brought up. The very place where I met the person who was driving us then! In those years they didn't yet have electricity like we had in Seoul and they had to manage with candlelight or kerosene lamps at night. The nights were scary for me being so dark, and the glare on the rice fields from the moon was spooky and any little noise outside made me jump in fear. Could I ever have thought the very person I had met then, the twelve year old young boy who had grown up isolated from the modern world and seemed to have very little opportunities in life, would one day run a large tailor shop in Seoul? His life certainly has evolved with time and I couldn't help but be happy for him and proud of him.

As we were driving past the main stretch through Norangjin, I looked out for where my father's garage used to be and where I had lived the last few years before I left. I recognized the railway station as well as the movie theater across the road from my father's garage used to be and I was excited to see they were still there.

We arrived at the hotel, New KukJe, located right in the heart of the city. A few of the staff knew my youngest sister, Myung Sook, well and gave us a personal warm welcome. I had booked us there for the first two weeks as I thought it would be easier for my relatives and friends to come and see us rather than having the impossible task for me to try to visit everyone. Not knowing the situation I didn't want to impose on anyone in the family either and it was Davina's choice to be with us in the same room.

My uncle and his wife dropped in with Myung Sook before they went home to make sure we were comfortable, and to see if we needed anything. Soon after Kyung Hee and her family arrived and it was obvious she had a lot to tell me, still in overwhelming emotion at seeing me again after all those years. She told me briefly about her life, how she had struggled to bring up their two little children mostly by herself given her husband hadn't always been faithful to her, and was in and out of her and children's life. At times he wasn't in contact for so long she didn't know whether he was still alive or dead. He was there with them but I was informed that he had only just come back into their life after he had disappeared for more than a year.

Korea has long valued the traditional family unit – single mothers in those years were often stigmatized and discriminated against and didn't have much support from the family and community. I was heartbroken and distressed to hear about her struggles in life. Although with very different circumstances, our lives isolated us far apart from each other, I couldn't help but feel guilty that I'd left her behind. Things might have been different for her if I had not left Korea. Kyung Hee was ashamed of how her life had turned out and most of the time she isolated herself from everyone whilst I was too busy establishing my life in isolation a world away.

Kyung Hee didn't enjoy school and had started to work already at age of fourteen. It might have helped her to mature much quicker in a tough adult world but as she grew older she wasn't able to be on top of the game due to lack of education, and it was obvious that she had struggled to survive. I didn't know anything much about her husband but I was distressed listening to Kyung Hee and thought about how I was going to talk some sense into her husband. He was standing there in silence and seemed to be in deep remorse about his wrongdoings. It was all too sad for Ki Hee and Sang Pil, seeing us talking in tears but not able to comprehend what the talk was all about. Ki Hee was just hanging onto her daddy's arm and had the insecure look of wondering what it was all about. But it was too much for Sang Pil and he kept on pulling his mother's hand, and wanting to go home, so reluctantly they all left. Davina also had no idea what it was all about and looked very concerned. I explained to her briefly about my sister's plight and she was very sympathetic and lent me her shoulder to sob on.

It had been all too much for Ed to comprehend as well; he isolated himself lying on the bed totally engrossed in a Korean children's program on TV.

The telephone rang, it was my other sister Myung Hee, I recognized her voice straightaway as we had been in touch in recent years on the phone, and she apologized and explained why she hadn't come out to the airport, and promised me that she would bring around her three little children and introduce her husband to me next day, and I was very much looking forward to seeing her again and meeting her family.

I woke next morning to the noise of the city traffic getting louder by the minute. I stood by the window and the first thing that caught my eyes at day break was the statue of - Yi Sun Sin, the famous naval commander of the sixteenth-century, who won the battle with Japan in a turtle ship, still standing at the same place as I remembered. It was overwhelming joy to see it there unchanged, given the rest of the city had changed so much it was not recognizable at all to me.

I took a deep breath in and exhaled in sadness, it was too sad to learn about the unhappy life my sister had endured and thinking about the reality of never to seeing my father or grandmother or my stepmother again, hit me hard like a lightning strike. I sobbed and sobbed as if the tears had been trapped in all those years since they had passed away and had finally found their way out. My energy was drained and I felt weak mentally as well as physically. I had to hold onto the window frame as I grieved, many thousand regrets crossed my mind. Gazing out the window I felt sad to my bones that they were no longer there waiting for me and I was lost in the emptiness. After a little while I regained my energy as I remembered my favorite place in the city, the Civic-center, that used to be in the vicinity and I had the sudden desire to locate it from my window.

While I was trying hard to find the old Civic-center the memories of yesteryears flooded in and thought of my school friends came to my mind. The friends I used go there with to watch many different performances. Although the old Civic-centre was nowhere to be seen the faces of my close friends flashed back in my memory and so clearly. I remembered the particular moment of my friend Chi-Nam giggling unstoppably one day as she was trying to hit me with her school bag as we walked out the school gate together. Her face was crystal clear! She used to wear a pair of thick glasses and had protruding front teeth. She looked much prettier now, she must have had her teeth straightened and she wasn't wearing the thick pair of glasses anymore - at last I was able to put the name, Chi-Nam, to the face and I felt so excited and happy, I shouted loud "A-HA, that's HER!"

I must have disturbed Davina because at that moment I heard her say, "Good-Morning Ann!" I sat by her bed and told her all about what had made me shout. Davina couldn't stop laughing and I was surprised that her peculiar and high pitched laugh didn't wake Ed up and he was still in deep sleep.

Mid morning Myung Sook came back with Myung Hee and Myung Hee's three little children, I was very happy to see them and Myung Hee's children were adorable being brought up very much loved in a happy family. The eldest girl five year old Se Mi looked the spitting image of Myung Hee when she was that age not only by her looks but also her bubbly personality, and the little boy four year old Se Yun looked more like his father I saw on the photo and I couldn't work out who the baby Se Ra looked more like as she was still an infant. My eleven year old Ed looked so grown up against his little cousins, although they didn't speak the same language it didn't seem to matter as they didn't waste a minute having fun together. It pleased us all to see them playing well together.

Amongst many things we talked about, Myung Hee was concerned about my not so perfect Korean and was trying to prepare me for the meeting with her husband later that evening. They had booked a table for dinner at a nice restaurant for us all and we were to meet him there after his work.

I asked her what I should call him even though he was younger than I, I must address him respectfully. Myung Hee was reminding me about the Korean culture, calling a brother-in-law by the first name was disrespectful and extremely rude and mostly called by one's family relational position instead of by his first name. Myung Hee was about to tell me what I should call him when the phone rang. I picked up the phone and said Hello, in Korean "*Yur-bo-se-yo*" I heard a man's voice saying, "*Yur-bo-se-yo, yur-gi-O-Sur-Bang-Yip-Ni-da!*" the direct translation word to word would be (Hello, this is Mr.O speaking) he said it in such an old ancient manner. By that I could guess it was Myung Hee's husband on the other end of the line, so without any hesitation I too responded in the same ancient manner in Korean "*O-Sur-Bang-Yi-Se-Yo?*" (So are you Mr. O?) My sisters heard only what I said on the phone but could guess who was on the line, and burst out laughing in unison, given what I said to him sounded silly and not appropriate, and they thought it was so funny and just couldn't stop laughing.

This episode made me feel rather uneasy speaking to him anymore and I passed the phone to Myung Hee and I asked what was so funny. Myung Hee tried to explain whilst she was still laughing with the phone in her hand so her husband could hear all that was going on. She said to her husband that if he had phoned one second later she would have prevented me from responding in such a silly way. She kept on laughing and said it was also funny that he rang the very second she was going to tell me to address him as "Semi-Appa" (father of Semi) – they were laughing so hard tears were running down their faces.

I couldn't help but think how easy it would have been if we could just call each other by the first name as I had become used to in Australia. I realized that to think and act like a Korean again I had to make a conscious effort. Davina's face was all lit up waiting to hear what the laughter was all about, and ready to hear another unbelievable and interesting story to be unfolded by me. She couldn't believe how different our culture was nevertheless she was enjoying every minute of it and I was so glad she was there with me.

Later in the day our cousin Kun Woo, the eldest son of my uncle, called in to see us. It was good to see him again, he was only a nine year old boy when I last saw him and he was in his mid twenties running a small business in Seoul, manufacturing all kinds of bags.

Early in that evening Myung Hee's husband sent two taxis to our hotel to pick all of us up to go to the restaurant for dinner. The restaurant in our hotel was a very nice up market one, the hotel being a "Four-star hotel". There were many good restaurants everywhere near our hotel but the taxis drove on through the hectic traffic for almost an hour, and finally stopped at the front of the famous "Sheraton Grande Walker-Hills hotel". It was such a big unexpected surprise for me as it was known to be the most up-market place in Seoul at that time.

Myung Hee's husband was there waiting for us, he was in his business suit and looked tall and very handsome. It was very nice to finally meet him. I am to him *Chur Heong* (wife's big sister) and he is to me *Semi -Appa(* father of Se Mi) and we knew how to address each other in the Korean way, without using each other's name. However it was very awkward to introduce him to Davina and vice versa so I introduced him to Davina as *Semi-Appa* and Davina to him like I would do in the Australian way, as Davina, because even my little Ed called her by her first name. No-one in my family could speak English well enough to either speak with Davina or understand the Australian culture and Davina couldn't speak a word of Korean let alone comprehend such Korean culture. This made it difficult to introduce them to each other not being able to do it the same both ways.

To add to the confusion I could introduce my younger cousin Kun Woo by his first name to Davina because I am his senior and he was still single. In spite of the initial awkward introductions everyone was happy to meet each other and looked forward to having meals in such a beautiful place.

We all followed Semi-Appa into the authentic Korean charcoal-grill BBQ restaurant in the hotel complex. We had to take our shoes off and had to sit on the floor on individual cushions around the two large low set-tables set with a charcoal grill each in the middle, serviced by a couple of waitresses from the beginning till we finished. The meals were authentic - table BBQ grilled meats served with many different vegetable side dishes called, *Na-Mul* and a variety of *kimchis* and also steamed rice. Not only the food was very delicious but the service was excellent. I thoroughly enjoyed the way we interacted with one another while we were having meals - it was intimate and caring. But sitting there with Davina and Ed I felt I had to explain to my family about the different table manners I had learned and made them aware of them, particularly in view of the imminent Olympic Games. I explained kindly to them that talking with a mouth full of food or chewing food with an open mouth, were not accepted in many cultures.

It was truly a very special treat for all of us to have a meal in such a place. I knew Semi-Appa was a bank manager of one of the large banks in Seoul, however I would hate to find out what he would have had to pay for the meals we had that night.

Davina was then forty-six years old, 163 centimetres tall and rather a large lady at about 90 kilograms in weight. It was not easy for her to have a meal sitting right down on the floor as she was brought up to sit on a chair. To be truthful sitting on the floor without the back support of a chair wasn't all that comfortable for me either as I was so used to sitting on a chair as well. Even though it was uncomfortable for her she seemed to be enjoying the whole experience. She even tried to learn to use chopsticks like we did and the children were only too happy to be her teacher. Everybody fussed around her to make sure she was enjoying it but she didn't complain.

When everyone got up ready to leave Semi-Appa and KunWoo noticed Davina was in distress, not able to get up easily, so they graciously assisted her to get up. The children thought it was very funny and they giggled and giggled even more watching me helping Davina do up the buckles of her sandals. The lovely autumn breeze embraced us all as we walked outside the hotel. We stood on the hill and exclaimed "Wow, How BEAUTIFUL!" The beautiful city, Seoul, sparkled by the river and high above the night sky was full of millions of stars glittering like diamonds and sapphires. The view from there very high up on the hill was absolutely breathtaking!

Standing there alongside Davina and Ed I was so very proud of my home town and I was very happy sharing such wonderful moments with my family. Semi -Appa once again ushered us into the hotel lounge for a cup of tea and sweets before he called a taxi for us and sent Kun Woo with us to ensure we got safely to our hotel. What an enjoyable evening it was! When we got back to our hotel even though we both knew Myung Sook would come early next morning to take us to Deok Su Palace, one of our five grand Palaces in Seoul, Davina and I were still wide wake and kept on talking about the lovely night until well into the early hours of the morning.

It felt good to be back at the Deok Su Palace. It hadn't changed much in all those years and I felt like I was there not long ago. But it sure had been a very long time because I was reading the information in English instead of in Korean as I used to. The palace is located right in the middle of the city, a tranquil place to escape from the hustle and bustle of the big city, where people can relax amongst well maintained lovely gardens or contemplate amongst many beautiful and historic buildings of yesteryear, or visit the national museum in the complex to learn about our interesting and rich history.

Unlike the breeze we had the night before there was no wind and the mid morning sun was getting rather warm. The trees in the garden had only just begun to show autumn colours and this made me concerned that we were there a little too early in the season and missed seeing the full autumn leaves display. Nevertheless the palace was a beautiful place to visit. Davina seemed relaxed and was enjoying every minute of the trip and no longer showed any concern at what some people in Mount Isa had said to instill fear in her with the preconceived ideas about the danger in Korea. We were often stared at by passers-by because Davina, Ed and I spoke English and stood out as there weren't yet many tourists in those years. It was a year BEFORE the "88 Seoul Summer Olympics", - The Profound Event when the South Korean capital, Seoul, opened its doors wide to the world and SUCCESSFULLY put Korea on the map.

We loved the street food, most of them were my favorite Korean foods especially the dish called *Kal-Geuk-Su* made with homemade thick noodles in a dried anchovy's broth. Pan fried or steamed *dimsums* and *binde dduek*, a kind of fritter were also delicious to eat. Not just for me who was brought up with such food but Davina and Ed liked the food as well and they were very cheap. For just $2.50 Australian per dish we had enough choices to please us all. The eateries were rather primitive but clean casual facilities designed to eat and run in a busy city life.

My family in Korea sometimes ate food outside in the evening in summer time, sitting on a straw mat laid down on the ground in our back yard, especially when we made a big pile of noodles and cooked a huge cast -iron pot full of the delicious soup *kal-geuk-su*, and when I was in mid teen years, I remembered the few times we had a competition - *who could eat most of the noodle soup amongst the female members of our family* - without fail, I always won the competition. I liked the noodle soup so much I could eat up to 4 bowls of it in one sitting. I would beat everyone, grandma in her late fifties, aunties in their late thirties, stepmother in her late thirties and needless to say all my little sisters. It never ceased to amaze everyone how I, as a small person, could eat so much. Each time I won, my grandma would wave her finger waved at me and say "Just as well you were born with a jutting chin!" What she meant by it was that I was lucky to be born with the look that indicated that I would never run out of food to eat and become hungry. She was not wrong; I have been very blessed indeed, I have been very fortunate to have a very healthy appetite to go with it as well.

When we returned to our room I received a few calls from my relatives and friends. It was nice to be reconnected with the people who were very dear to me. For some of them it was the first time ever we shared any conversations since I had left home. Late that night when I phoned Rolf and tried to talk my voice was noticeably getting croaky having been very emotional and talking so much. Rolf was somewhat intoxicated that night and he sounded as if he missed us very much. He said "Honey, please remember your home is in Australia with me and don't forget to come back home, I miss you and Ed so very much." I too missed him very much so I wrote a long letter to him that night to let him and Maurits know more about what had been happening and to let them know how much Ed and I missed them not being there with us. However I was very glad that I had come and was enjoying every minute and I told him that I should have come a lot earlier and with him. Davina rang her husband as well that night and informed him what a lovely time she was having. She spoke with her rather elated loud voice and I was very pleased to overhear that she was enjoying the holiday.

My aunt came and offered to take care of our laundry and bring it back for us. I didn't expect my aunt to do my laundry and felt uncomfortable accepting her kind offer, but not wanting to offend her I persuaded Davina as well to let my aunt do it for us all just for that one time. In a couple of days she brought our clean laundry back for us and we were very grateful. But a huge surprise and I was astonished when my sister, Myung Hee, later that afternoon phoned me and told me that my aunt was very concerned about me because she could tell by looking at our laundry that I must be poor in Australia. All of Davina's outfits were matching and had some kind of brand nametag on them but none of my outfits had any tags and that made her believe that either I bought cheap ones without any brand name or I made them myself because I couldn't afford to buy such outfits.

Davina also amazed to hear about it and burst out laugh when I told her and said, "Ann!" "That is the most ridiculous thing I have ever heard! If you would translate for me Ann, I will tell them how much I envy you because you are so good at sewing and look always unique and elegant." She said this with tears in her eyes from laughing so much. I was glad that she was there with me. Having lived for a long time in Australia where irrespective of rank in the society, people are treated the same and to dress extravagantly was not important. I felt a kind of a culture shock as if I had become an outsider in my own birthplace. Another one of my firsthand experience in life I must say - how attitudes and cultures can change when re-visiting families in overlong intervals.

I wanted to explain to them that my life is fine at least there wasn't any reason for them to be concerned about me, yet I didn't know where to start.

It's not easy to explain to people who have never been outside their country and are unaware of different values. I decided not to worry about it and pretended not to have heard it until I could figure out how to go about it.

My uncle's youngest son, Yang Woo came to visit us one morning. He was only two years old when I last saw him. He had grown into a very handsome twenty year old with a gentle and kind disposition. Ed was most pleased to find out he was able to speak some English and they became instantly best mates. He told me that he failed the exam to enter the university to study biology that year and he was studying by himself for the rest of the year to prepare for another chance to sit for the exam early in the following year.

He took us to the National Museum where we ran into a group of four men wearing clothes, from traditional costumes to modern day suits like the smart trendy off white suit Yang Woo was wearing; it was like a showcase of how much men's wear had evolved over the years. Those men's different outfits presented parts of our history on a par with the things we saw in the museum and I wanted to take a photo of them and asked the men if they wouldn't mind posing with Davina, Ed and Yang Woo for my camera and they agreed. Indeed they expressed how delighted they were to be asked to have the photo taken with such a lady (in their words, the American lady). This made Davina feel very special. They told us that they were from a small country town about 250 kilometres south of Seoul and they insisted that I send them a copy of the photos and they gave me an address. It was such a pleasant acquaintance for us all.

Another thing I was compelled to take a photo of was the public toilet facility there for females. It was a flush toilet but not the ones you can sit on. We had to squat down and to flush it we had to push down a bar with a foot. Not only Davina but I too panicked not knowing how to use a system we had never seen before. Furthermore because the facility was exceptionally clean the thought crossed our mind that it may be a part of the exhibit not for public use! Both of us were amused by the new experience and had a good laugh. The museum was an interesting place to visit and we enjoyed seeing it close-up with many wonderful exhibits of our precious cultural assets. Ed had such a lovely time talking with Yang Woo he didn't want the day to end.

Sometimes Ed got bored when I was busy speaking in Korean with the visitors in our hotel room and he would ask for my permission to go out to a computer games room to play some games. I gave him permission thinking that he must have found a game room inside the hotel, until one time when he returned from playing the games and I was free from the visitors he insisted that I and Davina to go with him to see him play a particular game he liked. We decided to go still thinking it was inside the hotel somewhere and followed him but when he led us out of the building I almost fainted to find out that the Games Room was not inside the hotel at all. It was frightening to realize how far he had been to play the games. He led us out of the hotel into busy streets and walked into an underground pass with numerous exits and walked on and on but he knew exactly which way to go.

As we were following him I felt cold sweat in the palm of my hands and a feeling of terrible fear that I could have lost him in such a big city by carelessly giving him permission to go and play the games and that I had taken it for granted that there was a game room inside the hotel. How lucky was I to have a child, at eleven years of age, who had such a good sense of direction and was confident how to go around in such a big city he had never been before. It was mind boggling that he didn't get lost. I kept thinking that he couldn't have read the signs to guide him in which direction to go as all the signs in the underpass were written in Korean only. Even for someone like me, who could read the signs and had used the underpass many times before, it was a daunting task to find my way around. Because many changes had been made since I last used it and it was easy to lose direction once you are down there.

The Games Room was more than a kilometer away from the hotel on the opposite side of the multiple lanes of busy roads. He didn't think anything of it at all and told me that he saw the Computer Games Room with lots of children playing games the day we visited Deoksu Palace with Myung Sook when we walked past it on our way back to our hotel. He just wanted to go back there to play the games when he could so he memorized the way. If the story was not surprising and frightening enough I was even more startled when we got there to find out that a couple of kids, who looked much older than Ed, already knew him and they were interacting well regardless of the language barrier. After all I must say, I was very proud seeing my little Ed so confident.

We stopped by a café for lunch on our way back to the hotel, while we were waiting for our meals to be served the noises of people in the café slobbering and chewing their food with their mouths open and talking loudly at the same time, disturbed not only Davina and Ed but me as well. Although I too was brought up that way and never thought anything was wrong with enjoying food in such a way, I must have been away from it for too long. It had got to the stage where I was getting embarrassed sitting there with Davina and Ed who were brought up to chew food with their mouth closed and eat meals without such noises. Given that the "88 Summer Olympic" games in Seoul were only a year away I was concerned that soon there would be a lot of foreigners amongst them, eating in public places like that and they would experience it and some might be offended or might even talk down about it.

Right next to our table there were three men wearing full business suits having their lunch in the same noisy manner, not only Davina but also Ed was feeling uncomfortable by the noises and winced and this made me get up and go to them. Out of patriotism I dared to express what was in my mind. I tried my best with scrupulous honesty, in the polite form of Korean, suggesting to them that it would be very nice if they could try to chew their food with their mouths closed and not talk at the same time, given that the Olympic Games are around the corner and there would be soon lots of foreigners who are not used to eating in such a noisy manner. One of the men got extremely offended by what I had said and stood up abruptly and angrily told me that it was none of my business how they ate, NEVER MIND the Foreigners, - so he said. I came back to our table somewhat scared knowing that I was wrong to tell them how to live in their own country. Nevertheless it wasn't completely without avail, as I saw that the other two men seemed to have taken notice and were eating their food more QUIETLY.

One late afternoon we met up with my friends Kyung Hae and Chi Nam at a tea room nearby our hotel. I had fun telling them about the morning when my memory flashed back and how Crystal Clear the memory was. I remembered Chi Nam's face of our school days and that I was finally able to put her name to the face. Chi Nam burst out laughing and told us that a long time ago she had her teeth straightened and had decided to wear contact lenses instead of glasses. It was good that Kyung Hae spoke fluent English and we were able to share lots of laughs with Davina as well about our schooldays. The more we talked the more it seemed we had never been apart.

Once again Ed got bored and asked for my permission to leave the table and wander around the place. I gave him permission under the strict condition that he would stay very close to the tea shop and as I had entrusted him Ed was just outside the tea shop sitting on a little bench observing the passersby and the activities of the busy city streets and waited until we were ready to go.

Ed was hungry and asked if there was any burger shop nearby. The craving for a burger was understandable given we had been eating mostly Korean food ever since we got there. Davina didn't hesitate a minute to agree with Ed to have something other than Korean food. I knew we were not that far away from Myeong Dong, the well known primary shopping districts in Seoul, and I wanted to take us there thinking it would be the nearest place we would find a café that catered for western food. However on the way we happened to walk past a burger shop called *"Wendy's Hamburger"*. The smell of the potato chips frying was good enough for us and we were looking forward to have a nice hamburger and chips but when we got our burgers we found out that it was not like the hamburgers we get in Australia made with minced beef, instead it was, literally, made with thickly sliced fried ham. Nevertheless the French-fries we had were nice and thin and crisp.

I could tell that Ed was satisfied and very eager to learn from me how to order the burger in Korean and how much to pay as he was planning to go back there when he had the chance. I had no doubt that he would and was capable to find the way back there from our hotel. Needless to say that he was making some note of the way in his mind when we walked back to our hotel. The cool autumn night breeze made walking so much more pleasant and brought back some memories of the nights like that night I had walked past the vicinity, and being there with Davina and Ed was very lovely but I so missed Rolf and Maurits not being there with us.

Next morning Ed was sleeping in and Davina wanted to stay back in the room to phone her family but I had things to do at the post office so I went out all alone. I had a letter to post to Rolf that I had written the night before and I had to send a telegram to congratulate Robby, the eldest son of Frances, who was getting married the next day. Walking down town toward the Central Post-office, was unlike when I was with Davina and Ed, nobody stared at me which made me feel as if I was one of the locals. This made my mind wander like a teenager who had just returned home from a long trip. I felt the great city, my home town, pulsating with me in happiness. It was great to be back to the place so dear to my heart.

My uncle and aunt invited us to come to their home for a day and I was very much looking forward to spending some more time with them and to go back to the house where I was born and lived most of my life before I left the country. The place was our family home until our grandma passed away and my uncle inherited it. My memory of the place was so vivid that I could find it with my eyes closed if everything stayed the same but after all those years I had no idea what to expect. As my uncle had suggested I took a taxi and told the driver to take us to Itaewon, the address I remembered well, but soon I became disoriented as the taxi passed through the Nam San tunnel that was built since I left and everything had changed so much. The taxi stopped at Itaewon but I couldn't comprehend at all where I was. I didn't recognize anything that I could relate to my memories. I found a public phone booth and phoned my uncle for help and he sent Yang Woo to guide us. The narrow unsealed walk ways to our home from the main stretch in Itaewon were all gone and replaced with bitumen sealed streets wide enough to park cars outside homes.

Not only the whole area was unrecognizable but when I got to the place there was no trace of our old home that I longed to see again, instead there stood a very different new modern house. I heard that my uncle had the new house built on the spot that used to be our yard and the old house was demolished and became the new yard. Although I would have loved to show our old house and where I was born and brought up, to my son Ed and Davina, I missed not seeing it again for myself, I was pleased for my uncle's family. The old house had been badly damaged by bombs during the wars and I had grown up looking at part of the ceiling leaning noticeably toward one side and every time it rained heavily made me nervous that the stone wall adjoining the next property may collapse. The old house was built in early 1940s with mud and dry straw. It had a tin roof, there were three rooms and a small wooden veranda next to each one and a kitchen next to one of the rooms and another larger kitchen between two of the rooms. At one stage of its existence there lived ten of us in the place.

It was good to see the town water supply was connected and brought me back memories of the difficult times we had endured, not having such luxuries in the past especially during those years when I was thirteen to seventeen, strong and tall enough, to carry on my back the large wooden frame with tin water containers almost as high as my waist, suspended from a hook on each end of the frame. I had to fill them up with water at the nearest neighbour who had the town water connected, and carry them home about 80 metres, mostly uphill, on my back.

The job had to be done often and very early in the mornings before I went to school. During summer time the chore was not that hard but in winter going uphill on snow-covered and frozen slippery walk ways, with such heavy things pulling on my back. No matter how hard I tried to be careful, I fell backwards at times and regardless of the pain I had to go back in tears and do it again because if I spilled too much water there may not be enough water for the family to use for the day. Not to forget to mention what a terrible embarrassment it was for a young teenage girl like me if any boys saw me fall. Moreover some mornings the tap was frozen and water was coming through so slowly that I had to wait in the queue forever in the freezing temperature. Now I think back it was perhaps another building block that was necessary to prepare me to be resilient.

Remembering that, all the more I appreciated the running tap as Davina and I hand-washed our laundry ourselves, whilst my aunt prepared lunch. My uncle and aunt were very concerned about seeing Davina doing her own laundry and they asked me why I would not do hers as well. I had to explain to them that they shouldn't be concerned about it at all as

Davina wouldn't expect me to do her laundry and I knew she'd rather do it herself. When we went up to their roof-top veranda to hang up our laundry I was amazed how far I could see and how much had changed. It was unrecognizable; it was nothing like how I remembered.

When my uncle's wife invited us around she also asked me if there was anything special that I would like her to cook for me. I didn't hesitate to let her know a dish that was cooked with the by-product from making bean curd, called *biji-jjige*. It was a very cheap dish to make in the olden days and a dish I missed quite a lot and also I thought it would be an easy dish for her to prepare and shouldn't cost too much for her. But the truth was quite the opposite. How surprised and obliged I was to find out that she had to soak the dried soy beans overnight and practically had to go through all the tedious process of making the bean curd at home to get the byproduct called *biji*, because she could no longer buy such a thing at a store, like we did in the olden days. The living standard in Korea has gone up so much that it wasn't viable for stores to sell it as not many people needed to eat such food anymore.

The lunch was ready and it felt good to sit around a table together with my uncle and my aunt. My uncle tried to teach Ed to call him in Korean, *hal-a-ber-ji* meaning grandfather and all of us burst into laughter when Ed repeated after my uncle with a different accent *ha-rab-ji*. It was very loving and precious moments for Ed and I.

The *biji-jjige* was nice but in honesty it wasn't as delicious as I thought. I guess my taste buds weren't the same anymore, and some other dishes were more delicious as my aunt thoughtfully prepared many other dishes to make sure Davina and Ed would enjoy as well. But when they explained to me what kind of hassles I put her through, I was obliged to eat more than I wanted, to show my appreciation.

My uncle's wife told me what had happened with people in the old neighbourhood and the many changes that were made in Itaewon over the years since I left the country. I was very sad and shocked to hear what had happened to my friend, Young Yi many years ago. Apparently no-one knew the real reason why she had slashed her wrist and killed herself. She grew up with much love as an only daughter and the youngest child of twelve children and was protected not only by her loving parents but also by her eleven older brothers. Perhaps having been brought up, wrapped in cotton wool, she was not prepared for the outside world, which at times can be very tough. The last time I heard from her would have been when she was married and sent me some lovely photos in the spring of 1975. She seemed very happy then.

I heard about my uncle's second son who was killed in a car accident early that year but I didn't want to make them sad by talking about him, and I was hesitant to express my sadness, but my uncle started to explain to me what actually happened on that day. I was more sad listening to them as I could feel their pain in their voices, and when my uncle started to talk about my father's passing my sorrow became too much for me to contain and I burst out crying and fell into my uncle's arms like a child. The sadness of my father's death had been bottled up inside me and once again it exploded; my uncle held me tight and let me cry in his arms for a while. He was concerned how Davina and Ed would feel whilst I was sad and crying, and to help me compose myself he began to tell me the story he has told me many times before, and asked me to translate the story to them.

The story was about when I was just an infant, about 7 months old. In the midst of the Korean War whilst our family was running away together from the enemy to hide. My uncle was then in his early twenties. While they were running by the stream I didn't stop crying, and to save the rest of the family from the enemy my mother didn't have a choice but to leave me behind a large boulder, but my uncle just didn't have the heart to run past me and leave me there in harm's way so he picked me up, at great peril to himself and the rest of the family. I wouldn't be alive today if he hadn't picked me up then and taken his chances not to be caught. Davina and Ed too became sad and emotional just listening to the story.

Yang Woo took us to Itaewon market after lunch; it was only a walking distance. I have lots of memories of the market. I would never forget the last few months before my little sister died, how Kyung Hee and I tried our best to buy food there to feed her and keep her alive. The market has evolved to a well known market for foreigners over the years. Many of the vendors there could speak English and it is the place where people can buy things in larger than average sizes, thus it is a popular market for foreigners like Davina. It is also known as a home for the majority of expatriates in Korea.

Davina and Ed loved the market as there were a lot of foreigners like us from all over the world shopping and socializing at many of the wonderful cafés. We could hear people speaking in all different languages and there were many of the authentic Korean culinary delights to try. The vicinity is especially dear to my heart as my father used to have a garage there on the main stretch, an automobile repair business, for many years until my first stepmother passed away.

It felt good to be back there and I enjoyed walking around reminiscing, and it was surreal knowing that I was there as a visiting expatriate. We all had a lovely afternoon there and enjoyed walking back together to my uncle's place. We picked up our laundry that was all dried and already nicely folded by my aunt. I thanked my uncle and aunt for their warm hospitality and I took the chance and explained to them, that I had learned to sew and I enjoyed making my own outfits very much, and most of all I love to look – unique! Furthermore I told them that wearing designer outfits was not necessary in our life style in Mount Isa where I lived. They were rather surprised to hear that it was not necessary to wear labelled designer clothes in a rich country like Australia. Nevertheless my aunt seemed relieved to hear that I was not financially struggling, and loved sewing for myself.

Before we left, my uncle was glad to tell me about the upcoming sixtieth birthday celebration of one of my aunt's husband who lived at Anyang about 20 kilometres south of Seoul, and wanted us to meet them at his place again in a few days to go with them. I looked forward very much to such family gathering.

One morning Davina was looking out the window, and called me to come quickly and have a look outside, as she pointed her finger to a lady walking below on the street and asked, "Ann, have a look at what that lady is wearing! Is she dressed to go to a wedding or going to work?"

I saw a lady dressed in an elegant cream lace dress, long sleeved and below the knee, with matching high heels, and carrying a business case. So I said "Who would get married at this early hour of the morning in the middle of the week? She is carrying a brief case she is probably going to work - maybe in a flash office?"

Davina burst out laughing as she couldn't believe anyone would wear such an extravagant outfit to go to work in an office, and told me that such a dress would be more suitable for a wedding, and she was ridiculously overdressed. She told me that she saw others in overly glittering outfits she would only wear when going out at night in Australia.

I explained to her that I believed it had lot to do with where we were, Seoul being such a large crowded city where competition was very high in every aspect of life; looking your best always was VERY important. Therefore the mentality of the people is SO different to us, from a small mining town where there wasn't much competition as most people were earning a good income from the mine and lived life relatively well. As Davina was listening to me with interest she put herself in a different mood as she laughed ironically at herself, and pointed out to me also that she was amazed to see how slim most people in Seoul were, and she tried but she couldn't count many overweight people like herself.

I saw a fortune teller sitting by the street waiting for someone to ask what he sees. Davina couldn't resist finding out what he may tell her about her fortune so I sat with them to interpret for them. The fortune teller began with telling her about her married son which she didn't have, and this put me straightaway in an awkward situation, so I interpreted to Davina as if he was telling about one of her married daughters, and I wanted to hear how the story would unfold but it only got worse. Everything he said didn't make any sense and was not relevant to her life. I had to try very hard to interpret in a way that didn't make her sad or unnecessarily disappointed. As we stood up to go, I let the fortune teller know how hard a time I had interpreting it, to save him from the embarrassment of telling such an irrelevant story, and that we both were very lucky that Davina didn't understand a word of Korean, - he just stared at me with empty smile.

We went back to my uncle's place in Itaewon to go to the birthday party in Anyang together. I was excited to see my younger aunt who came there as well, it was the very first time I had seen the aunt since I came back.

When I saw my elder aunt at the airport, I was happily surprised to see she hadn't aged at all and looked the same as I remembered her. Therefore I was very surprised to see my younger aunt looking much more aged than I ever expected. But later I found out the reason, - her son gave her a lot of heartaches in the past. She used to be like an older sister to me rather than an aunt and we were very close when I was growing up. She lived with us most of my childhood and I wore a lot of passed down clothes from her.

She used to work as a dressmaker. I would never forget the beautiful outfit I got her to make for me with the fabric and design I had chosen at the boutique where she had worked. I had paid for it with the prize money I had won from one of the mathematic competitions at my junior-school. It was a two piece sleeveless outfit, with a very short A-line skirt in multi pastel colours of polyester fabric. My father was so proud of me to have won the prize and allowed me to spend the money as I wished and all of it went to pay for that one outfit! I wore the outfit with pride for a couple of summers until I grew out of the size.

All seven of us went together by bus then tram and walked some distance between many of the lookalike tall apartment buildings. Everywhere we went in Seoul we saw "*Hodori*" the stylized tiger, the official mascot of the upcoming "88 Seoul Summer Olympics". The excitement of having the Olympics in Seoul was felt everywhere we went. To be there and being able to share such an atmosphere with my relatives was indeed very special. I was as excited as a child, no more grown up than my own eleven year old son walking next to me.

My elder aunt lived in one of the large apartment buildings on the third floor, with her husband and their eldest son, Han Young and his family. It was great to see everyone. My aunt's husband looked the same, didn't look a day older and it was so good to be there to celebrate his sixtieth birthday with him. My cousin Han Young was only a thirteen year old boy when I saw him last and not having had any interaction in all those years, it was unreal seeing him all grown up and married with two boys of his own; and seeing his eldest son who was the image of him was a magical moment. As I had expected two of my aunt's daughters-in-law were there all busy preparing the lunch, but the other two sons weren't there as they were at work. There was a lot of food prepared enough to feed an army and I was sure the celebration would continue well into the next day. Davina sat with me around the "all-female table" and Ed sat with the males around another table set next to us. They were the very special guests to all my relatives who were only too happy to have their company, even though they couldn't communicate with them.

As I walked past the bathroom I saw Han Young had the left the door ajar and was hidden inside smoking a cigarette. Being curious I reached for his arm and tried to pull him out of there as I asked him "Why are you hiding?" He quickly jerked himself back in and said *"Nuna* (big sister) Don't You Remember it is a breach of our etiquette to smoke a cigarette in front of the elders?" Yes, he was right I had completely forgotten about it but I remembered it the second he pointed it out. We can drink alcohol with older members of the family but it is not appropriate to smoke with them.

That being said it was still surprising to see a grown man abiding such an old etiquette, to show his respect to older members of the family. Although I thought it was rather a silly etiquette I was very proud of Han Young who still took such etiquette seriously and showed his respect to elders of the family and kept the tradition alive. I am afraid I have lost too many of the protocols I was brought up with, and not only that I don't think like I used to, but I don't behave like I used to in many ways. The realization made me more conscious about my behavior in front of them and somewhat insecure. I was afraid that I may be regarded and treated as an outsider from my own family, which was a worse feeling to realize than being mistreated or misunderstood by foreigners in a foreign country. My subconscious mind started to affect me with the stress and my voice was getting more croaky.

There is a big age gap between my two aunties, the elder aunt was married when I was very young and her family lived very near us. We practically grew up together with their three boys. Until I shared such an intimate time with my relatives again I did not know how much I really missed them.

Soon after we arrived back at our hotel Kun Woo dropped in to see us on the way home from his work. Ed suggested that we should all go back to "Wendy's burger" for dinner. The late afternoon air was rather chilly but walking together through the city streets filled with many excitements was much fun. On the way I enjoyed telling Kun Woo all about our visit to our aunt's place. I am the eldest of all my siblings as well as of all my cousins on my father's side. I am the big sister to all and they are all very dear to my heart.

Myung Sook would drop in almost every day on the way from her work to see if we needed anything. She worked as a shop assistant at a large up-market bakery in the city, near the hotel. She took a special day off from her work and took us all to the famous "Folk Village" in Suwon, about 37 kilometres south of Seoul. The countryside looked ever so beautiful with autumn leaves which had begun to colour the landscape and in the distance here and there my favorite flower, cosmos in full bloom, and their tall stems swayed gracefully in the wind. My heart danced with them with joy.

The Folk Village was an awesome place to visit not only to show our past to the visitors but also for the locals to revisit yesteryear. It is a huge living museum set in over 240 acres of land. It is a recreated village of the natural atmosphere of our late "Joseon Dynasty" period, the last and the longest lived imperial Dynasty (1392-1910). Over 250 traditional houses of that era from many different parts of the country were relocated and restored in one place, to preserve our way of life of the past. We saw many different kinds of houses that would once have told one's position in the society and they were furnished appropriately for that era, and people were actually living there doing things for a living just like then. The craftspeople were at work making pottery, straw sandals and baskets, etc. providing a showcase of all the crafts of that era. There were also many demonstrations. We saw a man walking on a tight rope, dressed in old traditional outfit and wearing a pair of shoes made of straw, dance groups in colourful traditional outfits dancing traditional farmer's dances and we saw also fully costumed a traditional wedding ceremony as well.

I really have enjoyed reminiscing and re-living the past I could relate to, given when I was growing up touched some of the old ways of life.

At the amusement park curiosity made us all walk into a haunted house together and like children we all ran out scared but laughing. We had a ride on a dodgem car and we enjoyed swinging on a very old swing made out of a rope with a wooden board for a seat, but the best of all for me was to stand on one end of an old wooden seesaw and teeter-totter with my little son, Ed, standing on the other end. The seesaw play of the bygone era warmed my heart, something that I never thought I would have the chance to do again, let alone doing it with my little son and it was such a satisfying experience.

I had been very busy with my camera capturing as many photographs as I could, and I ran out of film even though I had taken many rolls with me. I was waiting in the long queue at the kiosk to buy some more of the Kodak films for my camera, when I saw in the distance Davina was completely surrounded by a group of women. They seemed to be crowding her and becoming too familiar, even touching her hair. Although it wasn't anything odd for me to see, I was worried at how Davina would handle the situation, and I panicked and ran down to her as fast as I could. To my surprise she was just happily smiling from ear to ear, and said to me in her high and peculiar voice "Ann, don't worry, they make me feel as if I am a Queen and I feel so Very Special Right Now!" I sighed with relief and I was pleased.

The women came from a country town where they have no chance of seeing such a foreign mature lady who looked so different from them, and they couldn't just walk past without welcoming her with their kind gestures and to have a close-up look. Luckily Davina had spent enough days in Korea and was able to tolerate their unusual behaviour of overwhelming joy at seeing her. The hair tints weren't yet widely used as they are now, and seeing such reddish hair, other than black or gray hair was so unusual especially for those from the small isolated country town in Korea. All in all it was a wonderful day for all of us! I left there feeling extremely proud and grateful of everyone who made such a place possible and maintaining it for all to enjoy.

My friend Kyung Hae phoned to let me know that Chi Nam had organized a day to have lunch with us at her home and invited some other friends from our middle-school days as well, and she would pick us up in a couple of days. She mentioned the names of two of the other friends we were going to meet there but once again the names were crystal clear in my memory, but not the faces.

One huge mistake I made when I left home to go to Australia and which I do regret very much, was that given I was the first one in the family to graduate from high-school, I thought my father would be proud to keep my graduation-papers. I entrusted them with my parent, together with the graduation commemoration-albums of both schools in the hope to get them back in later years. Unfortunately such unexpected sad things had happened to my parents since I left, that my things had become lost. No-one knew what had happened to them and sadly they were nowhere to be found. I was hoping to ask Chi Nam to show me hers when I saw her at her place and couldn't wait to see our commemoration-album again. I would not have forgotten any of the faces if I still had the album with me.

It was good that Kyung Hae knew where we were going as we had to change busses a couple of times. The public transportation system in Seoul was great and plenty of choices as ever, but the city had grown so big I would have had a lot of problems to find the place without Kyung Hae's help.

Chi Nam lived in an apartment in an opulent neighborhood. As soon as we got out of the lift Chi Nam and her three daughters were waiting for us. Her seven year old middle daughter looked at me with a big smile and amazed me; she was the image of Chi Nam as I remembered her. She wore a pair of thick glasses and had protruding front teeth just like her mother had. Chi Nam married relatively late in her life to an older man who was a very successful developer. Their four-bedroom apartment was very spacious and luxurious, beautifully furnished with up to date mod cons. Keum Sook and Heung Cha had arrived together. Both were dressed elegantly and the minute I saw them I remembered them and we were very glad to be in each other's arms hugging and laughing.

Keum Sook was married with children but was working full time in an office in the American base in Seoul, whilst Heung Cha was still single and was a pediatrician and had her own surgery. All four of them had similar hair styles, short but with a trendy cut, and were extreamly well groomed and rather extravagantly dressed, and all looked so much younger than their age. Davina was very pleased she could join in the conversation with us as Kyung Hae and Keum Sook spoke very good English. Ed had all the attention from Chi Nam's three daughters. I couldn't help but notice that Ed was getting very good at miming, thus the language barrier seemed not to worry him and they played well together. The lunch was very delicious, traditional dishes with modern twists to suit everyone. I was very impressed and proud to see how much of our Korean cuisine had evolved and was truly ready for the international guests for the Olympics.

We have had such good laughs seeing the old photos of ourselves in our 22 year old middle-school commemoration-album, reminiscing and sharing some of the mischievous stories with Davina was very enjoyable. As we were all ready to leave Chi Nam suggested getting together again one night and going out to a night club to have fun. It was so funny that our married friends including myself thought it was a great idea and readily agreed, whereas our single friends were hesitant and were not as excited to go. This made all of us burst into laughter again. We had such a lovely time and I hoped that we really would have the chance to get together again soon and I was also hoping to see some of my friends from High-school days, but didn't have any contacts.

Wan Soo, a friend I used to know in the neighbourhood in Itaewon, not only phoned and surprised me but wanted to treat us all to a lunch and take us out to a nice outdoor restaurant, to catch up with me and I was very much looking forward to seeing him again. He was about a year older than I and we enjoyed being around each other when I lived in Itaewon. He drove his own car to pick us up. He looked very different to how I remembered him as a teen, his face was broader and his voice sounded more matured, he was proud to tell us on the way that he was married with three children and he was running a successful construction company.

The up-market restaurant was set in a beautiful garden and catered for authentic Korean cuisine, but we didn't have to sit on the floor or take our shoes off and sat on chairs as in western style, which was welcomed by Davina. While we were having lunch Wan Soo as a very proud dad, showed us his family photos and it was good to hear that his parents were well also. I mentioned to him about the wonderful luncheon we had the day before with my middle-school friends and not yet having had any chance of meeting any of my high-school friends. He was very surprised to hear that and told me about one of my close friend, Jung Moon who then had a hairdressing salon where he often went to get his hair cut, and he gave me her number.

I was so happy and over the moon to hear about her and very excited with the prospect of seeing her soon, and she may lead me into seeing other friends from our high-school days as well. Jung Moon was my best friend all throughout our middle -school to high-school days, not only because she was the only one I knew who went to the same high-school from the same middle-school as I had, but also she was the only friend of all my school friends who I felt totally comfortable to invite to my home. As I always felt I could trust her and never kept any secrets from her, all through our difficult and sad years of my stepmother's illness with cancer and her passing, and soon after losing my little sister. We often slept over at each other's home to study together and we were treated by each other's family as part of the family. It was unfortunate that we somehow were disconnected and lost many long years of our lives. I suppose it isn't all that surprising as we both frequently changed our addresses during the past seventeen years. Not that long after we arrived back at the hotel I had the phone call from Jung Moon that she was coming around straightaway to see me.

We were very excited to see each other again. She looked exactly the same as I remembered, even her hair style as if I had seen her only yesterday. She was happily married with three children and her husband also ran his own small business. Jung Moon explained that her husband's business was a kind of an education centre, where high-school graduates who had failed the exam to enter the university of their choice, could study on to prepare for the next exam. She told me also that running the two businesses and attending the needs of their three children kept them so busy; she hardly ever saw any of our old school friends even though they still lived in Seoul. But we promised each other that we would make time for each other while I was in Seoul.

One evening I had to catch a taxi to see another person I used to know from Itaewon. I found out from Wan Soo that she was working at a store a short distance away from our hotel and I couldn't wait to give her a quick surprise visit, and I went out alone. At the roadside I waved my arm at a taxi approaching my way. When the taxi stopped in front of me I looked in the taxi and I asked the driver, in Korean, if it was Ok for me to get in and he said yes, so I opened the door and sat on the passenger seat next to the driver like I would do when my husband drives our car, and I told him where to go. The driver was very quiet and drove without saying another word but when we were held up in a traffic jam, he broke the silence and suddenly asked me how long had I been living overseas. I was very surprised with his question and I asked him what made him think that I have lived overseas. He said with a smile that it was very easy to pick by three things.

He explained to me that he knew straightaway I was from overseas the minute I asked him the strange unusual question if it was OK for me to get in, because on top of the taxi there was a clearly lit-up sign showing it was vacant, as well as a card on the windscreen that indicated it was empty and then I sat on the front seat next to the driver, not at the back like any other local respectable woman my age would do. Lastly he couldn't help but notice that I was not extravagantly dressed like local woman, my age, in Seoul would wear to go out in the evening.

He asked me if his guess was wrong so I told him in amazement that his guess was right and that, indeed, I had been living for more than seventeen years in Australia and that this was my very first visit home. He also explained that during the last ten years or so he had been on and off in Tokyo in Japan and Shanghai in China, it was easier for him to tell that I was a foreigner. He went on to tell me that driving a taxi for a living in Seoul, he saw too many of the local women wasting their husband's hard earned money on gambling and on wearing showy clothes.

He told me that more and more housewives were into gambling on the Share Market which they don't know much about. He was not at all proud with the prosperity and seemed rather disappointed and spoke to me as if the rapid economic growth of the country had created some unwelcome headaches.

But as a woman I didn't share his opinion by listening to how he talked down about women in Korea. It sounded to me more like an opinion of a chauvinistic male and I couldn't help but think that Korea was still a very long way off for women's liberation.

He said that he had heard nothing but good things about Australia and asked me if Australia is really that good a place to live in. I didn't hesitate to tell him that I was very happy with my life in Australia and that it is a wonderful country to live in, especially for those like me who have an international marriage because being a multicultural society people are more open-minded and relaxed, without being locked in any old culture. Having said that I was very pleased and proud to see how much Korea had changed over the years, for the better. I had already observed at firsthand, having visited relations and friends' homes that the standard of living in Korea had improved enormously.

I told him also that it was good to see that there were no beggars on the streets like there used to be - no more of the injured and disabled people from the wars begging to survive on the streets. I presumed there must be a support system well in place to take care of them. But he said there was a huge gap still between the rich and poor, the support system had a lot to improve.

He said that he had heard that Australia is a large country with a relatively small population and rich with natural resources unlike Korea which is small, highly populated without many natural resources. He was envious that I lived in such a lucky country like Australia and he was hoping to go to Australia one day with his family to live. Our conversation was cut short as we arrived at the place where I had to get off. We said 'good-bye' to each other and I wished him that his dream would come true one day.

Wan Soo was very pleased to hear that I had caught up with Jung Moon and he was ever so kind to take another full day off from his business, to take us for a drive and show us some interesting new places in Seoul. At first he took us to "63 Building", the new 249 metres tall building built to overlook the Han River as the land mark for the "88 Summer Olympics", and was opened in 1985, less than two years before we visited there. It was in the vicinity not far from Norangjin where I used to live for about three years before I left Korea. The skyscraper looked awesome and made me very curious to find out what it's like to be on the top floor. We rode up to the top sixtieth floor by an external elevator, built with clear glass on all sides, for a full view of the area as we went up.

I didn't know I had such a fear of heights. My legs were wobbly in no time and felt weak and dysfunctional and I had spinning sensations in my head, not being able to maintain my balance when I was looking down, but I didn't want to miss out on the experience of seeing the view of the city from it as we went up. So I held on tight to the rail and tried to look down as much as I could. As we rode up everything below us became very tiny and seeing the grandiosity of the panoramic view from it was an incredible experience. The thrilling scary experience made me imagine the fear of looking down from a plane flying high up, but standing outside. Davina screamed loud as if she was experiencing the panic attack most of the way up. It was only about a minute ride but it sure was a very memorable one. Ed giggled as he thought it was rather funny to hear such a grown woman screaming like a child, and he looked down with ease as the height didn't have much effect on him.

Davina and I sighed and were most relieved when we got out of the elevator on the sixtieth floor. The top floor was the observatory and there was an art-gallery as well. I tried to take some photos of the magnificent view from the observation deck, as I felt it was a safer place to take some photos, but I was soon told by a guard that taking photo was prohibited. We didn't have time to go into the art-gallery as Wan Soo was hoping to show us some other places on the day but before we went back down we had our lunch at the "Sky lounge restaurant" on the fifty-ninth floor which catered for western food. The Fillet-mignon I had for lunch was an identical dish to the Fillet-mignon we had at "Copper Grill" in Mount Isa where I used to work and to my surprise even the price was almost the same.

It was truly an awesome experience also to have a meal at such a classy restaurant so high up, with the magnificent view all around. From there we went right down to the basement which had three levels. There in the basement was a large aquarium called "63 Sea World" and IMAX Theater, as well as lots of shops to look around. The aquarium was then said to be the largest indoor aquarium in all of Asia. It had 20,000 aquatic creatures representing about 400 different species as well as crocodiles, penguins and fur seals. It was an amazing place to see up close and personal with so many of the wonderful creatures of the underwater world.

Seeing the movie called "The discovery of the Grand Canyon" at the IMAX Theater in the basement was another awesome experience. The theater had over 500 seats with a full surround sound system. The overall effect was like watching a 3D movie we see nowadays. While we were watching the movie we often screamed in fear because of the sheer frightening sensation that you are inside the movie, and experiencing the awesome drops in "The Grand Canyon". It was the first time in our lives that Davina and I experienced such sensation and we weren't any different to the little children sitting next to us, and we screamed loudly. Watching such a movie from the IMAX theater where the sensation was intensified by the surround sound system was truly frightening and a heart-rending experience, not just to hear and see but feel as if the river in the Canyon would burst out of the screen and rush at us.

From there he took us to the "Seoul Sports Complex" built in 1984 which served as the main stadium for the tenth Asian games in 1986 and was well and truly ready to serve as the main stadium for the "88 Summer Olympics". I was very proud to witness how beautiful the complex was. The spectator's seats were said to be for 70,000, were in two tiers of a totally covered area. I left the complex with a huge pride and prayed that the Olympics would be a great success, and that all would go without a hitch or threat from North Korea.

On our back to the hotel we saw a large parade on the street to commemorate the day of the beginning of the countdown for the Olympics, as it happened to be exactly 365 days to go from that day. I was emotional, to say the least, to be actually there and seeing such a parade. The countdown has begun in my heart as well, with the very best wishes.

About a year earlier I met a man in Mount Isa who was sent by one of the refineries in Korea for a six months' work experience with Mount Is Mines. We called him Mr. Park. Rolf and I got to know him well and before he left Mount Isa he gave me a beautiful single stem copper rose he had made by giving a fresh rose an electronic current treatment through a copper solution. It was his first experiment to preserve a fresh rose forever in copper solution, but it turned out very successfully as he had wished and he was very happy to give it to me as the departing gift and I will never forget what he said to me when he gave it to me "I truly Hope that Your Korean Identity will be Forever Protected as the Fresh Rose Preserved Forever in this Copper Rose." The copper rose is still with me to this date and reminds me to never forget that I am a Korean, foremost of all.

Mr. Park was delighted when I phoned him as he was expecting the call from me when I arrived in Korea in September and he was looking forward to playing tenpin bowling with me again. He took time off from his work on the next day and took us to a bowling Alley in Itaewon because he knew I used to live in Itaewon. It was very thoughtful of him. Ed liked the game and had a natural talent and played well but it was the first time for Davina to play the game, and her bowl headed to the gutter almost every time, nevertheless she too thought it was lots of fun. After the games he took us for lunch at one of the nice restaurants in Itaewon before he drove us back to our hotel.

I phoned one of my father's cousins, the older brother of the one who picked us up from the airport when we arrived. His name is Jong Auck and he is my favorite amongst my father's cousins. I dialled his number thinking of him of the days when he used to work for my father as a young man. His voice on the phone was exactly the same as I remembered it, for the moment I had completely forgotten that he was married a couple of years before I left for Australia. It was embarrassing that he had to help me to remember about it by describing, little by little, about his traditional wedding ceremony which had I attended, which was held in the country.

My memory about his wedding day was very faint; it was floating around in my head in small lots. Although somewhere in my memory I always remembered a wonderful traditional wedding I attended in the country but I couldn't remember clearly whose wedding it was until that moment, and as soon as he started to explain to me about it the pieces were linked up. I was rather embarrassed about not remembering properly. I couldn't picture him as a married man because I had hardly ever seen him since he was married and moved away, and we were not in touch even in those years I lived in Australia. It's been almost 20 years since I had spoken with him let alone seen him or his wife. He was very excited and he promised that he would come in a couple of days to take us to his home for lunch. By then luckily I remembered his wife's face and I was looking very much forward to seeing her again and meeting their children.

His elder brother heard that I was coming to visit and he came around with his son as well, it made an extra nice get together. The food was delicious and the company was very loving. Their second daughter, who was in the second year of high-school, enjoyed practicing her English with Davina and Ed, which was fun at times for everyone else to listen and made her parents very proud. Jong Auck's wife never sat still and was always doing something whilst she was in the conversation with us. I saw her peeling a large bowl of fresh garlic still in a very old Korean way. She was peeling garlic soaked in the water one by one by hand which was a tedious thing to do, I showed her how to make the skin just fall off by hammering them with a wooden mallet which was much easier than peeling them in her way. We shared lots of laughter and had a really enjoyable day.

I had not seen my full sister Kyung Hee and her family since the day we arrived, but she didn't have a phone to contact her and no one knew where she lived, so I was very relieved when she finally phoned me and let us know where she lived. We went to her home by taxi. It was very far out of the city. She was renting a small place but kept very nice and clean and she had prepared a table full of very delicious food for all of us to enjoy. It was so good to be with her and her family and to have the chance to open up our hearts and have a good talk, especially the chance to find out, from the *horse's mouth,* so to speak, from her husband's side regarding the reason why he had been neglecting his family from time to time and giving so much heartache to his wife my sister Kyung Hee.

He was an ex-Vietnam soldier who was lucky enough to return home without any injuries, and had brought his hard earned money back with him, and was proud to have given it all to his poor mother and had to face the real world empty handed. He struggled to survive not having the money nor a good education or any qualification. He and Kyung Hee met and fell in love starting their life together in a society that demanded good qualifications or a good education. They worked hard together at whatever work they could find, but the problem only became worse when Kyung Hee became pregnant. To find the way to make better money he started to sing in the night clubs as he was good at singing, and in turn he was led away from his family at times to go distances to find the place that would pay better for his singing, which caused big arguments between them. At times he was not allowed by Kyung Hee to return home and he had no choice but to stay away. I felt sorry for his misfortune but at the same time I was somewhat relieved because I could see they both were still very much in love and he was back at home. I hoped he would stay with his family from then on and work things out between themselves.

I had searched all over Seoul for some months prior to leaving for Australia, to find our relatives of our birth mother's side for Kyung Hee, as I thought that she would be feeling very lonely without me. Unfortunately all of them had moved away from Itaewon and ever since my father remarried we were disconnected from that side of the family, and we grew up missing them not knowing whereabouts they were because no one in our family wanted to talk about them. I went to various census offices in different suburbs all over the city and searched for their names to find where they might live. It was such a daunting task as too many people had the exact same names, but I was so lucky to find the family record of my mother's only brother. Our uncle by then had already passed away but we were reconnected with his wife and their three grown up sons. Chang Seuk, the second son of the uncle, is only a few months older than I and I missed him most as we used to play together a lot when we were little, and we were very excited to see each other again. From them we found out where two of the three aunties lived. I had just enough time, before I left the country, to go around seeing them with Kyung Hee and got her reconnected but I didn't have enough time to search where our youngest aunt and her families were. Apparently she was separated from the rest of the relatives. The only thing I heard about her was that she was very well educated and was teaching piano for a living.

After we had lunch Kyung Hee told me about our cousin, a daughter of our mother's second sister, who had been very kind to her since I left and played the rôle of a big sister for her for many years. But as they moved many times from place to place to live, Kyung Hee was somehow disconnected again from her, and she wished to find her again. The cousin, Keum Auck was also married to an ex-Vietnam soldier but they started their life together reasonably well with the money he had earned from the war, and I also discovered that Keum Auck was one year senior to me at the Su Do High but we didn't know about each other while we were attending the school, and we only found out about it after we were reconnected.

On that afternoon I went out with Kyung Hee to help her to find our cousins again and went to the census office of the last place where Chang Seuk used to live, and tried to find out where he had moved to. We were lucky to find the record and that his new address was in Incheon, 45 kilometres out of Seoul, but no phone number to contact him. As it was getting dark and all of us were tired from walking around for so long we returned home with the hope that somehow we will be able to contact him on another day.

On the next day Myung Hee was taken to hospital for an emergency surgery to have her appendix out. My uncle's wife rang me that she would pick us up in a taxi on her way to visit Myung Hee in hospital, so I went out and bought a bunch of fresh flowers to take with me. But to my surprise my uncle's wife didn't allow me to take the flowers with me so I reluctantly left them with the girls at the reception. Anyhow it was such a relief for everyone to find out the surgery went well and Myung Hee was Ok. The hospital looked very well equipped and clean and the staff were very friendly but Davina agreed with me that it was rather strange to see patients' rooms without any flowers.

Myung Hee asked us to move into her home a few times. But we remained staying at the hotel not only because it was conveniently located and well known to everyone, and it was easy for everyone to contact me, but also I was concerned that Kyung Hee might feel left out if we were to move into Myung Hee's place, because I knew Myung Sook lived there as well. However after the surgery Myung Hee refused to wait any longer and insisted for us to move into her place. So I explained to Kyung Hee and asked for her understanding before we moved. We stayed at Myung Hee's home for the rest of our holidays in Seoul.

Myung Hee's apartment was a large three-bedroom modern apartment equipped with all things modern and furnished as we would in Australia.

She prepared one of the bedrooms with two single beds for Davina and me to use, and took both her little daughters with her into the master bedroom, whilst the third bedroom was always for Myung Sook. Ed and Myung Hee's little son slept on a bed made on the floor in their lounge room. She had a house maid who came around a few hours every day to help her with the house work.

It was so obvious to see that Korea was in a cultural transition. Whilst older people's homes were still furnished like yesteryears as I remembered, young people's homes were furnished just like in western style as we have in Australia. Children ate cereal for breakfast at the table whilst older people still preferred to have leftovers with rice and kimchi for breakfast served on a low foldable table sitting on the floor.

I could see the huge change happening right before my eyes.

Myung hee's home was a comfortable place to stay for us, and we were well cared for by my sisters - at times perhaps too well. Myung Hee was concerned about the meals for Davina and Ed, and asked me every time their likes and dislikes, before she prepared the meals to make sure there was always something nice for them to enjoy as well. Furthermore while at the table eating meals my sisters literally would try to feed them to make sure they tasted everything they prepared. I was only too happy to see that, as I was brought up that way.

It was the second evening after we had moved in that Davina left the table while we were having dinner, without saying anything. I took it for granted that she needed to go to the toilet and because I was busy eating and so into our conversation that I didn't realize that she hadn't returned to the table for some time, until Myung Sook pointed it out to me and, concerned about her, I went to look for her.

I found her sulking, sitting on the edge of her bed, in our room and seeing her like that made me extremely concerned, and I asked her "Oh, what's wrong Davina why are you looking so SAD? Did anyone upset you?"

She had tears in her eyes and looked at me with a stare of sheer disappointment and said, "Do I look like an invalid, why don't they let me choose what I want to eat, instead of everyone trying to FEED me?"

I was astounded to hear what she had to say and only then did I realize that I should have warned her that we often do fuss around each other when we eat, to share food and show each other we care. Once I had explained to her that they were doing it out of their love for her to make sure she tasted everything they especially prepared for her, she seemed to feel a lot better. We went back to the table together. My sisters too were very surprised to hear what it all was about and they agreed with me to back off a bit, and sincerely apologized to Davina, but they were still in disbelief and couldn't get the awkward smile off their faces.

At the week-end all of us made a large amount of lovely Sushi rolls and went for a picnic in a park with our elder aunt, Yang Woo and Myung Hee's whole family - all eleven of us together in hired cars for the day. Singing along in the car with my little nephew and niece, the children's songs I knew so well, on the way to the park were such joyous moments for me.

There were lots of people at the park and we saw many animals from all over the world that were kept in different enclosures but as like in nature as possible. We had a ride together in a horse-drawn wagon and had the picnic lunch on the lawn. There I saw a monkey smoking a cigarette, sitting on a swing ladder made of ropes stretched high up between the huge big rocks that had very high peaks. It looked so funny smoking just like one of we humans. It was such a grand park full of interesting things to see and enjoy; we didn't have time to see everything there. Nevertheless we had a very lovely time with the children and it was great to see Ed having a great time with his little cousins. It was indeed a rare opportunity for Ed to have such an outing with his cousins.

One evening Myung Hee surprised me with a voucher valued close to $100 Australian from a shoe store in Myeong Dong, the very well known up market shopping district in Seoul, for international brand outlets. It's fair to say it is the shopping Mecca for fashion in Seoul. Given it was not any kind of special day to receive such a gift my instant thought was that Myung Hee too might think like my uncle's wife, that I couldn't afford to have nice shoes as I was wearing the same not so expensive pair of shoes every day and every night. I felt somewhat misunderstood and being meddled with, and I wasn't all that happy to accept it.

It was necessary for my job to be dressed up well and I loved to dress up and I sure had enough lovely shoes to go with my different outfits but I only took the one pair of shoes I felt most comfortable to walk in, as I had intended to buy a couple of pairs of nice shoes while I was in Seoul. Seeing me wearing the same old shoe day or night, I must have given the wrong impression again to my caring family, and made them concerned that I may not be able to afford many shoes, and they were trying to help me out, not knowing all the facts.

Having said that though in those years I never ever paid more than $35 Australian for a pair of shoes for myself, and most of the good shoes I had would have cost me around $25 to $35 because I never felt the need to wear any shoes more expensive than that, and I never had the need to have any more than five to six pairs of good shoes. I had to ask Myung Hee for what reason she got the voucher for me, she could sense by the tone of my voice that I wasn't pleased with her gesture of kindness. And she explained to me that there were no other reasons than her husband was given all sorts of gifts by grateful customers, and she happened to have more vouchers than she needed and she thought that I would be happy to have a good pair of shoes made to measure to my liking while I was in Seoul.

I reluctantly accepted it with thanks and agreed with her that I would get one pair made to measure before I left. Once again I realized not only had I become foreign to the culture I was brought up in, but also my mentality had changed so much, so that I was not feeling comfortable with it all. I felt like I had been meddled with and misunderstood by my family. Yet, I was not interested to explain in detail to them how everything was with my life, and make contradictory statements to what they may imagine. Because I was afraid it may sound to them as if I was making excuses in denial.

I guess I had lived away for too long from caring relatives and lived in isolation for a long time, so that I had to learn to survive without any help from anyone, and became even more protective of my own instinct and what I believed in.

Another thing happened while we were staying at my sister's place because of the sheer difference of the cultures. Se Mi Appa came home from work one evening and saw Ed lying on the floor. He walked up to him and sat beside him and gave Ed a gentle squeeze on his nose and a couple of gentle smacks on Ed's cheek and said "AREN'T you just GORGEOUS!" just like he would do to his little children out of love. I saw him doing it and I was rather happy to see it because to me he was showing his affection to Ed, that he was happy to have Ed around at his place and I never thought anything else.

However when my little niece Se Mi was very worried and told me that Ed was lying there still, in silence, and very sad big tears were running down his face, it took me by surprise not knowing what made him so sad so suddenly, so I asked him. By then everyone in the room was concerned about Ed including Se Mi Appa and waited for his answer. He burst out crying then and said to me "What Did I do Wrong, Mum, Why did he SMACK me? I haven't done ANYTHING Wrong…." Listening to what he said we realized, it was just another misunderstanding because of a different culture, and all of us including myself burst into laughter because only then we realized that Ed was not brought up like we were in Korea. I explained to Ed that Se Mi Appa did it to him out of love because he didn't know that in Australian culture no one would do that out of affection. Se MI Appa was VERY surprised to learn that, and felt bad for making Ed so sad, and he held Ed's hands and gave his Sincere Apology. Davina too laughed loud when she found out what the commotion was all about and realized it wasn't just herself having such an experience because of the different culture in Korea.

There was a technical high school teacher who used to live with his mother near where we lived in Norangin. Both of them were very fond of me and so much so that at times I had to avoid seeing him. He was a gentleman about ten years older than I, tall and handsome. Naïve as I was at nineteen years of age and had my heart already set on Rolf, I was rather troubled by his affection toward me. More so when I became aware of my stepmother and his mother who were making it easier for him to drop in and see me at home, at times, I had to get help from my sisters to hide from him. I heard from my sisters that since I left the country he fell in love with someone else and was married and moved away from Norangjin, but he still kept in touch with my youngest sister Myung Sook and wanted to hear about me.

He heard from Myung Sook that I came back to Korea for a visit and phoned me. He was by then a professor at a university. He wanted to treat us all to a nice lunch somewhere and take us all afterwards to show us the university where he worked. But it happened to be on the day when a student riot against some new government policies had just flared up at the same university, with tear gas and all. Davina was petrified of the riot and didn't want to go anywhere near it and I postponed seeing him until another day, when the riot was over and it was safe.

After a couple of days the riot became just a demonstration, he phoned me again to tell me that it was not as dangerous and he was anxious to see us soon as possible, as he was free from lectures while the demonstration was on. I asked Myung Sook if she could take a day off from work and come with us, so she did on the very next day. He was wearing a suit and looking as handsome as ever. Davina was very impressed with him as I was in every way, and was looking forward to his company. Davina seemed smitten by him and even forgot all about her fear that the student demonstration was still going on.

He drove us in his flash car to a lovely outdoor restaurant and needless to say we had a delicious lunch. After lunch we were driven through the streets where the demonstration was, outside the university grounds, yet there was absolutely no apparent danger for passersby. No one in the street looked scared about it at all and it surprised Davina as we were driven right through it. She sighed with relief and even had a laugh at the media in general, how they may exaggerate the event for the news report. All in all we had a lovely day together. Especially for me and him as it was like a very lovely closure to an episode of my teen years as we were able to talk about it openly, and it was fun sharing our fond memories together with Davina and my sister Myung Sook.

Finally we were able to contact my cousin Chang Seuk, and Myung Hee organized for us all to meet at her home. She invited Kyung Hee and her children, Chang Seuk and his wife, as well as Keum Auck and my friend Jung Moon. It was a very rare event to say the least seeing that Myung Hee and Myung Sook hardly knew those cousins on my birth mother's side. It was very kind of Myung Hee to organize such a get-together for me and Kyung Hee at her place. And it was the first time for Kyung Hee to be invited to Myung Hee's place, as they haven't been much in touch all those years since they were married. Seeing Ed playing with all five of his little cousins was very pleasing for everyone and I was having a wonderful time with all of my sisters together with our cousins and my friend Jung Moon. The feast prepared was scrumptious. Davina was overwhelmed with the warm hospitality wherever we went and she told us many times how grateful she was that she came with me and met my relatives and friends.

We had to give ourselves a couple of days free from meeting people and just go shopping and have a look around the wonderful department stores we have in the city as well as the big markets, as we were yet to experience the well known, "East Gate Market" and the "South Gate Market". We were lucky being there early in the autumn as we could buy lots of good summer clothes in "going out of season" prices. There were many wonderful gift items to choose from, from the famous international brand names such as "Pierre Cardin" to very cheap but exotic handcrafts. We literally shopped till we dropped! Arriving home very tired, we couldn't wait to go shopping again the next day. Davina learned fast and loved to bargain the prices at the markets and enjoyed the street food there. She was truly wonderful company to be with no matter where we went, what we did or whomever we met. So was Ed, he loved every minute of it also, he was the man to protect and guard us both – he thought.

We went to Myeong Dong finally and I got a pair of high heel made to measure in expensive snake skin, and paid $98 Australian with the voucher Myung Hee had given me as a gift. Davina was very excited to have the opportunity and happy to get a pair of classy open summer sandals made to measure.

Mr.Park contacted me again and took us to his home one afternoon and introduced us to his wife. She was a small person with many creative ideas, seeing that I am also interested in art and craft, her works inspired me a lot and it was very interesting to talk with her. She served us some green tea in tiny cups without handles, on a low table, together with some cut fruits beautifully arranged on a platter, which was different to the afternoon tea we would normally have in Australia - coffee and tea in a mug with scones or sweet cakes. They have been married for many years but no children yet. The place was beautiful and delicately decorated with many handcrafted ornaments she had made.

The last Sunday before we left Korea a get-together was organized by Keum Auck at her parents' home, who lived with her brother at Suwon, about 34 kilometres south of Seoul. Together with Kyung Hee, we followed Keum Auck. We got off the train and walked past the road that had many stalls of fresh fruit and vegetables. I wanted to buy some beer or fruits to take with us but Keum Auck suggested to me to buy a few kilograms of meat instead and this instantly reminded me of another Korean way of life that I had completely forgotten, and I felt inadequate thinking that previously I went to many other places and brought, perhaps, the wrong gifts and hoped that my relatives would have forgiven me. It felt strange walking with a bag of meat to visit people but at the same time I was rather happy being a Korean again, doing what was respectable and expected by our elders and for that I was grateful to Keum Auck for giving me the advice.

The lovely garden at the entrance to my aunt's(my birth mum's elder sister) place was full of my favorite flower, cosmoses in full bloom, dancing elegantly in the autumn breeze and seeing them so close, I felt great joy! We heard a couple of dogs barking as Keum Auck opened the tall gate, and as we entered, my aunt and uncle rushed out of a lovely two story brick home and welcomed us with open arms and we hugged. Although their faces were not familiar at all to me I could faintly remember my aunt's voice. Given she would be the closest person to our mother, the joy of seeing her again for the first time in such a long time made my heart beat fast, and had me in tears and then, seeing Kyung Hee crying in our aunt's arms as if our aunt was our mother, made me cry as well, in empathy. Our other cousins Chang Seuk and his younger brother Jung Ho and their families arrived soon after, and then came Sang Gil, the only brother to Keum Auck, who had just returned home from his work. I was pleased to notice that Kyung Hee and Sang Gil knew each other well and they seemed so happy to see each other. All fifteen of us were together and all of us stayed there over night. We ate delicious food, drank beer, wine, and *soju*, the Korean spirit. We played Korean card games. We shared some tears as well as lots of laughter as we sang many old songs together.

Kyung Hee loved singing and could sing well, and so could my aunt. It was merely a faint memory but there was a similarity in our aunts' voices. How faint memory was maybe it was a precious one and I was happy to hold on to it.

Davina and the little children went to bed by midnight but the rest of us stayed up into the wee hours of the morning and shared the precious and wonderful time together with our aunt and our uncle. I heard more news about our eldest aunt and her family, who had migrated to Chicago in America some years prior, but for some reason no-one seemed to be in touch with our mum's younger sister who still lived in Seoul.

Next morning before we left, Davina took a photo of all of us together. The fourteen of us were ever so happy to pose for the camera, feeling the great sense of belonging, to remind us all of the wonderful time we had shared, for years to come. Chang Seuk was very happy to give us a lift all the way back to Myung Hee's place, in his mini bus, and we shared more of the laughter all the way.

I received a call from Pil Hyeo, another friend from junior-school days. She heard about me from Kyung Hae and was desperate to see me as soon as possible because I was leaving the country in a few days and if we didn't meet that afternoon we wouldn't get to see each other. That afternoon we met at a teashop near Myung Hee's place and she brought one of her friends, who was a teacher at the same school where she taught, but was in the process of emigrating to Australia with her family and wanted to meet me to talk about Australia.

I couldn't ever forget Pil Hyeo because she used to be the shortest person in the class and had lots of freckles on her rather pale face. I recognized her very quickly but I was very surprised to see that she had grown taller than I am, and she also recognized me very quickly even though she hadn't seen me for a couple of decades. As soon as we saw each other we pointed our fingers at each other with big smiles on our faces and rushed to each other. She was happily married with two children and loved being a teacher.

Her friend Jung Sook was also married with two children. Jung Sook and her husband had just sold their import and export business and were looking forward to going to Australia. I answered to the best of my ability, the questions she had about life in Australia. I told her that they would be just fine as they both were very well educated and they would not even be lonely, as they have each other, and there were already lots of Korean migrants living in Sydney, where they were planning to live. We gave each other contact details to stay in touch before we said our good-byes.

Two days before we left Korea we planned for another get-together with my school friends. Most of them were busy working and we were also very busy every day, it was lucky that we found the time to suit everyone.

We were to meet Chi Nam at the "Sky Lounge" at the "Lotte Hotel" in the city and have lunch there with her, and follow her to meet others at a well known night club called "Hollywood" that evening. I was told it was a fancy exclusive night club! My youngest sister, Myung Sook, wanted to join us there as well after work. The thought of meeting with my friends there and having fun was all good, but when I actually got there and saw the place, I didn't feel all that comfortable to go in, as I had never been in such a fancy, exclusive night club before either in Korea or in Australia. I felt it was an improper place for a married woman without her husband to go to; I was rather a little hesitant for a minute, but as more of my friends started to arrive, I was back in the mood of *Why not just be in the moment and have fun with my friends.*

I walked in there with an attitude that nothing was going to worry me at all and seeing Davina smiling from ear to ear I knew Davina was with me all the way. We were seated at our reserved table and I sat there pretending there was nothing the matter with me, as if I was used to such a life, while we were waiting for the rest of our friends to arrive. I watched others in the room with interest to see how they behaved. The grand place had two big round spinning stage sets under lots of fancy, dim lights.

Soon everyone arrived. We all settled down for a drink. Some of us had alcoholic drinks and some just had juices and we joined in the crowd and danced together. It was the very first time ever I had danced with Davina, and I don't remember if I ever danced with any of my friends or my sister before.

Dancing in my brand new snake skin high heels, I felt very feminine!

As the night deepened there were the stage shows, a man on one stage and a woman on the other stage. Each of them appeared on their stage fully dressed in beautiful traditional costumes made in many layers of soft fabrics. They danced in individual styles but to the same beautiful sensual music and as they danced they stripped off their clothes, piece by piece, until they were naked, and then, in his nakedness, the man left the stage to loud applause from the room packed with people. But the woman danced on even more sensuously and slowly with a live snake thick and long, longer than her height wrapped around her body. The beautiful soft curves of the naked female body entwined with the curves of the ever so slowly moving snake, in time to the music was something very exotically beautiful and sensual.

It was just mesmerizing!

I started to take some photos to show Rolf but soon I was stopped by a guard.

Followed by such a sensual strip show, the very famous, my favorite old singer named Hyun Mi, appeared on the stage. Just seeing her again after such a long time was enough to fill my heart with emotion, being in the same room with her for the first time was truly an overwhelming experience. She was the most famous singer from way back when I was living in Korea. When she started to sing one of my favorite of her old romantic songs, entitled *"Bam-An-ghe"* (Night fog) I almost died with emotion and the song made me miss Rolf all the more, as I had the urge to dance with him to the song.

But then, her next song! She was singing another one of my favorite of her old time songs, song of all songs, a romantic farewell song as if she was singing just to me. As she sang the song, *"dder-nal-dde-neun-mal-i-yup-si"* (Say no word… if you must go…) my heart went all to pieces!

What a night!

I was emotionally wracked but I loved every minute of it. After all that we had to say farewell to one another, - hadn't we?

It was again one of those rare and wonderful experiences that will stay with me forever.

My voice became croaky within the first few days I arrived in Korea from the numerous emotions I was experiencing and talking too much perhaps, and it never had the chance to get better. Whether I had yet seen some of my relatives or friends I hoped to see or not, the time had come to get ready to leave, and put me in total emotional disarray, knowing that I wouldn't be back for a long time. I was only just beginning to feel comfortable again with the Korean way of life but it had to come to an end, as Rolf said, my home is with him and our sons in Australia, and I must return home. I have told my friends in Mount Isa I was going home to Korea but needless to say the true home for me now is in Mount Isa in Australia, - I must leave.

I am surely out of touch for the life I was brought up by and felt somewhat inadequate which was heart-breaking at times, but I must accept it as it is the reality of life. Not much time left to say good-byes to everyone let alone to find more of the people I hoped to find.

Davina has enjoyed the time in Korea very much but she couldn't wait to go home to tell everyone about the many interesting experiences she has had in Korea. It being the first overseas country she ever visited she had many first-hand experiences to tell them, especially those of her friends who had misconceptions about Korea. Ed was just happy no matter what each day brought. Why wouldn't he be, he was with his mum, - wasn't he?

Chang Seuk came to pick us up in his minibus to take us to the airport. Myung Hee's whole family and Myung Sook came with us in the minibus. Arriving at the airport I saw my other cousins, Kun Woo, Yang Woo as well as Doug Young, who I hadn't had the chance to see until then, who is a youngest son of my aunt who lives in An Yang. It was nice to see them all there and my friend Jung Moon came out as well. I was hoping to see my sister Kyung Hee and her family there but they didn't come and I missed very much not seeing them there, - leaving without saying Good-bye to her again.

It was different from the arrival day - no one was sad and crying - we were emotional to say good-byes again, but at the same time we were all in a happy mood as we were reconnected and looked forward to the future. We hoped to stay in touch and see each other again one day soon. Ed shook hands HARD with everyone and promised positively that he will come again very soon. I too really hoped that it's not going to be too long before we will see everyone again.

Davina couldn't resist shopping and had bought too much to take home. Her suitcase was way over the limit and she ended up paying close to $400 Australian for the excess weight. It taught her a big lesson but she was not all that disappointed and only happy that she was allowed to take them all home.

We boarded the Singapore airline and as we flew high into the sky I thanked God with all my heart for the wonderful time I'd had in Korea and I prayed that the upcoming Summer Olympics would be a GREAT SUCCESS!

We changed our flight at Changi airport late that night and flew back to Brisbane overnight. We arrived at 6.00am local time. I had promised one of my friends, Carol, whom I hadn't seen for a while since she and her family moved to Brisbane, that I would telephone her to let her know that we had arrived back.

As she was expecting my call on that morning she had the day planned to spend time with us and sent her husband straight away to pick Ed and I up from the motel and took us to their home. Davina also went out to socialize with her friend again who lived in Brisbane. Carol is a good friend of mine and a pretty talented potter and her husband Don, a manuals art teacher, used to teach Maurits at the Kalkadoon State High School. It was lovely to catch up with them; we were there all day until late that night. The following day around mid morning, we flew back to Mount Isa.

While we were busy in Korea the time passed so fast it felt like it had been a very short time, but arriving back in Mount Isa it not only felt like I had been away for a very long time, but also to another world. Nevertheless I was very glad to come home. The trip was very emotional from the start to the finish my croaky voice was yet to recover. Just by hearing my voice Rolf was sympathetic as he could imagine how emotional the trip would have been for me and it was so nice to be in Rolf's loving arms again. The three of us were re-united in tight hugs and in happiness. All the way home from the airport, Ed talked non-stop about the trip.

Davina also looked very happy to see her husband and they left the airport just before us, but soon after we arrived at home a large see-through box of a beautiful bouquet of fresh orchids in full bloom was delivered to me from a local florist, and surprised me. Davina didn't waste a minute to express her gratitude to me, and with the bouquet there was a little handwritten card, *"To Ann, Many thanks for the wonderful time I had & the wonderful friends & relatives I was privileged to meet." From Davina.* It was a very pleasant surprise and I was very happy to know that she has had a lovely time and that she enjoyed meeting my family and friends. I phoned her straightaway and thanked her for her kind words and the lovely flowers and let her know how much I enjoyed her company on the trip.

Davina often talked about the wonderful experiences she had in Korea and she made me proud of my family and friends and where I came from.

Chapter Ten

I have worked over 4 years for Frances until Frances and her family moved away from Mount Isa to the Sunshine Coast. Soon after that I got a job at the Carpentaria Buffalo Club and worked there almost 10 years as a *maître-d'* until I retired from the work force in 2001. The environment of a Club Restaurant was different again to what I was used to but it was the perfect job for me to use all my knowledge I had gained from the experiences working in the hotels and the Chinese restaurant. I enjoyed the live entertainments we had over the weekends although it brought many different challenges. There was always something to learn and grow as we had the regular management meetings and set goals to achieve. I loved my job so much that nobody, including myself, ever thought that I could give up and walk away from it, but I did.

It is true to say that our heart had left Mount Isa ever since we bought the acreage property on the Sunshine Coast for our retirement and the dream of our next chapter of our lives had begun. Also there were big changes in the company Rolf was working for and all the small diesel operated power stations in Rolf's care around Mount Isa, were about to be taken over by the company's Cairns Division. Rolf had a couple of options, ask for a redundancy package or move to Cairns. Moreover around that time Rolf was not feeling well and often experiencing irregular rhythms in his heart. Therefore moving to where our heart was, - was a far better option. Rolf took the redundancy package and left the company.

Therefore, for me to resign from my work was inevitable. Once again in my life I was faced with the profound moment of **WHAT IF** - what if anything bad happens with Rolf's health whilst I was enjoying my work and delaying to leave… I knew I will never forgive myself. It was best for me to resign and leave.

By then our boys, including my brother had already left Mount Isa as they all advanced in their chosen careers. It was only a matter for us to resign from our positions at work and sell the two properties we had in Mount Isa and go. By then I had worked nine years and nine months, to be exact, for the Club. Given you had to work a full ten years before getting the "long service leave pay" in those years, friends at work thought I was silly not to work three more months and miss out on receiving the extra pay. But it wasn't important to me as Rolf was feeling unwell and he had already resigned from his work and was waiting for me to do the same. I told myself that money isn't everything and I'd made up my mind to leave therefore I wasn't expecting to get it. However the Board Directors and the Manager of the Club had agreed and then surprised me with the full entitlement pay, which was unheard of in those years, and surprised everyone including myself.

I had a wonderful time working for the Club and the Club has been wonderful to me. Even though I often reminded everyone that I was getting ready for retirement in the near future for the past three years, ever since we bought the property in Pomona, no one of the management team ever tried to replace me with someone else. They included me in the various courses to upgrade me and supported me until I gave them the actual written resignation. I felt I was appreciated by all right to the last minute when they sent me off with a big surprise party and wished me well.

We had to sell our rental property before we could sell our house to save us from moving twice unnecessarily but it was not selling for a long time. Originally we had bought the house because I wanted to have Maurits living closer to us after Maurits left home to gain his independence. When I had heard about the house in the same street as ours, that was soon to be on the market for sale, I did not hesitate to take the rare opportunity to buy a house so near to us. Whilst the rental market in Mount Isa was doing very well and was not affected by the down-turn of the economy the real estate market for selling was badly affected and wasn't moving at all.

There was another issue blocking the sale of our rental property and it took a long time to sell. It was located near the racecourse and there was a horse stable next to the property belong to a neighbour, which created bad smells and flies. At the beginning I was led to believe by the neighbour that the stable was legal to be there, but long after I found out that it wasn't. I contacted someone I knew well who was in the position to have it removed. Soon after that we were offered a price we were happy with and at last we were able to put our own house on the market and be serious about selling it.

We were extremely lucky one of the regular customers of the Club, who knew me, had one look at our house and gave us an offer. We couldn't have been any luckier to have the settlement days for both of our properties in the same week.

We had to hurry and pack and send away most of our belongings by a removal company and told them to hold onto our things until our tenant in the Pomona property had the chance to find another place to live and move out. We had to vacate our place by the last week in June but I wanted to work into the first week of the financial year to take advantage of the taxation rules. Therefore we had to look for a flat to live just for two more weeks in Mount Isa. Knowing there was such a high demand for rental properties, no land-lord in Mount Isa would let anyone rent a flat for just two weeks, I rang Peter: the land-lord of the flat we used to live in some 28 years ago back in 1973 when we first moved to Mount Isa from Darwin, and explained my situation to him and asked if there was one vacant flat of his that we could rent for just two weeks. He was happy to hear from me and told me, that it may sound unbelievable but the flat we used to live in had just become vacant and he was happy to let us rent it for the two weeks without the bond money or the contract. How lucky we were again! We were so happy and felt somewhat sentimental that we moved back into the same flat where we started our life in Mount Isa and finished with the same flat. We thanked Peter very much for his kindness. Once our properties were sold everything happened so fast we didn't have time to say our farewells to everyone we knew, - and I knew so many ... so I wrote our last farewell for everyone and gave it to Liz, the editor for the local newspaper "The North West Star" and asked her if she could publish it ASAP for me.

It was in the paper the very next day.

"Letter to the Editor" Page 6, "The North West Star" Friday, July 6, 2001

She subtitled it, "Sorry to leave"

In November 1973 on the way from Darwin to Mount Isa, the conversation I overheard in the ladies room at the "Three ways road house" Northern Territory almost got me worried.

(The stranger A) "Which way are you going?"

(The stranger B) "We are going back to South Australia to live. We've lived in Mount Isa for the last two years, it's not a bad place to live but two years were enough for us"

(The stranger A) "What's it like to live in Mount Isa?"

(The stranger B) "People are very friendly and all that but Mount Isa is a place either you love it or hate it."

I still remember the conversations like it were yesterday and how it made me feel reluctant to come to Mount Isa. All those years of our young and productive years we have worked and lived in Mount Isa and as we are preparing to leave town in a few days, looking back, I know how wonderful Mount Isa city and its people have been for us.

I'm glad we came. Having worked twenty-five years in the hospitality industry, the last ten years at our wonderful Carpentaria Buffalo Club, I've been able to play a big part in our community and enjoyed every minute of it. I am very proud of our city, our friendliness, close-knit community. I hear often tourists commenting on how friendly we are and how Mount Isa is a bigger and better place than they ever imagined. My husband Rolf is retiring from the workforce, we need to start another chapter of our lives elsewhere. We are leaving with very happy memories of Mount Isa. It is sad to leave and at the same time it feels like we're recharged, ready for our new beginning, new challenges.

Thank you so very much Mount Isa for the wonderful life we have shared.

So long everyone, all the best wishes!
Ann Gustavsson

On Monday morning the last thing I had to do before we finally drove away was to call in at the Buff Club and pick up my work reference from my boss. I had never asked anyone for a reference before that time, as I never needed one to get a job in Mount Isa, but as we were moving to a place where no-one would know me I felt it was necessary to have one in case I wanted to work again, so I asked him if he would write one for me on my very last day at work.

The reference was written on the Club's official paper.
Dated,

Monday, July 9, 2001

To Whom It May Concern

This is to confirm Ann Gustavsson was employed by The Carpentaria Buffalo Club from October 1991 until July 2001 as the Maitre De in our Bistro and function area.

Ann has always given 110% and it has been a real pleasure to have had her working for us. Ann knows the hospitality industries very well and she has an attitude that makes customers feel welcome, important and comfortable. This of course led to a lot of repeat business for our club.

We are sorry to lose her, she is a rare find in this industry and I recommend her without any reservations whatsoever.

Yours faithfully
Signed, R.A. Jacobson
Executive Manager

I thanked him sincerely for having given me the wonderful support and guidance to do my job well and helped me to grow as a person. I also let him know that I have loved every minute of my job and I wished him and The Club my best wishes. It was very emotional to say the final good-byes to everyone as I walked out of The Club. But every step I made I knew I was a step closer to the life we both looked forward to – moving to an acreage property in greener pastures and to do what we want to do when we want to do it and hope together to create a place of our dreams, a paradise, not just for us both but to share with our family for many years to come.

It's hard to believe but another long 27 years have passed since the first visit I made to Korea in 1987.

The journey of my life has had its many "ups" and "downs" just like anyone else's. My rôle as a wife, a mother and now a grandmother, also has had many challenges but I am always willing to learn and improve and I am not afraid to challenge myself to achieve what I want to achieve.

Writing my story in English has been something I wanted to do for a long time, yet did not have the courage to do.

Yet again I dared! And I am glad that I did.

It is needless to say how satisfying the experience was!

I feel not only the sense of wonderful accomplishment that I have it done finally but also having the experience in re-living the past again I have learned so much more about myself to be able to put my future into perspective. I only hope the rest of my twilight years will be filled with more of the discoveries of the wonderful experiences a life journey can offer.

I must say though without a doubt that my best achievement so far is that I am still in love with the man who made it all possible and he is by my side.

www.ingramcontent.com/pod-product-compliance
Lightning Source LLC
Chambersburg PA
CBHW060113170426
43198CB00010B/874